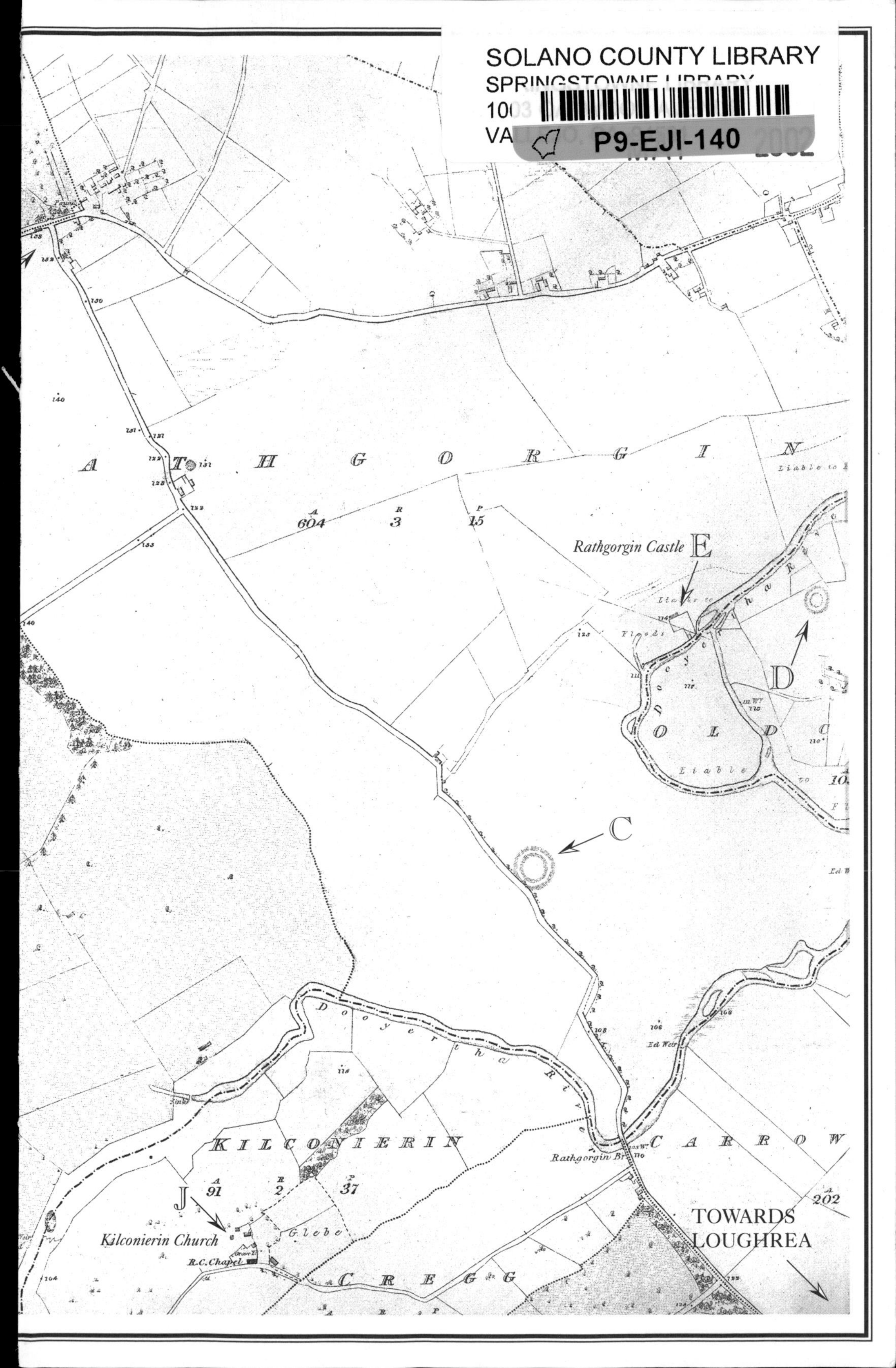
SOLANO COUNTY LIBRARY
P9-EJI-140
A T H G O R G I N
604 3 15
Rathgorgin Castle
E
D
C
O L D
Dooyertha River
KILCONIERIN
CARROW
CREGG
91 2 37
202
J
Kilconierin Church
R.C. Chapel
Glebe
Rathgorgin Br.
TOWARDS
LOUGHREA

The Fields of Athenry

William de Burgo, "the grey"

Also by James Charles Roy

The Road Wet, the Wind Close: Celtic Ireland (1986)

Islands of Storm (1991)

with James L. Pethica,
"To the Land of the Free from this Island of Slaves": Henry Stratford Persse's Letters from Galway to America, 1821–1832 (1996)

The Vanished Kingdom: Travels Through the History of Prussia (1999)

The Fields of Athenry

A Journey Through Irish History

JAMES CHARLES ROY

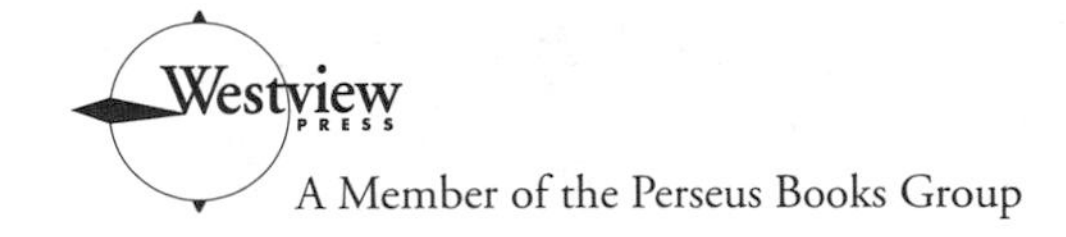

A Member of the Perseus Books Group

Published in 2001 in the United States of America by Westview Press, 5500 Central Avenue, Boulder, Colorado 80301-2877, and in the United Kingdom by Westview Press, 12 Hid's Copse Road, Cumnor Hill, Oxford OX2 9JJ

Find us on the World Wide Web at www.westviewpress.com

Library of Congress Cataloging-in-Publication Data
Roy, James Charles, 1945–
The fields of athenry : A journey through Irish history / by James Charles Roy.
p. cm.
ISBN 0-8133-3860-3
1. Ireland—Social life and customs—20th century. 2. Roy, James Charles, 1945– . Homes and haunts—Ireland. 3. Castles—Conservation and restoration—Ireland. 4. Ireland—Civilization—20th century. 5. Ireland—History. I. Title.

DA959.1 .R69 2001
941.5082—dc21

00-048473

Design by Heather Hutchison

The paper used in this publication meets the requirements of the American National Standard for Permanence of Paper for Printed Library Materials Z39.48–1984.

10 9 8 7 6 5 4 3 2 1

This book is dedicated to the memories of

Penelope Preston
Gormanston Castle
County Meath

Sans Tache

&

Robert Brown
Ballyportry Castle
County Clare

There were yielded out of Connaught violent men,
keenness, great deeds.

—Irish, c. A.D. 700

CONTENTS

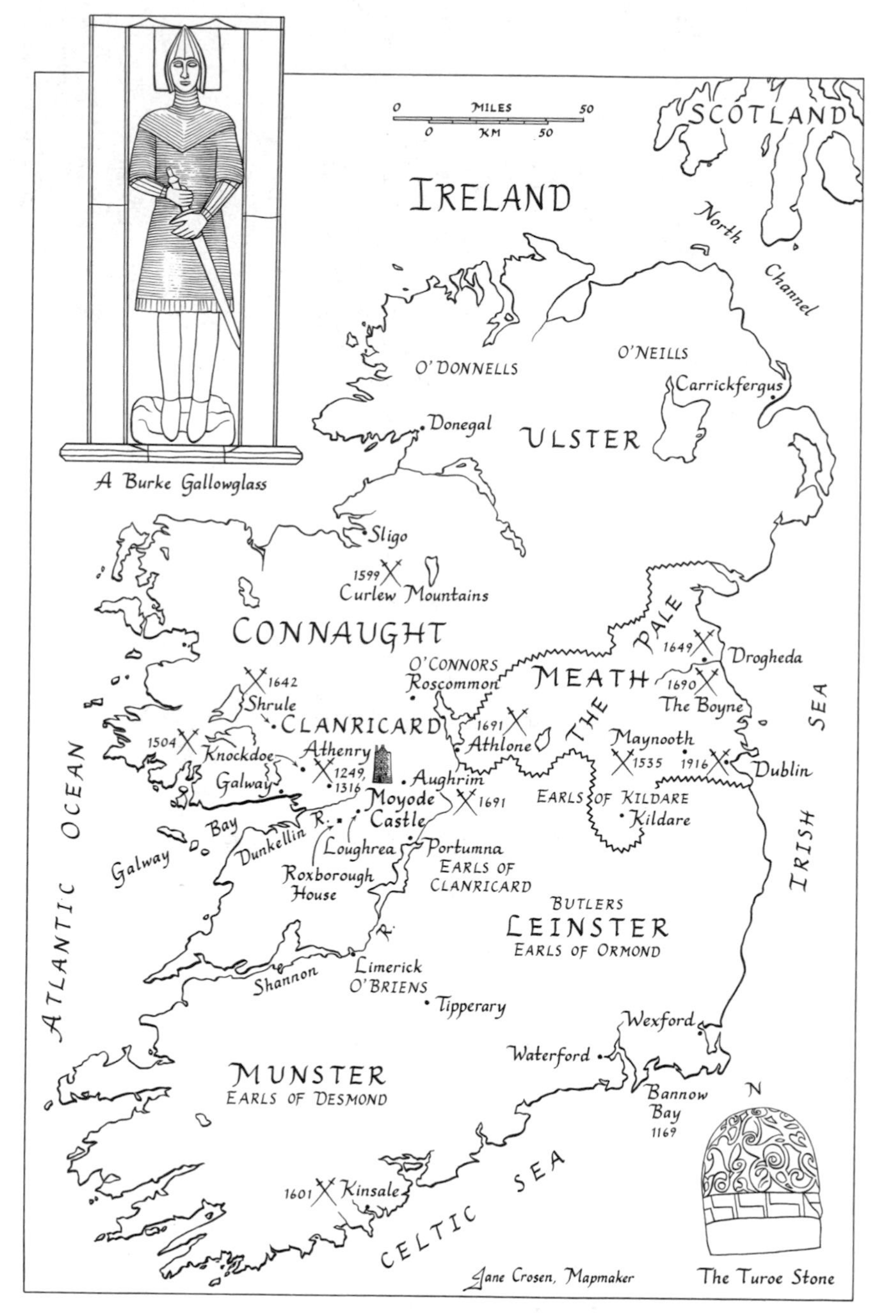

Ireland and Connaught

INTRODUCTION

He smelleth the battle afar off, the
thunder of the captains and the shouting.

A friend of mine once asked me, "Why Ireland?" He had just returned from two weeks of misery in the Emerald Isle: atrocious weather, abominable food, expensive drink, and historical remains whose shabby, unkempt, diminutive personality had betrayed all the praise lavished upon them by myself and others. "The next time I want to see the sun, I'm going to Spain. For a good meal and a glass of wine, to France. And for something extravagant, Rome. They say the Colosseum is quite a sight."

There is little doubt that Ireland is different from other European countries. A peripheral kind of place—"a pimple on the chin of the world," according to an ancient cleric—it has never been at the cross-roads of life, is always off to the edge. In modern times the country has lagged behind the Continent both materially and culturally, only now losing that sheen of innocence so long its special preserve. Out-siders such as myself lament this transformation, much to the annoy-ance of progressive Irish friends. "You people who have everything never want to share," I've often been told over argumentative pints of Guinness. "You come over for the melancholy Ireland of songs and ballads, the donkey cart and leprechaun. The last thing you want to see here are fast cars or people using computers."

This book records, on two separate levels, my own loss of inno-cence regarding Ireland. I initiated this experience, unwittingly, in 1969 by purchasing the ruins of Moyode Castle, located on the great eastern plain of County Galway in the province of Connaught. For over fifteen years, the aura of that desolated sixteenth-century shell infected all my thinking, mostly superficial, on Ireland and its extrava-

Moyode Castle, 1969

gant history. I wallowed in all the great blarney of saints and scholars, Wild Geese and rebels, the "terrible beauty" and "Celtic Twilights" of William Butler Yeats. When I began working on Moyode in the middle 1980s, these perceptions inevitably changed.

"Familiarity breeds contempt" runs the old saw, and though my affection for most things Irish remains as strong as ever, the mundane reversals of fortune that plague any substantial building project—and especially those of a Third World nature, as County Galway revealed itself to be—can strain the credulity level of any would-be zealot. Shards of Elizabethan prejudice infected my vision: delays, procrastination, financial sleight of hand, interminable tea breaks, the gush of brave talk unbacked by resolution, all caused me to think as "a foreigner." Moyode became in many respects more of a burden than a respite.

But familiarity also breeds knowledge. Submerging myself in the details of Moyode Castle and the few immediate acres surrounding it inevitably transformed the obsession I had cherished for so many years. As the scattered physical remnants of this landscape revealed themselves to my wandering eye, as their essentially nondescript and often pedestrian character became apparent, I found myself overwhelmed at just how unglamorous, violent, grubby, and desperate so many details of this history indeed were.

With increasing fascination, moreover, I discovered that just about every phase of the Irish saga had left its physical imprint on Moyode Castle and the fields over which it stood. From the unrecorded blur of pre-Christian Ireland to the Norman invasion of 1169; from the murderous passage of the great de Burgo barons of Connaught to the wild Celtic Burkes into which their line degenerated; from the ravaging Tudor wars to the Confederation of Kilkenney to the fiasco of the Boyne; to the coming of the Protestant Ascendancy to revolt in 1916 and the ensuing "Troubles"—all these events dispersed their generally catastrophic marks on this seemingly bucolic site.

Arnold Toynbee had it all wrong. History is never neat, never concise, never predictable. Generally speaking, it is never fair either. I came to understand, rummaging about the environs of my new home, that Ireland's story is a hugely disorganized froth, and that attempts to sanitize the incoherent shambles of its surge through the centuries benefits the country's major growth industry (tourism) but little else. The personalities, pressures, events, and incongruities of fate all burst our desire for a clean summation of trends and fortunes in what is, I believe, a tragic story and certainly a tragic land. It is easy to bog down in chaos, but no more apt metaphor for the Irish saga is available than in that single word.

The rebuilding of Moyode Castle seemed to me at times a reflection of this lurching narrative that constitutes Irish history, and I record the ups and downs of that experience in this book. I have also attempted to relate Ireland's past through what I know happened here in these fields, pastures, ruined buildings, all so amply watered both by sweat and blood. Familiar individuals will enter and leave various scenes in this chronicle, but for the most part the reader will meet characters whom records and annals have tended to ignore. It has been my happy task to bring them, I hope, to life, giving the lie to my friend's sarcastic inquiry, "Why Ireland?" with the rejoinder, "Is there anywhere finer?"

Moyode Castle

1969

A castle of many rooms, but very filthy and full of dung.

The Quest

The complexities of an Irish landscape remind me both of a family tree and a skeleton, where all parts interlock or connect in a seemingly ordered whole but, when looked at from different angles, reveal bewildering levels of meaning. No country in the world is as delineated and defined, down to the last square inch, as Ireland, yet boundaries of different sorts divide and confuse the various allegiances each seems to require.

Moyode Castle stands on the southern portion of a large, open piece of grazing pasture in the townland of Moyode demesne, land long valued as "champaign country" by farmers and herders of cattle, sheep, horses, and pigs. The townland is one of thirty-two that make up the parish of Carrabane, itself a part of the old Norman barony known as Athenry, after a town of that name roughly 3 miles to the north. This Norman delineation of power and, more important, possession, approximates the territorial boundaries of what it replaced, an ancient Celtic *tuath*, or kingdom, called in Gaelic Uí Mhaine and situated in the county of Galway, which, along with seven others, makes up the province of Connaught, one of the "Fifths," or Cóiceda, of Ireland, a broad geographic designation that predates recorded history.

The term "castle" as an architectural description for Moyode has always seemed to me slightly hyperbolic. Moyode is actually a rather small and lonely tower house built around 1550 by a minor vassal family known as the Dolphins, who had held this patch of land off and on for three centuries, ever since the Norman incursion here that started in the early thirteenth century. Such an ancient pedigree strikes the modern visitor as substantial and noteworthy. But to the native Gaelic *filid*, official custodian of a clan's lore and genealogy who disdains the use of pen and paper in favor of that more trustworthy calculator, the human brain, any boast of 300 years' possession would be ridiculed as vain and preposterous. Celtic septs, whose lineage a *filid* could recite from memory to the back of beyond, had been here through three millennia.

In Irish terms, Moyode Castle is hardly unusual. If you were to sweep your hand in a large horseshoe curve beginning in Galway and heading south through Clare and Limerick, turning eastward over the Golden Vale of Tipperary and Cork, then coming back north over the province of Leinster into Meath, the shadow you'd leave behind would cover the remains of over 1,000 similar buildings. Some few, a handful, are occupied, either by ancient Irish families who never left or wealthy foreigners who have restored them to a degree of luxury never imagined by their original builders. Still others, open to the sky, stand in decent enough condition, taken over by the Irish government and minimally maintained, a rather recent preservationist impulse dictated more by the desire to promote tourism than to honor their builders, French-speaking Norman squatters. But most others lie scattered to the winds in fields and woods, farms and villages—deserted, cracking, falling apart, home to cows, pigs, chickens, mice, bats, crows, pigeon coops, peat piles, rusted farm tools, straw, refuse, and plastic feedbags. The smell of manure is their hallmark, the dank of slop and dripping ivy their atmosphere.

Of these cadavers, the majority have only a wall or two still standing, what the writer Sean O'Faolain called "broken tooths of masonry," seen from the train or car. Hundreds more are merely piles of stone, perhaps stumbled over by antiquarians trying to pinpoint some reference to a stronghold in a moldering charter or monastic chronicle from days long gone and forgotten. Yet some, by miracle, retain the semblance of their original condition and survive relatively intact, their circular stairways in place; carved window mullions, doorways, and fireplaces just where medieval masons set them; chimneys and gables erect, though tilting. That was essentially the condition of Moyode when I first saw it in 1969.

I had not come here by accident. Maps had led the way. In 1826 the British government commissioned the first ordnance survey of Ireland. Army engineers measured, plotted, and documented the entire island, producing hundreds of elegantly appointed charts that noted not just the geographical lay of the land but also human impressions, both ancient and modern. Old abbeys, monasteries, nunneries, saints' wells, sacred groves, cemeteries, round towers, megalithic graves, and castles, irrespective of historical era, were all marked, and when the Irish government issued a more broadly based series of thirty-two individual maps after World War II many of these identifications remained. I noticed them almost accidentally. I had purchased what I thought was a road map for Limerick. What I ended up with was a maze of castles.

I think back on those months of discovery in 1969 with great affection. I had never quit a job. In September of that year I did. I had never dropped everything, packed up, and run away from my responsibilities. In October of that year I did. I had never learned to operate, to say nothing of own, a motorcycle. In November of that year I did. For $550 I bought something in London called a Royal Star. It was a BSA, the initials standing for Birmingham Small Arms, the company that had made it. In just a few weeks I understood why so many other people called it Best Scrap Available. But it ran, most of the time.

In London I affected the current air—leather jerkin from Royal Navy surplus, flyer goggles, cowboy boots, blue jeans. In Ireland, where I went for cheaper living, all this was replaced by necessity: oilskins from a Dublin fishing gear shop, rubber Wellington boots from a grocer's; heavy winter underwear, socks, and gloves from secondhand clothing sales run by nuns. It was cold and wet in the countryside.

I was roaming. I had been to Ireland twice before as a child, but with little lasting impression. My mother was of purely Irish Catholic heritage (O'Brien and Hennessy). Her forebears, with the odor of rotting potatoes in their nostrils, had come over to Boston during the nineteenth-century Great Famine. They ended up in nearby Marble-

Gutted interior, Knockgraffon Castle, County Tipperary

head, but not as masons or fishermen. My grandparents were lace-curtain Irish, he a small-town lawyer and politician, she a lady of airs, many of which my mother inherited. When we returned to Ireland as visitors in the 1950s, we did not come to kiss the sacred land of our ancestors or to eat soda bread and drink stout in thatched pubs out in the bogs. We came to socialize at the Dublin Horse Show; to drink tea and eat enormous dinners at the Russell, Hibernian, and Royal Marine Hotels; to stay on as paying guests at Glaslough Castle, where Sir Shane Leslie, childhood playmate to Winston Churchill, bored everyone to death (even me, a child of seven) with his ghost stories. The only relations we thought to look up were the Blennerhassetts, an old Protestant family whose lineage, much to their regret, had included a wayward son in Tralee who went out slumming one night and ended up marrying a Catholic O'Brien, remotely attaching himself to our family tree. Come to think of it, we came to Ireland as the Normans had, as conquerors. Instead of swords and coats of mail, we had money.

The castle disease began modestly. The first tower I took the time to record was in County Limerick. I had seen it from the road, a sudden glint of gray, suddenly standing full in my sight, then hidden again just as quickly in a copse of trees as I motored by. Although I must have passed dozens of similar buildings on similar rides, I stopped for this one out of simple curiosity. It was lunchtime, and I picnicked there at the top on a bed of soft earth and grass that over centuries had settled, seeded, sprouted, and taken hold over the ramparts. The view remains in my mind's eye even now: scraggly, barren fields of autumnal yellow and green; stone walls speckled white zigzagging down hillsides and across pasture; rusted iron gates tied shut with twine; long, sloping vistas down a valley to the sea.

I camped out that night and lit a small fire in the old hearth on the top floor, open to the sky. It attracted the attention of a neighboring farmer who thought his cattle were being stolen, a pastime I imagined had gone out of style since the heroic days of Cú Chulainn and his Knights of the Red Branch, semimythical Celtic marauders celebrated by Yeats and other romantic Irish poets. "Ah, the days of Holy Ireland are long gone," he told me apologetically. "St. Patrick would curse our race if he were here again." Later he brought me over some tea and bread.

In the morning I looked at my map to see generally where I was, but no approximation was necessary. There, on that minor unnamed road, no more than a cow path really, on the backside of a deserted moor and mountainside, beside a little swollen stream of brown, chilled water, stood in bold Gothic type my definitive location: **CAS**.

Looking around, however, I had to ask myself—pinned down as I was by the cartographer's pen—just what was it here that made this barren place so worthy of attention, no matter how long ago in the ancient past? What led to this building, this strange mark of possession, authority, force, and anger in a kingdom worthy of nothing but the view, a place, as the farmer told me, where he could hardly make a living? Was there gold here long ago, silver, precious metals, slaves, plunder? All I could see or smell was dung.

In looking over the map, I noted two or three neighboring **CAS**. I went to see them. One reminded me of an inverted pyramid, a four-story-high corner of a wall precariously attached to earth by a course or two of eroding stone rubble. Not long for this world, and I put an

"R" for "ruin" next to it on my map. The second had disappeared entirely: no mound, outline, cache of loose stone, uneven ground surface, or ruptured earth that might, in a ghostly sense, reveal where it once might have stood. Next to that I put a "D" for "disappeared." That night I camped again at the ruin of the previous evening. The farmer laughed at me, said I was trespassing. An American had bought the castle from his cousin a decade before.

For the next three months, my collection of maps grew. One or two here, three there, eight at one shop, until I had all thirty-two covering the entire island. At night, in hay sheds, open fields, pubs, or wherever I happened to be, I pored over them, circling every notation I saw for these buildings. By day I traveled to search them out. There was not a dirt track (what the Irish call a boreen) I didn't follow, a bog I didn't slog through, a stream I didn't cross, or a bull I didn't challenge if a CAS lay alongside or at the finish. Where and when I determined to purchase one I cannot say, but my notes grew more detailed and critical. They took to pointing out negatives such as proximity to busy roads or unkempt farmsteads, cracked walls, smashed stairways, shattered vaulting. There could be only a single explanation for doing all this. My final list had forty to choose from.

It came down, in the month of November, to two sites. The first was on the shores of Lough Mask in Galway, looking across that great lake toward the incomparable collection of mountains in Connaught called the Twelve Bens of Connemara, "a grand soft spot" as one local put it, and unrelievedly dramatic. I camped there for a couple of days, the farmer eager to sell. Storms came and went, passing showers and sometimes hail from above. The wind never ceased its pleading whine from the nearby Atlantic, lake water at the castle base relentlessly slapped the masonry.

Nietzsche wrote that a bold man must always build his house at the base of a volcano, but the tumult of this desolate, wild scene I judged to be too much, a decision I look back on as remarkably mature. Besides that, the farmer wanted too much: £5,000! He couldn't believe it when I left. "I thought all you Germans had money," were his last confused words to me.

In the dusk of a late fall day, I returned to Moyode and reconfirmed my initial attraction to it. Far away from any road, the building had few neighbors nearby and no annoying disfigurements to intrude on an otherwise unblemished vista. Clambering again about the ruin, I judged it sound and asked about its owner. It turned out he lived 3 miles away, a not uncommon occurrence in Ireland, where farmers may have several small holdings scattered about the neighborhood. I have often wondered what he and his wife really thought when they saw this motorized wonder in their yard, a John the Baptist in animal skins perhaps, swaddled in several layers of unwashed and now torn rain gear, four months' beard, wild and dirty hair, making inquiries about something that they had never in their lives given a moment's thought to. We arranged to meet the next morning. He must have tossed and turned all night in questioning amazement.

It was very cold that evening. I do not remember it as such, but I find the comment in my notes of these events, with an added remark in the margin that I was running out of money. It was becoming awfully raw for camping, the fresh hay in farmers' sheds too wet or clammy to sleep on. So I went to find a bed in the nearby town of Athenry. My journal entry says only, "a dank place." I recall sitting in a cold, dark pub drinking cold, dark porter.

Rain was falling when I went out to see Thomas Uniacke at Moyode. Athenry, an old Norman frontier settlement—a marcher baron town with grim castle, grim gate, grim walls—seemed to me a lumpy piece of black coal as I left it, an unnatural blot on this otherwise deeply green, though sodden, landscape. I felt alien as I put the place behind me, a stranger, a Norman, going out to grapple with the native Gael. Instead of riding a warhorse, however, I came to bargain on Best Scrap Available, its deep-seated roar reverberating through the empty streets of Athenry.

I arrived first and waited on the little lane that runs by the entryway into Moyode demesne, one portion of which is the great 30-acre pasture, on the furthest edge of which stands the tower. Until the 1920s or so, a formal and rather grand set of wrought iron gates had stood here, held up by two imposing cut-stone pillars with pyramidal capstones. To the left of these was a handsome custodian's cottage of Georgian design. Both ostentatious statements were meant to inform visitors that they had reached the grounds of Moyode House, a neo-Gothic assemblage of nineteenth-century baronial castle, courtyard, stable, dairy, school, cattle shed, smithy, dog pound, vegetable plot, and formal garden that was the nucleus of a 3,000-acre estate of the Persses, a once prominent family of the Protestant Ascendancy. The

The town of Athenry, County Galway

little tower I was here to purchase had been a folly or ornament for the Big House, a few hundred yards to its west. But in Yeats's phrase, all turns to ruin once again. The Big House was burned to the ground in the "Troubles" of 1922, the Persses having fled three decades before, ruined, as they would claim from faraway Westminster. The gates were sold off and removed, the lodge beside them deserted, turned into a storage shed.

I saw Thomas Uniacke a good several hundred yards away through the morning drizzle, certainly before he saw me. Thomas Uniacke never learned to drive a car, but the miles he pedaled! He had come from the opposite direction, Loughrea, another former Norman outpost some 7 miles to the southeast. He coasted noiselessly down to me, small sprays of water shooting off to either side. We walked into the field together.

He owned all of this pasture, inherited from an uncle, once the formal lawn of Moyode House and surrounded by a sunken wall of about 6 feet in height to keep livestock out and tame deer in. These are the famous ha-has of Ireland, so called by huntsmen who, at full bray on a chase, gallop along and suddenly find themselves confronted with a 5- or 6-foot drop to an adjoining pasture and no time to stop. The avenue to the old mansion was the property dividing line. Everything to the west belonged to Gerald Harty, another farmer, whose house from the 1930s we approached; everything to the east belonged to Uniacke. The one exception to this was the mansion ruin. Uniacke owned what was left of this and a decrepit coach shed. The rear yards and outbuildings, the residue of decay, belonged to other assorted individuals, farmers and day laborers whom I would come to know well in future years.

It was clear from the start that Uniacke cared nothing for the castle—"I'd give it to you for a shilling if ye'd take it away"—nor indeed for the old mansion, the rubble of which he sold off to the road commissioners whenever they needed fill or crushed stone. It was the land that counted, and it was the land he wouldn't part with. I explained I was interested only in the tower and a small right of way leading up to it, feeling reasonably secure that way back in here it would be unlikely that anyone might build a house. We stepped off a rough calculation as to how much land this really involved. Very little, we judged. However, it would cut a swath through his field and technically separate it into two portions. We agreed to no fences along the right of way that could interfere with the desultory wanderings of his cattle. All of a sudden, we had nothing more to say. It was Uniacke's decision whether to sell.

His mind was churning. Was this a good deal or not? Was he being made a fool of? Could the tower truly be worth anything? He couldn't believe it was, nor his uncle, who had held it since the Troubles way back in the 1920s, and his wife had said to him just last night it wouldn't fetch a farthing. Yet someone else's interest in it had suddenly made it valuable. How valuable? This was bad terrain for Thomas Uniacke. This was not trading cattle at the mart in Athenry. He knew the rules there; he knew what a beast would bring; he was famous far and wide in the parish as a canny man of business. This, however, was different. This was dangerous.

"What's it worth to you, then?" His first venture.

"£500," I said.

"£1,000."
"£700."
"£850."
"£800." A long pause here. A very long pause.
"Done."

We shook hands on it, in the by now pouring rain. Three days later I was back in New York, looking for a job. I sold the BSA.

THE IRISH WAY OF DOING BUSINESS

The deal for Moyode was clinched via Western Union many months later, a delay that, in retrospect, should have come as no surprise to me. I had hired a solicitor in Dublin, an Anglo-Norman eccentric of the first order, Godfrey Skrine, who informed me quite early in our friendship that he began each day standing on his head, naked, for three minutes. Godfrey's office, an impeccable address next to the old Parliament building and Trinity College, should have warned me that Ireland does not work like other countries. Stacked to the ceiling were scores of ancient metal bins, painted black, with stenciled names of famous Protestant Ascendancy families printed on each. These boxes were packed with papers, often to the bursting point; wills, deeds, codicils, and property maps—the documentation of countless lifetimes—spewed over the edges of their containers, barely kept in place by straining padlocks. This was a Dickensian nightmare, a hell on earth for some filing clerk in need of punishment.

"Will I have a box here with my name on it?" I asked Godfrey.

"Oh heavens no, not unless you get a title from Buckingham Palace. But the paperwork will be just as grubby and tattered, maybe even singed from a fire or two in the past. But we needn't worry about that for the moment. The first task is to get Uniacke's agreement in writing as to what you discussed in the field."

"That's no problem. We shook hands on it."

"That's what you think, my American friend. Let's wait and see if Mr. Uniacke reconsiders."

Godfrey, of course, was right. Just as English kings and queens received, to their growing annoyance, dispatches from generally hapless lord deputies describing the vagaries of extending law and order to the unruly Irish, so too did my loyal solicitor send one report after another with generally gloomy tidings. "Uniacke back-peddling," said one. "Mr. Uniacke very inclined to run out on this," said another. "Uniacke having second thoughts altogether," and so on, said many more. Thomas himself even sent me a note. "You will be surprised to hear from me," he wrote, and I was. The difficulty seemed not so much about money as about judgment and reputation. "Mr. Uniacke has a sinister acquaintance who is telling him not to sell," one of Godfrey's letters said, "and this mug is dead right in my opinion. The value of property in this country is soaring, and what you have to realize is that whereas Moyode Castle doesn't mean a row of beans to Uniacke, such men as he count their land by the square inch."

Thomas was later to tell me, after we too had become friends, that he never intended to welsh on our deal. "I was happy enough with the price, and we had agreed to it face to face so I felt bound to keep my word. It was all so unusual to me, to be honest, and when you're dealing with the unknown you have to step back and see if you've made the right choice. I never decide anything with cattle until I know it's what I want to do. Same thing with getting married, for that matter! Once I thought it through and heard some opinions, I saw no reason not to do it."

Many, many months later Godfrey sent a telegram: "Uniacke has signed at last." Five or so years after that, having negotiated the anarchistic maze of Irish legal custom, I finally had a deed, "a scruffy piece of paper" in Godfrey's words, "by no means to be lost as we can never bespeak another. You're welcome to Ireland!"

LOCAL DETAILS

In the fifteen years after, Moyode remained in much the same condition as the previous three or so centuries. Cattle came in when it was raining hard, hundreds of generations of crows and mice made the place home and reared their young, and locals still came to court on the top floor over the arch, known as "the Green Field," where a large tree took root and a fine bed of grass grew luxuriantly from wall to wall.

My own emotional response to the place was neither calming nor rhythmical, but rather displayed a typically American aptitude for impatient naiveté—I would restore the place, and soon. Labor in the early 1970s was £14 a week, which seemed affordable, and by my calculations the place could have been done up in three to four months' time. I burned to start, but an architect I knew, my old friend Bob Brown, advised calm. "You haven't a clue as to what it's like here. You cannot delegate authority on the job. You can't say, 'Do this and that. Have it done by the time I come back next summer.' The minute you leave, tea is served and a song—out of sight, out of mind. The wages are cheap, but spread them out over many years and the whole thing becomes very dear indeed."

I eventually reached a Zenlike level of acceptance and compatibility with the building. Moyode was there, going nowhere. As my mother used to say, "I'll never spend a night in that place," and she was right. She died sixteen years after I bought it. I still went by every couple of springs or falls. I brought my wife-to-be, an artist. She loved France, Italy, Portugal, even England, but Ireland seemed pretty crude by comparison, and the tower house left her cold. "I'll never spend a night in that place," she said, but her reasons were different from my mother's. It was just too gloomy. How could anyone come here after Tuscany or Venice or the Alentejo and love a place that had no light? Dungeons just were not for her.

So after a while I generally went by myself. I'd camp in my car or pitch a tent out in the pasture, visit with all the locals until another cup of tea would almost make me sick, rummage through the neighborhood on the old bridle paths, putting my nose in whatever pile of ruins came my way. Naturally enough, I also spent hours just sitting on the ramparts, sharing the ravens' view of open countryside for miles around, and one thing I noticed was that no matter the season, no matter the weather, no matter the year, my view never changed: to the south, stretching 20 or so miles in open, wide, green fields, the champaign of what the Gaels called O'Kelly's Country, dominated by a modest but attractive mountainous ridge of 1,200 feet known as Slieve Aughty; to the west, toward the Atlantic (only twenty minutes' drive away) were the Persse ruins with Harty's farmstead to the right of it, fields and forests beyond; northward, Thomas Uniacke's pasture and the broken gatehouse, followed by a long, indistinct blur of woodland, mostly pine; facing east, a panorama of irregular, slightly rolling fields and stone walls, plenty of livestock, and just about the only mark of modernity around, an inconspicuous set of high-tension wires. In there somewhere, if you looked for them, were the ruins of Rathgorgin Castle, built in the thirteenth century by Norman invaders.

The impress of man, from up here, anyway, seemed then and still does relatively slight, and yet the entire compass of Irish history can be surveyed and noted and verified within walking distance of Moyode Castle. Such a claim seems pretentious, but two points of contrast come to play here. The lore and recorded passage of people and events through Ireland's past are lengthy and hyperbolic. At times, in the telling or listening or reading of it, one receives the impression that this small island has forever been at the center of great deeds and events from which spectators around the world can only stagger back in awe and stupefaction.

In fact, Ireland has always been the back page, most of its recorded history of more import, quite naturally, to the Irish than anyone else. It has never ever, I can say with confidence, affected the greater, wider world in any fashion other than annoyance. The Romans knew the place existed yet found it too poor to bother conquering. Christian missionaries paid it little mind, sending over to Ireland the least of their brethren, ill-used zealots like St. Patrick, on woefully unsupported missions that were more concerned with stanching the sources of bloody raids than with saving souls. Pope Gregory the Great had no knowledge of Ireland: It was Britain he cared for, and he knew little enough of that country. The Vikings, fellow outcasts, did make a play for the place, but their interest in the Continent and England, where prosperous societies had produced considerably more attractive pickings to steal and plunder, was far more pronounced. The twelfth-century Normans were vagabonds for the most part, penniless descendants of William the Conqueror's warriors whose glory from the single Battle of Hastings has eclipsed for centuries the nameless skirmishing that constituted the invasion of Ireland. The First Crusade, a cataclysmic event in European history, contained but a smattering of "naked and savage fanatics" from Ireland and was ignored in Irish monastic chronicles. And no matter what parochial writers from Ireland may say, English kings and queens, be they Plantagenets or Tudors, Stuarts or the House of Orange, never spent more time or attention on Irish details than they had to. No matter the Irish headache, greater fame or disaster always lay to the east of them, on the Continent, than over their shoulders out in the Atlantic. Rarely was there glory to be won in Ireland. The country had potential; it was there to be plucked, harvested, or planted with unwanted populations from England, Wales, Scotland, or Flanders, but no one's British heart was ever really in the place.

And so the legendary battles of Ireland, the armies and conquests, with their attendant great threats and parleys and treaties, all taking place in venues of monstrous castles, abbeys, and cathedrals are all really rather mundane when taken in the context of wider European history, as indeed the physical remains testify. The armies in Irish conflicts were never so very large, the battles not nearly as immense, nor the castles ever so grand as all the old sagas relate. Just walking about these few Irish acres around Moyode will show us that. But this must not disguise what were large and grand: the people, their unbounded desires, the depths of tragedy that often engulfed them.

This is what makes Irish history so attractive and compelling, its utterly human scale. Moyode Castle (and the other artifacts that lay a mile or two in any direction) by its mere inconsequentiality gives substance and authority to the multiple dramas that played out here. Warriors fought and died on this field not by the hundreds of thousands, not by the thousands or even hundreds, but more likely ten or twenty, fifty or eighty in any given battle. But the death rattle of one man, with our attention solely on him and his miserable, tortured demise, may grip our hearts more than some anonymous, impersonal conflagration where uncounted souls have fallen. Moyode removes the hazy myths of Arthurian fantasy, the kind of romantic posturing that I grew up on reading adventure stories by Robert Louis Stevenson and, later, J. R. R. Tolkien.

By concentrating on the view from Moyode and what it includes, we focus our attention on the few. The story is here to see in small decrepit ruins, in boggy fields and forests, at a crossroads here or a river crossing there. None of it is on a grand historical scale, but the familial dimensions are the stuff of Shakespeare. One wonders at the capacity of the heart for suffering. This is one dimension where the Irish do not exaggerate.

SELECT CHRONOLOGY

C. 3000 B.C.	STONE AGE.
C. 1800 B.C.	BRONZE AGE.
C. 500 B.C.	IRON AGE.
C. A.D. 475	PROBABLE DATE OF ST. PATRICK'S MISSION TO IRELAND.
C. 520–620	CONVERSION OF IRELAND TO CHRISTIANITY.
C. 700–800	HIGH POINT OF IRISH MONASTIC TRADITION.
795 AND ON	VIKING RAIDS, MOST INTENSE 837–876.
C. 841	DUBLIN FOUNDED BY VIKINGS.
1006	BRIAN BORU BECOMES HIGH KING OF IRELAND.
1066	NORMAN CONQUEST OF ENGLAND.
1166	MACMURROUGH OF LEINSTER FLEES IRELAND.
1169	ROBERT FITZSTEPHEN LANDS IN WEXFORD TO ASSIST MACMURROUGH.
1170	STRONGBOW, WITH A LARGE FORCE, LANDS NEAR AND CAPTURES WATERFORD. MARRIES MACMURROUGH'S DAUGHTER.
1171	DEATH OF MACMURROUGH. HENRY II CROSSES INTO IRELAND WITH EXPEDITIONARY FORCE. STRONGBOW SUBMITS, IS CREATED EARL OF LEINSTER.
1176	DEATH OF STRONGBOW.
1189	DEATH OF HENRY II.

Celt and Norman
1166–1185

A race madly fond of war.

The Gael

During the nineteenth and early twentieth centuries, people of rural Ireland were much sought after for bits of local color and history. From John O'Donovan, the legendary Gaelic scholar who first made his mark during the ordnance survey of the 1820s, to the poet Yeats and Lady Gregory in nearby Kiltartan, antiquarians, artists, sociologists, storytellers, and ordinary tourists walked the lonely byways and sat at the hearths of shabby cottages to mine as much as possible from the peasant consciousness. Most of what they found were embellishments: sagas, tall tales, myths, and fireside fairy stories only remotely related to fact. In modern times not even these sources are easy to ferret out, as people born in the 1920s and 1930s pass from the scene, their memories unshared with the young of today who show meager interest in the subject. Just a few years ago, in County Donegal, I was looking for a cultic stone called in Irish Cloghaneely, located as I thought on the grounds of a private school. I recall approaching a group of boys playing soccer. Of the fifteen or so, none had heard of it. I went into the faculty lounge. The six or seven teachers there hadn't a clue. The headmaster was summoned to no avail. Finally, I went down to the kitchen. An old scullery woman washing pots led me out the

Mary Coen with Stone Age ax head her parents found while plowing

backdoor. In among some bracken and stunted trees, not 40 yards from the school, stood "Balor of the Mighty Blows." She regaled me for about thirty minutes with all manner of entertaining nonsense about this one-eyed giant until the headmaster, clearly bored, bundled her back to the kitchen. By now that old woman is dead.

Beyond the trimmings—the Gaelic frosting, as it were—many of the local people around me have little reliable knowledge of the remnants in our neighborhood, though artifacts from as long ago as the Stone Age routinely turn up in the course of plowing fields and building new sheds. The Normans built Moyode, they tell me—"the foreigners put it up." In fact, the story was long advanced by the time Moyode appeared about 1550, the pure-blooded Norman adventurer pretty much a dinosaur at that point. The Norman mark is not here, but a few hundred yards to the east.

Just a short walk over several pastures brings me to the Athenry and Loughrea road, a normal Irish thoroughfare, narrow and winding, originally a cattle drive curving its way along the path of least resistance between two dots on a map. When I first began coming here in the 1960s, you could stand in the middle of it and barely see any traffic for thirty minutes or an hour at a time—only a few bicyclists perhaps, a horse and cart or tractor, the occasional trap, lorries now and then. Private automobiles were certainly not rare, but the Irish farmer in a Morris Minor usually saved his petrol for a run to the pub of an evening, not for cruising about the countryside on a whim or to pass the time. But nowadays there's trouble on the roads: too many fast cars driven with utter recklessness and abandon. With real care I cross this road to Rathgorgin on the other side.

Rathgorgin is a townland. Ireland has several hundred of these, a civil division dating from the nineteenth century, and most are minuscule. To my eye this particular townland consists of about thirteen pastures of varying size. In one of these, the one I'm standing in, the remains of a Celtic earthwork commonly known as a rath are barely visible. In another is an old mound, the motte of a Norman motte and bailey. Two hundred yards from it, in a third field, are the scanty remains of Rathgorgin Castle, built in the early 1200s, again by the Normans. We should begin, I think, with the rath.

When the Normans came to Ireland in 1169, they came as adventurers, as pure a collection of freebooters and opportunists as any country has seen. They had no foresight into what they were doing, no consciousness as to the change they were bringing with them, no idea their impact on this island was to be more profound than any other in its history. They were unreflective fighting men who would leave an indelibly physical mark on the land with castles, towns, and abbeys that dwarfed in number and size what they found here. To their minds they had entered a vacuum. Aside from the native monastic centers, some with round towers and a few small stone churches, but most consisting of wood or mud-and-wattle structures with thatched roofs (which they happily plundered and burned when convenient), the most common sort of habitation they saw was the rath.

In Rathgorgin's field we see the only mark of the pre-Norman Gaelic clans anywhere around here, and it isn't much. Local people used to call these earthworks "forts," but in fact their defensive capabilities were meager—a circular ditch with two ramparts on either side (fill dug up from the trench), the inner sanctum a cramped 50 feet or so in diameter. The rath may have had one or two little huts inside it, perhaps an outer wooden palisade, but it was essentially a livestock pen, a place where the farmer who worked these fields gathered together his prized bulls or calves every evening, and perhaps his family and dependents as well, for safety. This particular rath, along with an estimated 30,000 or so whose traces still exist, is in a much-degraded state. Even if it served a chieftain, there is little about this site that could seem to justify the accolades that many of the sagas lavish upon them. The royal rath of Tara Hill near Dublin, for example (Ireland's equivalent to the mythical Camelot), exudes nothing but an everyday aura. There is the usual tourist fodder from the nineteenth century about the superstitions attached to these long deserted "palaces" and the reverence given them, but out of thirty-six raths that I found enumerated on the 1839 map of this area (24 square miles of territory) most have disappeared under the plow or bulldozer.

At the beginning of our narrative, then, we have this rather slight statement. It tells us something, but not too much, about the Celtic tribes who lived here for countless generations. It probably told the Normans nothing at all, except perhaps that they had nothing to fear, a great mistake, as things turned out. The Celts were formidable foes in many unexpected ways.

Normans found in the Gaelic warrior a high-spirited, emotional, reckless, suspicious, acquisitive, devious, conservative, valiant, bombastic, and often cruel opponent who delighted in all things that made heroic life worth living. He loved to eat and drink (both in excess); he loved to court, abduct, or possess as many beautiful women as possible (married or not made little difference); he loved to hunt his game on foot and anything to do with the out-of-doors; he loved praise and vain decoration; he loved to see his enemy skewered to earth, writhing in agony, a sword or spear plunged through his body, blood splattering all over the victor's face. His society was simple though complicated in many ways, barbarian in the Roman sense of the word but actually quite cultured in its love for erudition and learning that few other Germanic or Scandinavian tribes could equal. A densely formulated legal maze that elaborated many scales of social rank, along with a tribal structure whose leadership depended on rules of lineage and genealogy to function, supported an entire class of hereditary scholars and lawyers who, being illiterate, performed all their tasks orally and from memory. Similar discipline governed bards and poets who entertained the common people with long tabulations of ancient battles and noble kings from the past. This respect for scholarship and the strictures of academic training transferred itself to the clergy as Ireland converted to Christianity in the sixth century. Though monks and scribes often denigrated the pagan sagas as "delectations for fools," they could not themselves resist from turning many a pious Christian saint into a bloodthirsty, though still holy, warrior. St. Patrick was often depicted in Homeric rages, where the dead and injured littered the landscape, yet also in calm and earnest conversations with God, a chat between equals in most cases. Irishmen had from the earliest times a firmly established foundation of self-regard.

In pre-Christian times, life revolved around cattle. There was no money in Ireland; there were no towns, markets, stores, or trade of any meaningful sort. Cattle provided all: meat, milk, butter, hides, simple barter, and, most important, glory. Irish men were idlers. They barely practiced agriculture, were essentially herdsmen and pastoralists. This gave them time, time that weighed heavily with many. Time to think, to plot, to scheme, to leave behind their raths in search of plundering far afield. Their women, after all, could do the herding.

Marauding was a treasured, often dangerous way of life. We should not be totally swayed by the old Celtic annals that seem to chronicle an endless cycle of bloodshed and petty warfare—"The year of Christ, 1070: Great destruction was made by various distempers," a typical entry of the times—but they certainly do reflect a commonplace of Irish existence. The famed Cú Chulainn sagas, an assemblage of stories created before the birth of Christ, glorified the great bulls with their trailing herds and the exploits of heroes who sought to steal them. The bards recited or sang these tales nightly around the fires. Young men eager to prove their worth could not be restrained from raiding and thieving, nor could those from plundered raths be dissuaded from revenge. Add to this mixture women and the occasional murder, and you had the long memory for which the Irish are so famous.

Complicating life for these warriors was the question—or more properly expressed, the allure—of kingship. Ireland was not conceived by her inhabitants as a nation, a generic "kingdom of the Gael" yes, but not what we might consider a modern state. The Celt was parochial; he felt a member of his clan, or his *tuath* (the petty unit of kingdom), but he had no feeling for Ireland as a whole. Fortunately for the Normans, there were something like 150 *tuath*s scattered about the island, tangled in often strange and conflicting allegiances that could include *tuath*s in Scotland, the Isle of Man, or even Scandinavian colonies in Ireland itself or the Hebrides, Shetland, and Orkney. The notion of the single strongman, a unifying high king, was certainly well documented in the Celtic system, but no individual warrior ever established his might to convert such theory into fact.

On the local level, every man with a sword in his hand aspired to the exalted status of king, no manner how puny the *tuath*. The Celtic tradition was not that of Norman primogeniture. The net of candidates for a crown was cast wide, an encouragement to fratricidal outrage. A man who took the wand of sovereignty on a dung-littered coronation mound had two immediate concerns. The first, to secure his position, required him to eliminate or maim every rival. That usually meant brothers and even distant cousins. One can stand on the rath here at Rathgorgin and imagine the fear that some lad keeping watch over cattle must have felt when he realized that the five or six young men—his brother and cronies, closing in on him from all sides, out of the gorse and mist or nearby trees—meant to gouge out his eyes or, worse, stab and hack him to death, perhaps to hold him down while one slit his throat. "Woe to brothers in a barbarous nation," as a Norman wrote. And then second, once these purges had been achieved, the king had to prove his mettle by leading a host of followers on raid and pillage, for in Caesar's words what the Celtic race "most greatly admires is that lands surrounding them should be devastated and laid solitary to the farthest extent. This is the true test of valor." If successful, the king could then mate with sovereignty.

The underlying theme was vanity. All the classical reporters, Greek and Roman, who studied the Celtic Gauls in the first and second centuries A.D. noted with wonder their habitually boastful, preening, and bombastic personalities. Beauty of threat, beauty of body, and beauty of sword stroke clearly carried the field. No wonder the emphasis on disfigurement. Blind men could not be leaders, insults were enough to raise a blister on your face, the perfect king satisfied his kingdom (always feminine) by making love to her. Celtic coronations were profoundly sexual. In some primitive rites, sovereigns mated with cattle or horses, surrogates for sovereignty, in front of the gathered tribe. In

The Turoe Stone

others great phallic totems such as Tara's *Lia Fáil*, the penis of Fergus, played some part in his initiation. Nearby to Rathgorgin is the Turoe Stone, standing on the lawn of a farm once owned by a Dolphin, in fact, which, to judge from its shape, likely played a similar role out here in Connaught.

This ostentation greatly favored the invading Norman, for its effects on the battlefield were disastrous to the Irish. Celtic warriors disdained death, "regarding their lives as naught," and often behaved with such reckless abandon during combat that many observers felt they had taken leave of their senses. Easily worked up and gathered together for a hosting, egged on by the stirring old stories of bard and *fili*, protected first by druidic spells and then by relics of the saints, and, finally, taunted by their women, Irish warriors rushed off to battle pell-mell. They wore no armor and thus were extraordinarily nimble, a bonus in Ireland's boggy terrain, but out in the open in the face of arrows and mounted horsemen they were little match. They carried swords, axes, short spears, and slingshots. If two bands of warring Celts met in a field, they would simply clash together in a confused melee, victory achieved when one side broke. Tactics did not exist. Great terror fell to any army that ran away in disorder, as the Irish were fearsome in pursuit, being natural scavengers. But superior technology or any stratagem that proved novel and frightening in either sight or sound was more than sufficient to dissolve them utterly into a witless rabble, for behind the facade of bold and prodigious bravery ran a streak of melancholic foreboding. They were easily disenchanted in a hard fight and could flee suddenly in many directions at the greatest speed imaginable. Unlike Viking or Saxon warriors, the notion of a last stand for its own sake was foreign and appalling to the Celts. They always ran first, to annoy and pester again some other day.

Unfortunately for their many and separate struggles with the earliest Norman adversaries, the Irish also proved incapable of change, not surprising for a rigid society that had followed the same timeless path for centuries. They fought as they had since well before the time of Christ, with enormous impetuosity, lack of foresight, and ignorance. Norman techniques were straightforward. The Irish, over time, realized what was happening but still could never exercise the patience required to sift through options for an effective response. When they stripped the bodies of their Norman enemies on the battlefield, they took swords, daggers, and spears as spoils, but they left the chain mail and armored pieces to rust away, deeming them the badge of cowardice instead of the martial advance they represented. It took generations for the Irish to catch on. Their society looked back in time, never forward. In the end intermarriage did more to blunt the Normans than battlefield heroics by their opponents.

This is not to say the Normans were invincible. They were checked, beaten back, often annihilated by the Irish on many occasions, despite their superiority in arms and military skills. Yet they did possess inflexible willpower and a formidable greed that proved beyond the understanding of even the normal Irishman, who ordinarily was the equal of anyone in the medieval world for covetousness. The Irish loved plunder; they adored gold and precious stones, particularly if they had once been the property of someone else. What they did not comprehend was the Norman passion for land. When the Irish won a field of battle, they scavenged for booty, collected the heads of their fallen foe, and turned back for home singing songs of victory. When the Normans took to battle and emerged on top, they did not leave for anywhere but stayed. A Norman motte is the mark of conquest.

You can see the motte here at Rathgorgin from the road, but only with effort. It is not the sort of feature in a landscape that startles one by its presence, nor does it kindle emotions of King Arthur or heraldic banners. A Norman motte is simply an elevated mound of dirt surrounded by a ditch. In many English sites, and some Irish, a catwalk connected the motte with another mound, lower but also elevated, encircled by another ditch, usually dry but sometimes flooded by adjoining streams. This lower mound was called a bailey. Both were probably surrounded by a palisade. The bailey, often of considerable size, contained sheds or lean-tos and was meant for livestock, farmworkers, and retainers. It was also the first line of defense. The steep wicker stairway up to the higher motte where the baron and his closest knights lived had a gap in it, traversed by a moveable insert that could be pulled behind at night or during an attack, hence the term "drawbridge." Both the motte and bailey were susceptible to fire, and during any prolonged siege the attacker would probably deduce, after a while, that flaming arrows shot into these enclosures would eventually flush its defenders out to open field. But "siege" implies patience; it suggests the will to possess something fought for. The Celts had neither. When they took a motte and bailey, they destroyed them. The notion of living inside something enclosed was distasteful to them.

In rainy weather one cannot walk these fields without rubber boots or waders. I certainly have rarely seen this place dry to the foot. The ground is low, liable to floods, marshy, and often submerged in mire, all of which encouraged the Normans to site their stronghold here. The motte itself is about 15 feet high, and like its neighbor, the old rath, it measures internally about 50 feet in diameter. The bailey is harder to figure, but dimensions taken at the turn of the nineteenth century by a local antiquarian gave it at 134 feet long by 50 wide, narrowing down to a width of 33 feet at its farthest edge. The owner of this field greeted me here one day with the information that it was 3,000 years old. A more likely date is about 1232, when the *Annals of Lough Cé* report that Norman barons were building castles here against the men of Connaught.

MOYODE, OVER PAM'S HEAD

I next saw Moyode in 1971. Although money had changed hands between myself and Thomas Uniacke, I had no title to the place nor legal right to begin any work. Even so, I thought a few housekeeping chores were called for, in the process of which I met my immediate neighbors.

Seamus Taylor, for instance, helped me block up the main staircase of the castle with a neat little dry wall of Galway limestone, to keep inquisitive cattle from climbing to the top, as they were alleged to desire. Before my biyearly expeditions to Ireland, he and his wife, Nancy, lived at the Georgian gatehouse that one passed when entering the demesne (three still stand). They had pulled the usual Irish maneuver of building a new house for themselves immediately adjacent the old and letting the latter cave in and generally decompose in a mass of vegetation. This has always surprised my sense of aesthetics—why live next to a ruin? "You're a fine one to ask me that," Nancy once said, "You being the prince of ruins."

Jerry Harty, down the road a few hundred feet, solved the dilemma with a curious sort of logic. He built himself a very fine house right in front of his older one, then decided he wouldn't move the few yards over. His wife refused to join this sudden nostalgia for the ancient hearth, however, reasoning that new is better than decrepit, and crossed the marital divide. Now the Hartys have two fine homes, each with a warming fire in the kitchen to welcome visitors.

The Harty clan, I came to realize, were thickly settled in Moyode. Gerald Harty owned the large house I looked over to from the top of the castle, located right next to the former Persse mansion, Moyode House. His farm of 100 acres is the closest to me, and it was his door that proved my immediate destination—and still does, now that his son Alphonsus has inherited the place—whenever things went wrong or I had to borrow something. In 1971 I decided to test the draw of my enormous medieval fireplace, building a quaint fire of neat wood chips and peat, all provided by a bemused Gerald Harty. In about five minutes, with smoke going everywhere but up the chimney, I ascertained that Moyode's ancient flue was blocked, and further poking around revealed the cause: several thousand generations of densely settled crow debris and nesting material. Figuring that the base of this mass was probably dry, I ignited it in the expectation that the resulting inferno would clear the chimney, quite a ludicrous expectation as things turned out.

"You have to understand the weather over here," Gerald Harty said later. "It's a wet land. Nothing ever dries. You could build a bonfire in there, and the upper 30 feet would never spark." The castle billowed dank, odoriferous smoke for a solid, smoldering day. Out of every crack, every crevice, up through the open roof—everywhere but the chimney—clouds of black swirled to the heavens, a veritable recreation of some page in Moyode's no doubt disaster-filled history.

The next week I asked Gerald what to do, and he went out to his shed and gave me a chimney sweep kit left over from Dickens's day, a rickety collection of twisted and bent 3-foot sticks that you screwed together piece by piece and shoved down the flue—or in my case, up the flue, as it was too dangerous a proposition to lean a ladder against that fragile protrusion 50 feet from the ground.

Standing there in the castle's old fireplace, I extended the brush almost 30 feet, pushing, pulling, heaving, cajoling that tangled and by now sooty mass of bird dung and twigs to break free. When it did, bit by little bit, it fell on my head or down my shirt neck and sleeves, into my pockets and even my socks. No more bedraggled figure had ever been seen by day's end. I begged Gerald to let me have a bath. "Well now, I'm sorry Jim. We have no indoor plumbing yet, but you're welcome to the pump outside."

On my next visit to Moyode, the crows had neatly plugged the chimney yet again. I left them undisturbed then, and for the next twenty-three years. In 1994 I asked Alphonsus Harty the same question as before: What was I to do about the crows? He went out to his shed and pulled out the same relic his father had. "Spot on, Jim, and good luck to ye!"

In the ruins of old Moyode House lived the Brodericks, Patrick and Bridget, with three of their children, a brood of grandkids, and various other relations. Patrick and his wife were old even then, and although I stood there many times listening to their talk about the Persses and grand living at Moyode, I never understood a word they said. I grew to know instead Mick and Frank, two of their sons. Frank took a weekly check from the forestry department most of his adult life, felling scrawny pine with ax and saw, hauling them out by horse. "I'm only a lodger here," he said once, pointing to his parent's house, formerly the dairy, "and I own only three things in this world: the clothing on me back, my wristwatch, and this old bike. But you know, Jim, we have an expression here in Ireland, 'I'm as happy as Larry.' And so I am."

Mick, the eldest son, was in his fifties and presented a more elusive figure. No one was, or for that matter is, quite certain what he did for a living, beyond the general consensus that it seemed to involve the barter of horseflesh. Mick fell out of the cradle with that uniquely Irish virtue, the appreciation and knowledge of handling horses. When the late John Huston lived near here on his Georgian estate of St. Clerans (replete with its own tower house, I must add) Mick had a job there in the stables, and often went to France when Huston shipped his horses there to hunt ("A queer country, that place"). Other than this, I never heard of any steady employment that Mick ever had. He deals in a few sheep now and again, but more often I saw him earn a few shillings at weddings and country fairs with his sidecar, giving rides.

Sidecars are pretty much a thing of the past in Ireland, but Mick has driven one all these years. In his wallet he must have the dog-eared photos of a dozen brides and grooms, all of whom he had driven to the altar, usually dressed in a top hat and various pieces of a morning suit he held in reserve for just such formal occasions. His horse, Pam, usually had her mane braided as well.

Mick greeted me one morning early on in our friendship as he was hitching Pam to her ancient harness. "Ye be home again, Jim."

"Yes I am, Mick."

"And how was the weather out there in America?"

"Hot this summer, Mick, very hot."

"We'll take that out of ye, never fear. Are you up for a spin then?"

"Indeed I am, Mick. Where to?"

"I'm in a roaming mood. I'll show you Moyode."

For the next three hours I enjoyed the Galway of a century ago, along the back lanes and narrow roads that few if any automobiles ventured along those twenty-some years ago. Stretches of field that I had never noticed, buildings and artifacts that had been just a blur when I might drive by, stood out in clear detail at the leisured pace of Pam and her master. Unlike many theatrical Irishmen that I know, Mick is not a talker, and for the most part our progress was marked solely by Pam's shoes clicking along over the road.

"She's a fine mare," I said indulgently, knowing nothing of horses.

"Not going on so bad now, not so bad," Mick replied. He told me she might fetch a good price, as she was only nine years old. Later I found out that Pam was over twenty.

We stopped, inevitably, at several pubs along the way. Mick disdained porter, being what the Irish call an "upper-shelf" drinker,

Mick Broderick and sidecar, c. 1958

whiskey with a dollop of port wine being his preferred poison. At the end of day, I tried to slip Mick a few pounds, but he wouldn't take them, ruining another stereotype of the Irish, their greed for money.

"I'm not surprised Mick wouldn't pocket the fiver," a friend said later. "He took you out for the honor of it. He enjoyed the fact ye had a grand time."

"FOREIGNERS IN ONE MASS OF IRON"

Of what character were the Normans, these "heroes," as the Irish annals called them, dressed in gray? Again, it would be best to put out of mind the preconceptions we may have gleaned from years of Sir Walter Scott and, more pernicious, the glorious images of cinema. The Normans may have been dukes, earls, and barons, but their lineage was hardly royal. A Viking outlaw known to history as Rolf the Ganger, along with a group of other berserkers and renegades, having exhausted the potential for continued terror and spoliation along the coastline of Ireland, rowed up the Loire as far as Chartres in the year 911. There they joined battle with the Franks and were defeated, though they left the field intact, thereby maintaining themselves as a threat to order, agriculture, progress, and the peaceful worship of God and king. We next hear of Rolf in the vicinity of Rouen, where, either through treaty or bribe, he had been baptized a Christian and recognized as vassal to the Emperor Charles III. This was a classic solution for the French, to place barbarians on their farthest border, denying other freebooters entry to the interior. Over time Rolf and his descendants consolidated, then expanded their holdings to approximate territories we associate with today's province of Normandy.

The process was not, in many ways, a pleasant spectacle. Rolf, on the counsel of his religious advisers, no doubt, made arrangements that mass be sung perpetually for the safety and repose of his soul, but when the day of his death finally arrived he ordered 100 Christian slaves massacred to appease his Nordic gods of war. As far as the exasperated monks of Rouen were concerned, the progeny Rolf left behind were no better than their father, simply a collection of unregenerate pirates.

Out of this stock sprang, most famously, William the Conqueror, who was born in 1027, over a century after Rolf's defeat at Chartres. The Vikings were by then thoroughly Gallicized. They spoke French, had put away their pagan trappings, and adopted to some degree the political persuasions and habits of their neighbors, particularly the King of Île de France, to whom they continued at least in nominal vassalship. But something in their makeup, something in their gene pool or psychological profile, made them different. There is no other way to explain the impact they made on Europe during the eleventh and twelfth centuries.

On the most obvious level, they gave up the primary weapon of their ancestors. Whereas the Irish found in the Viking battle-ax a tool for gore much to their liking, the Normans turned instead to the horse. The use of cavalry in warfare was certainly nothing new in the year 1000, but the Vikings, old sea dogs, had had little experience with horses either in Scandinavia or the countries they seasonally raided and sometimes settled. Viking strategy had always been wrapped up with long ships and rivers, quick strikes then a retreat to a fortified camp or out to sea. They might spy an occasional scrawny nag now and again, carrying a local chieftain and perhaps a few of his men, responding to their latest depravation, but those opponents would dismount before engaging in hand-to-hand combat. When the Vikings settled in Normandy, however, it was the chase, I think, that began their affair with horseflesh.

It would be difficult to overestimate the love affair medieval man had with stalking, flushing, pursuing, and then killing wild game. William the Conqueror, it is said, cared more for beasts of prey than he did for his children. The hunt, as old as time, became a faster game with horses, which enabled men to keep up with their hounds, most particularly as virgin forests diminished through the decades of the 1000s and the chase took to crossing at high speeds the open fields that were springing up between stands of wood.

The chase hardened these men, especially those of the warrior class who found themselves supported by the emerging system of feudal obligations whereby all their material needs were supplied by villeins and serfs. In wintertime they could be found out on the hunt every day of the week, usually mounted. The results were a people superbly attuned to the skills of horsemanship and the agile use of weaponry, particularly spears, while on the move. Technological innovations, refined repeatedly, such as stirrups and saddle accoutrements, provided even more leverage for the horseman, allowing him to deliver sword strokes more powerfully and to utilize his spear for thrusting as opposed to throwing. The famous kite-shaped shield was also developed as a function of purely mounted defense, and soon the shirt of iron mail ringlets began to cover the more exposed portions of a warrior's body, his arms and legs. To the usual conical helmet of the times, Normans added a nose bar, to protect their faces from the longer bills and pikes that enemies began using to unseat them. From the master of chase, the Norman emerged as master of war.

The horse that carried him about evolved as well, becoming a tougher, weightier animal, pampered by its newer status. Bloodlined horses, unlike oxen or ordinary cattle, were exempted from the mundane realities of farm chores and plowing. They found themselves removed from the system, taken out of their agricultural context, to become the prerequisites of the nobler classes. No longer were they animals that suffered through a winter, losing body fat and tone, awaiting spring's grazing to replenish their strength. All the resources of the land were put before them. Peasants went hungry, but seldom the warhorse, fattened up and bred for heavy lifting as men ladened themselves with new, costly, and more burdensome armaments.

All of this required land. A warrior in Normandy, as elsewhere in France, was nothing without it. The feudal arrangements of tenure and service to king were by this time well-formulated principles. The Roman example of centralized empire had dissolved to a dream, its remnant to the average man perhaps some figment of an ostentatious title appropriated by the local despot. An Irish king of Connaught could even do that, styling himself "the Augustus of the West of Europe." But these semibarbarian societies of mainland France had lost sight of everything else. They hardly had roads, cities, commerce, coinage, or even the remotest idea of where they were. Land and security were the two assets most firmly desired. Feudalism tied the two together.

At first the equation was simple. For lack of an emperor and Roman senate, to say nothing of a provincial governor, men sought protection together around anyone strong enough to secure their local holdings from brigandage or subjugation. In times of alarm, this petty warrior could call his people together to join him for battle and would conduct a foreign policy of sorts with neighboring strongmen by offering alliance and the promise of mutual help. Through greed or treachery or simply more men, one of these associated powers would bend the wills of the rest to him. Petty kingdoms have developed in just such a fashion since the beginning of time.

In the absence of coin or treasure, the commodity of value became land. A small-time king, through his sword, held the land in his own name but parceled it away to his closest supporters, who peopled the grants, farmed them, and lived off whatever crops they generated. In return they offered the lord service in times of war and, later, a percentage of their yield. This local noble lived but little better than his workers with one exception: He would rarely starve. His barn would be full, or at least fuller, than those of the serfs who toiled for him. Because he no longer tilled the soil himself in order to survive, he could give himself over to the pleasures of idleness, the hunt, and war.

Men are rarely satisfied when it comes to power. Kings want more lands, more subjects, more authority. As little islands of sovereignty develop, they seek to spread out, usually in the direction of people who want nothing to do with them. To the borders kings sent their more aggressive henchmen with these instructions: Keep the neighbor out, harry him, go into his domain should you see the chance, expand. Charlemagne called such areas "the marches," and each baron he sent to run one became a *Markgraf*, or count of the march. Far from the center of things, out of the immediate control of his king, the marcher lord could suffer delusions of grandeur. He could become a rebellious sore point, ill disposed to pay heed to royal summons. He was winning the new lands, after all, why should they belong to the king?

As Normandy and the other provincial kingdoms of today's France and Belgium—Flanders, Brittany, Anjou, Poitou, Maine, Aquitaine—emerged as political entities at the turn of the millennium, many kings or local magnates sought to tighten their control. Primogeniture was a logical result. The Frankish kings in particular had seen that a multiplicity of semilegal wives with their assorted "royal" progeny proved a danger to their single source of wealth, the land. They sought to curb divided legacies by regularizing succession to one heir, customarily the eldest son. But if that son did not have an arm of steel, he was destined for a short and tragic career. Feudalism favored the local point of view. Men's loyalties were generally directed to the sword they feared the most, and that was usually the one they saw every day, the local lord's. This is one reason contemporary annals mention so many traveling courts. Kings had to be seen as much as possible, especially by restive barons. Otherwise the latter grew insolent. Even so, in 1150 the Count de Champagne delivered to his lord, the king, ten knights for service. He had at his disposal, through feudal obligations within his own domain, 2,300 knights but deemed the ten sufficient.

At the time of William the Conqueror's coming of age in 1047, the Norman duchy was a kingdom of modest dimension. It spread from east to west, from Eu to Mont-Saint-Michel, for a distance of only 200 miles, and nowhere in that span was its southern border more than 70 miles distant from the sea. Physically and politically it resembled, in many respects, the kingdoms of its neighbors. They, however, were not Normans.

What made the Normans different? Certainly they were deemed "different" by those who came into contact with them, whether French speaking or not. Most societies were martial at the time, dominated by violence, greed, flowing blood. What was it about the Normans that made them stand apart from the Bretons or Flemings or

A Norman knight, c. 1066

Lombards? Anna Comnena, a Byzantine princess whose family suffered mightily from the Normans, said very simply that it was their "untamable temper." Around their persons, as she wrote in her historical memoir, there seemed always to be "a general air of the horrible."

The Normans of the eleventh century were by and large illiterate savages. There is nothing in the historical record to make us think otherwise, no glimmer of romance or chivalric notions that might justify a flattering portrait. They were venal, treacherous barbarians who lived little better than wild beasts in their gloomy, smoke-ridden hovels. They were merciless in battle, their natural pursuit, and rarely magnanimous in victory. Towns or strongholds taken could expect the most brutal treatment; Normans routinely slaughtered women and children, often after torturing them. They butchered prisoners taken on the field if they were worthless as ransom, taking them apart limb by limb until the knights grew too fatigued with their bloody sport. Count Roger of Sicily, deviously seizing his father-in-law over some long-forgotten dispute, pulled his teeth out over time, then personally gouged out his eyes before dispatching the wretch with a sword. William the Conqueror, when he "harried" the north of England following rebellion in 1069, killed every male creature he came across and destroyed all in his path. The Domesday Book, a tabulation of the entire conquest, put £73,000 as the annual income of William's newly conquered kingdom. Yorkshire and Lancaster were good for a paltry £1,200 after the Conqueror was finished with them, and they took a generation to recover.

Some very few of the Normans found their way into service to the Church; fewer still of these were able to read or write. Many were simply warriors in cleric's robes who, whenever their ill moods overcame what modest powers of reasoning they possessed, hardly hesitated to kill recalcitrant monks of their own order, sometimes at the foot of the very altar "so that blood ran down the steps of the sanctuary."

Of the very same implacable nature came as well their undaunted bravery. No one, not even their bitterest foes, ever faulted the Normans on this count, and history is too full of legendary examples to single any out for particular note. Instead, I am reminded of one inconsequential episode involving the minor knight John Marshal, father of the infinitely more famous William Marshal, earl of Pembroke and lord of Leinster, the truest "flower of chivalry."

John, a crude and boorish thug of little conscience, had played near the center of conflict between Stephen of Boulogne and the Plantagenet factions during the civil wars that began in England in 1138. In one particularly desperate episode of those tumultuous times, Marshal found himself protecting, in flight, the Plantagenet queen Matilda. Riding sidesaddle, Matilda hindered the retreat. Grabbing her bridle, Marshal yelled to her, "By the love of Christ, Madame, either ride like a man or we are lost!" Helping her remount, he sent the fleeing party along. Then, standing with one companion, Marshal defended the road. Driven back by the pressing enemy, the two barricaded themselves in a nearby church. The sanctuary was set afire and began falling in. Lead sheathing from the roof melted, splattering the knights with molten metal. One glob burned out Marshal's eye. His companion suggested surrender. Marshal, turning his empty, bleeding, smoldering socket on the wretch, threatened to kill him instead. They stayed in the conflagration until the building collapsed around them. Their enemies, thinking them dead, left the scene. Three days later, John Marshal was recorded in another fight.

No matter the odds, Normans did not hesitate to charge forward—*Boutez en avant!* as the war cry of the Norman de Barry family had it—Keep pushing forward! What differentiated them from opponents like the Irish, however, was their ability to think and fight at the same time. They always had a feeling for terrain, both the physical and mental. They had it in their minds to manipulate their foe, whether by strategy or deceit, into a position where the peculiar strengths of Norman character could be applied. In battle, this usually meant open fields where their horsemen could maneuver and charge; in negotiation, it entailed a diplomatic persuasiveness that would lead opponents to a parlay, which often resulted in villainous betrayals. For Norman courage extended to treachery. Many men quail from murder. The Normans never gave it a thought. Peter de Bermingham invited twenty-four Irish chieftains to his castle at Carbury in County Kildare, 1305. By the end of that festive occasion, all had been slaughtered at the dinner table. Bermingham himself took one young son of the O'Carrol and flung him over the battlements of his castle to the ground below. This little boy was his godson. Bermingham boasted of the deed to his dying day.

In the final reckoning, what seemed most dangerous about the Normans was their unremitting determination. A rebuke on the battlefield was merely an excuse to attack again; a whole campaign in shambles was but encouragement to plan another. Anna Comnena saw this trait as a cancer, "an incredible sore and incurable disease." The Normans never went away; they did not allow for obstacles.

This accounts in large measure for the wild extravagance of so many Norman expeditions. Nothing was too far-fetched for them, no goal so absurd as to be unthinkable. William the Conqueror's expedition to England, though full of nerve, peril, and desperation, is pallid in comparison to Norman adventures in southern Italy, Sicily, and Antioch, and in particular to the at times fantastical careers of Robert Guiscard and his son, Bohemund. These warriors of "insignificant origin" were to style themselves the duke of Apulia and Calabria and the prince of Antioch, respectively. These titles alone indicate the breadth of their activities, though not the treks, skirmishes, assassinations, naval engagements, sieges, famines, hostings, negotiations, marriages, traps, rapes, excommunications, and plots that all of these entailed. When they marched together, father and son, Anna Comnena called Bohemund "the pungent smoke that precedes the fire."

Controlling these men was the major headache of their overlords. William the Conqueror was said by one Master Wace in his *Chronicle* to have thought that Normans "must be bent and bowed to their ruler's will; and whoso holds them always under his foot, and curbs them tightly, may get his business well done by them. Haughty they are and proud, boastful and arrogant, difficult to govern, and requiring to be at all times kept under." This was a lesson the kings of Normandy and England were to heed. All Normans seemed to have the character of marcher lords. They were too wild for bridling.

Because the Normans were barely rational at times does not mean they were stupid. Unrestrained they could be, blind with greed or rage they often were, but their powers of common sense proved formidable. They were a very concrete kind of people who would formulate goals and then pursue them unwaveringly. In the military sphere, they were great colonizers. They knew how to take land and to hold it. In the political arena, they could organize all levels of societal interaction to a point where they were the primary beneficiaries.

Their manipulation of the Church, courts of justice, manorial contracts and charters, papal legations, and the royal court itself all reveal what amounts to a single-minded pursuit of order and reward. They marked every transaction with stone reminders of their authority: Their castles and cathedrals symbolized for everyone fear and power. Their kings and leaders were rough men, but they were not arbitrarily egregious. Most of their maneuvers, however ugly or morally misshapen, had a point to them.

Nowhere is this more evident in their lives than the sphere of religion. Even Roger Guiscard believed in God, or at least Dante thought so. He is certainly recorded as attending all-night vigils before a full day's battle ahead, a physical feat of some note. Many writers, chief among them the distinguished historian David Douglas, have made much of the "contrasted emotions" of these times, perhaps best expressed by the Norman Crusade of 1099, where butchery and piety shared the same sword. This expedition is interesting on several counts, the first being the Church's explicit sanction of war, a notion quite alien to Jesus and the Apostolic theology of primitive Christianity. Even St. Augustine, threatened by Vandals, found the notion of holy war somewhat indigestible. But the papacy had reasons for blessing the Crusade. It was hoped that every Norman with a weapon and horse would pack his belongings and go, thereby sparing Europe, and particularly Italy, from their unwelcome enthusiasm for mayhem.

More intriguing, however, the Normans had a literal perception of life around them. God was a real being, as was Satan, and the nails that were hammered through the body of Christ were as real as the wood of the crucifix, the legionnaire's lance, the divine blood that poured into a precious chalice. The love and veneration for relics that could deliver heaven to their hands was indeed very strong. It offered the balance they needed to offset the many sins that even they recognized as stains on the soul. A Norman never hesitated to kill for a relic. What seems to us a contradiction was for them a brute fact, just as storms and hurricanes were seen as devils in flight, with the following calm God's cooling and blessed hand.

Fierce and savage Normans at the height of their powers could walk away from ambition and power without a word of explanation. One moment William's father, Duke Robert I, was busy purging his rivals and clawing about for his dukedom. The next he simply set out for Jerusalem on pilgrimage, casting his hard-earned spoils to anarchy and nothingness. Kings, dukes, barons, knights—they clogged the dangerous paths to the Holy Land. They saw their self-interest at stake, many times joining the two strands by becoming Templars, celibate monks dedicated to the carnage of war. Many other old warriors simply saw light at the end, joining monasteries or abbeys they had endowed as a pledge against the devil in the bloody prime of their careers. Satan was loose upon the land. The practical Normans realized this was someone even they should fear.

EARLY FRIENDS AND NEIGHBORS, NOW DEAD

There is no use in denying that at twenty-three years of age, at the time of my purchasing Moyode, I was a hopelessly muddled romantic, given to wearing capes with Celtic crosses stitched on the back and hiding portable cassette players in any of the various cavities of the castle wall, from which Gregorian chants could lend a properly medieval background to my readings in Tennyson's largely foolish *Idylls of the King*. The capes are long gone, and the hurly-burly of having young children has diminished my dependence on music.

Disappearing too have been overheated fantasies of Moyode as a point of departure for uncovering what Norman Mailer called the "unendurable Grail" of life's meaning. The place has a different context for me now, no longer the abode of a chivalrous Sir Gawain but more likely a glorified cattle station housing a nondescript collection of herders and armed landlords, most of whom were illiterate, bug infested, and hopelessly dirty. My promise to prospective visitors, who generally become unglued at the word "castle," is that the experience I plan to offer them some day will be a truly Norman one—come to Moyode and live like a pig.

Other things have changed over the years as well, no surprises here. Old friends die off, and the countryside, in the words of a neighbor, grows lonesome. My old friend Bob Brown, an expatriate from Manhattan who had purchased Ballyportry Castle in County Clare for £250 back in 1960, ended up in a nursing home somewhere in Limerick with incurable lung cancer. Ballyportry, an immense tower house with several grand halls and multiple staircases, had been an inspiration to me of all the possibilities that good taste, deep affection, and generous infusion of cash could do for an old stone building, but more valuably it served as a restraint. When the wild Atlantic winds drove ocean moisture right through the semiporous limestone walls and shorted out every electrical connection in the place, I decided against wiring Moyode. As Bob doled out hundreds of pounds for precious oak beams and flooring, I decided the cheap Irish pine known as deal was good enough for me. The day Bob reported that his boiler had arrived—"the size of a Fifth Avenue bus"—I began looking through my *Whole Earth Catalogue* for coal stoves. As I was taking a luxurious bath in Bob's immense tub (formerly a stone cattle trough) a group of uninvited tourists burst right in off the road to inspect the castle lavatory. I concluded that plumbing had unintended consequences and could be dispensed with.

Some cultural accoutrements I learned to avoid as well. Bob's baronial Great Danes developed an unhealthy appetite for sheep, causing acrimony among his neighbors. At that point, I abandoned my adolescent craving for an Irish wolfhound. I absorbed as well a lesson not to involve myself, as the "rich American," in petty village gossip or disputes. There were two pubs in Bob's locale where he was no longer welcome, an unusual ban for the reputedly avaricious Irish to impose.

Poor Cathy Cahill, who lived in the tumble-down cottage next to Bob, also died in miserable and lonely fashion. Cathy, a wizened spinster doomed to the traditional Irish martyrdom of caring for a large brood of unmarried brothers on the family farm, was a font of wit and wisdom (as well as a marvelous cook). I can recall countless occasions when, coming in through her open door wet and hungry, I found Cathy baking bread in the open hearth, carefully tending the peat fire and placing embers on the top of her old black pot to give the bread "an even bake." What a feast, with tea and her own concoction of jams and jellies, the conversation flooded with profluent gems of varied folkloric value. ("If you want to live and thrive, let the spider run alive," she once said, chasing one on her hands and knees to capture and release it outside.)

And then old Stokes, a farm laborer, sitting against the wall outside in the sun with two spindly canes, muttering about a life from the 1930s now all but forgotten. He too, like the times he lived through, is dead and gone.

My very oldest Irish friend, Penelope Preston, was run over and killed in the aptly named Donnybrook section of Dublin as she was leaving daily mass. "At least we know she was in a state of grace," her nephew said.

"She was in it anyway," I remember bitterly replying.

Pops, as she was familiarly called, was of a different breed than my Celtic neighbors, being of impeccable Anglo-Irish stock, though, like them, impoverished. She had run a genteel boarding house on Leeson Street for years, and my parents had stayed there whenever they passed through Dublin. Afternoon tea—itself a practice in decline—was a cornucopia of cakes and sweets presided over by Pops's indomitable mother, who disguised the family's wretched circumstances by continually stressing its social prominence. "Not just blue bloods, you know—holy blood runs through our veins!" The Prestons, of course, had sufficient cachet to overwhelm my mother. The minute she heard of Penelope's own ancestral castle, Gormanston in County Meath (from which they had long ago been evicted), and the legend that whenever the head of the family lay on his deathbed, the foxes of Gormanston came out and barked, she turned to putty and proved an easy mark for the Prestons as they sold off their silver and plate to remain solvent. I have to this day the Preston teapot.

One year in the early 1980s, when I was "in residence" at Moyode, camping in my old Citroën out on the great field, Pops paid a visit with her cousins and a local priest. A fervent Catholic and deeply superstitious—she had once seen Satan after a concert at the Georgian mansion of Castletown outside of Dublin, recognizing him by his cloven feet—Pops had an undeniably spiritual touch. She was, for example, a famous diviner, often called upon to locate the proper site for prospective wells. I noted her feeling for Moyode in my journal:

> The priest remarked that a house that's lived in has a spirit or a life force that evaporates immediately when and if it's deserted. "This place here now, it's dead. There's no life or any hope of it to these old stones." Pops begged to differ, something I have never seen her do with a clergyman.
>
> "Not so, Father," she said, patting the old keep. "I can feel this place vibrate. It's choking with life. It has a story that would flood us if it could."

I recall having dinner that evening with Pops and her relatives, who had a seaside cottage overlooking Clew Bay in County Mayo. Pops's intuitive appreciation for Moyode should have moved me more, and I wondered why it hadn't. I came to some sort of awakening that night that partially explained it for me: I had grown up. I was already a decade and more removed from the banter of her young nephews and nieces, all university students in London and outraged over censorship in Turkey ("Can you believe it? Plato's *Republic* has just been banned!"). I remember being more interested in the poached salmon.

Inevitably during my comings and goings to Moyode I noted other changes besides those listed in the obituary columns of our local newspaper. For one, area farmers were getting used to me. When I camped in their fields at night, they seldom rushed out to see whose headlights were illuminating the dumbstruck faces of their cattle. Gerald Harty had once accosted me in the middle of the pitch dark as I was setting up my tent, suspicious of foul play in the demesne. But thereafter he told me to come into his house anytime I wished to warm up or have a cup of tea, which of course I did over the years.

I witnessed as well the diminution of both the Catholic religion and Guinness stout, which seem utterly unrelated pieces of business, though insiders used to think of them both as the glue that kept everything together. The new mass was bitterly resented, especially by the older generation, who considered what was going on up at the altar a succession of Protestant-style "pranks." "To go to mass on a Saturday, it feels all queer to me," said one old man. "And the Friday fast, we never broke it yet!"

Penelope, predictably, had been horrified and disconsolate. "I feel sorry for Protestants," she said to me in 1984. "We have the divine presence, and they have nothing." But the ecumenical mass, in her opinion, diluted the mystical experience and made the entire ceremony High Anglican, meaning "fun, but not disciplined or important." Perhaps she died at the right time.

"I can remember when the mission priests used to come here," a neighbor told me. "They used to shake their fists at us till we'd be shaking in our pews, and yet there'd be no question of ever answering back to a priest, I can tell you. But the young people now, they'd never take that. They'd get right up and walk out. The God of wrath doesn't appeal to them, if you get my meaning. They're all into the new God, the God of love and all. And if the heat in church isn't on, holy Christ in heaven, they won't come in at all. It's a disgrace to the memory and torment of Old Ireland!"

As is the state of Guinness. As far back as the 1970s, many aficionados have noted the transformation of this storied drink. "It used to be you could tell the difference between various batches," said a barkeep in Athenry, "and the head, it came out so thick you'd think it was mother's milk. But as Ireland modernized and people started getting fridges, you could see the Guinness people trying to standardize their porter, preparing people to refrigerate it and drink it at colder temperatures, which of course kills the taste." I agreed with his assessment, adding my own impressions that Guinness seemed thinner these days, more watery. "Welcome to the new Ireland," he replied. "At least 'Guinness Lite' was a fiasco."

INVASION, 1169

Our spontaneous reaction to two dates of some historical significance reveals, I think, the degree of importance the wider world has attached to each—1066 and 1169. The former, of course, every schoolchild in the English-speaking world will recognize as the Battle of

Hastings and William's conquest of England. The latter is the year when Robert FitzStephen, Norman knight, along with 400 followers, first landed in Bannow Bay to begin the conquest of Ireland. It is an event that most general histories of Europe ignore, and for good reason. The enterprise was a rogue operation for the most part, of little immediate concern to anyone but the few individuals involved. Even the Irish at first paid it little mind.

I do not mean to belittle the significance of 1169, however, which in terms of my own involvement with Moyode Castle and its particular story is clearly an event of paramount interest. Rather, we should seek, in speaking of Ireland and its past, to put the matter into perspective. When William the Conqueror sailed for England in September 1066, he led an army of over 6,000 men. He was at the time already a fearsome and well-known warrior, an anointed duke whose domain on the Continent was universally acknowledged as a principality of worth, pedigree, and power. He met in battle the recognized (by the English, anyway) monarch, King Harold, whose army could be called, in all fairness, a national army as opposed to a provincial levy. When Harold died, an arrow through one eye, his cause was recognized as equally dead. Resistance to William's advance on the capital of London proved slight. When he was crowned in Westminster, even the Saxons had to acknowledge him as their lawful sovereign, and though justifiably bitter at their eventual ruin, as William rewarded himself and his followers with enormous landed grants, the native aristocracy rarely argued that any of it was not their proper due. They had not prevailed at Hastings; all that followed was their harvest.

To William, the increase in his own individual wealth and military authority was nearly beyond calculation. It has been estimated that by law and custom William had levied from his own Norman barons a feudal force of only 1,200 knights for the invasion. After the conquest, feudal obligations to the king from England alone totaled 5,000 knights. And whereas the dukedom of Normandy was smaller in size than the single county of Wessex, we can begin to understand the scale of William's newfound prosperity by noting that over 25 percent of all revenue from the newly appropriated farms and manors of England were reserved for use by the royal house. The important point to see here in relation to Irish history, however, is that William still cared more for Normandy and its affairs than he ever did for England.

William was French. His earliest career, with its well-catalogued list of horrors, reversals, flights in the night, and eventual triumph, was set against a Norman background and Norman perspective. The borders with Brittany, Maine, Blois, Île de France, and Flanders were the major points of concern, struggles with Kings Henry I and Philip I his primary causes for worry. No matter the later tangled succession whereby various of his sons ruled separately in England and Normandy, the attention of these rulers was always directed in an easterly direction. The Plantagenets who succeeded them—Henry II, Richard the Lion Heart, John—these men spoke and thought in French and were politically oriented toward the Continent, where they engaged most of their time and energy plotting or fighting. Richard, for example, after gaining his crown, passed only six months of his ten-year reign in England. John, his brother, spent more time there only because he had managed to fritter away the entire Angevin holding in France to Philip II by 1214.

In and of itself, Ireland meant little to these men. They eventually came to receive revenues from the place, of course, but these they largely squandered where their hearts lay, on continental adventures. The only aspect of this island that gripped their attention was peripheral. In Ireland wayward and difficult Norman barons played out their boundless ambitions. This was a characteristic Norman kings could recognize. They knew greed well, perhaps as a mirror to their own souls, and they feared it in their subjects. Most of the time, men like Henry II reacted to events in Ireland. When conditions warranted, the kings came, wreaked havoc or order depending on their personalities, then departed. English chronicles generally paid little attention. "King Henry crossed over to Ireland and made peace with the people there. He then returned," Florence of Worcester noted. Later he made a notation of equal importance: "All the world is afflicted with coughs and colds."

Robert FitzStephen, unlike Duke William of Normandy, was not at the height of his power and reputation when he landed in Ireland, on Bannow Island, in 1169 with a small Norman force.* As a matter of fact, departure on this Irish adventure had been a precondition for his release from a dungeon in Wales, his jailer delighted to have him

---

*The catalogue of given names in genealogical listings, whether Norman or Irish, can become extraordinarily confusing over the course of successive generations. Broadly speaking, "Fitz" and "Mac" should be read as "son of" and understood as proceeding backward in time toward a patriarch. Thus, hypothetically, Robert FitzStephen, is son of Stephen FitzRichard and grandson of Richard FitzRobert and great-grandson of Robert FitzWalter.

gone, hopefully to death, in a faraway land. After three years of imprisonment, Robert was a man without options, hope, or expectations. He had nothing to lose. He went as a hired sword.

His boon companions, the thirty or so knights who accompanied him, were family, dependents, and friends. They were all Normans of the rough, frontier variety. Sixty more of their number were men of sufficient means to afford a horse and some armament. Together, this meant a mounted force of about ninety. The remaining 300 or so were archers and footmen. Included in the band was a spy, Hervey de Montmorency, "a man of fallen fortunes, having neither armor nor money," according to a contemporary. He was the uncle of another ruined Norman, Richard FitzGilbert de Clare, known to us today as Strongbow.

STRONGBOW

The very name "Strongbow" is enough to lure many of us down the path to romantic ruin, but unfortunately for this man's checkered career, too often reality intrudes to cloud our picture. Even his grave is suspect, an effigy pointed out for decades in the nave of Christ Church Cathedral in Dublin but now clearly identified as that of some other baron. Was Strongbow a warrior of fabled strength, equal to his name? Apparently not. Contemporaries marked him as a stolid individual, more diplomat than soldier, never in the van of charges but in the middle of the pack, more relied upon for durability and self-control in battle than recklessness. Even "Strongbow" is a misnomer, a nickname coined for his father and an inheritance. Worse still, his title as earl of Pembroke was suspect, a grant from King Stephen during the civil wars of 1138 to 1153. The de Clares had backed the wrong side then and paid for that mistake when Henry Plantagenet, styled the II, took the throne after Stephen's death in 1154. Welsh rebels and Henry's vindictive hand then stripped the de Clares of their vast territories in Wales. Strongbow, bitter yet fearful, brooded in his castle at Strigul, on the march of Wales, across the Severn from Gloucester.

This is exactly where Henry II wanted him. If Henry could foil his marcher barons in this fashion, he would. It amused him. The king spent all his waking moments arranging just this sort of conundrum to keep everyone in check, everyone fretful, everyone frustrated. Marriages, treaties, expeditions, letters of instruction and warning, intrigues, and drunken têtes-à-têtes were all arranged to create a balance, one that by necessity required constant tinkering to keep meaningful but that rewarded his dynasty with wealth and expanding frontiers. When he thought of Strongbow, no doubt he did so with derision.

Henry, however, was mercurial and overindulged in that divine crop for which the choicest land of his French possessions was set aside, namely, wine. He made many remarks and gave many orders in the middle of the night when he was tired or inebriated. Most of these decisions cost him nothing. Even impaired, Henry was a match for most who opposed him. But some indiscretions proved costly, as in the unfortunate affair concerning Thomas Becket, when knights misinterpreted drunken remarks by the king and murdered the archdeacon in Canterbury Cathedral. Still others were horrendous policy at first but later, through luck and an iron will, salvaged to his benefit. Such was the case of his grants in Ireland to Richard FitzGilbert de Clare.

When a petty Irish chieftain from Ireland, Dermot MacMurrough, appeared before Henry at his peripatetic court somewhere in Aquitaine in 1167, complaining and posturing that he had been wrongfully expelled from the mighty kingdom he had ruled for decades, Henry listened, smiled, drank, gave gifts, and wished Dermot luck. He also gave leave that anyone Dermot could recruit to give him aid was free to go to Ireland.

Henry had certainly never heard of Uí Cheinnselaig, Dermot's *tuath*, though he knew well of Ireland and had once given thought to its conquest. This he dismissed from his mind until Strongbow approached him for permission to proceed across the Irish Sea in Dermot's cause. It was a delicious moment for Henry. The very request was a stunning humiliation for the de Clares, an admission that for all their titles and airs the Plantagenets had ground them so far down that they were casting off to fresher fields beyond. Henry told him to go if he wanted. What difference did it make to him if the earl of Pembroke wished to travel to Leinster? Strongbow was welcome to Ireland if he could win her. This was, in a contemporary's phrase, one of Henry's little jokes.

In 1170 Strongbow embarked from St. David's Head in Wales. His feudal levy numbered almost 200 mounted Normans, with another 1,000 or so archers and foot soldiers. These men, like those who had gone before, were looking for land and plunder. Hervey de Montmorency, in communication with Strongbow about FitzStephen's so far quite credible progress, warned him to hurry. Ireland, a kingdom with great potential, lay there for the taking, and in Ireland there was no Henry Plantagenet.

In his stead there was an Irish high king to deal with, Rory O'Connor of Connaught, but any comparison of Rory with, let us say, a King Harold of England, who died one hundred years previously at Hastings, would be misleading. Rory was a provincial king to be sure, but a high king in title only. His authority was diffuse—it hardly existed in many corners of the island—and like Irish chieftains before and after he spent inordinate amounts of energy quelling family feuds and conspiracies. Rory knew how to blind sons and brothers, the first lesson of any Irish king. He knew how to go on a hosting, how to gather together his levies for punishing expeditions, how to deal with minor chieftains like Dermot MacMurrough, who clearly deserved as many chastisements as possible.

For Dermot MacMurrough was a troublesome man who came from a troublesome family. His father had been a deceitful scoundrel who suffered the supreme penalty in Dublin town, where the Vikings had seized and murdered him. To show their contempt, they had thrown a dead dog into his grave. Dermot, through treachery and the usual depravations, achieved the leadership of his clan and expanded in a modest fashion through southern Leinster. His methods were crude. He settled one dispute over ecclesiastical appointments in Kildare by burning the abbey to the ground then abducting the abbess and giving her over to the enjoyment of a follower. This indignity removed her from office in the same fashion that gouging eyes from a warrior prevented him from attaining kingship. Dermot's abduction of Dervorgilla, the wife of his detested foe O'Rourke was another sexual card he enjoyed playing. When he tired of Dervorgilla or simply treated her so abominably that she could no longer stay, the affair was tidied up and the wayward wife returned. But twelve years later, through a complicated chain of events involving Rory O'Connor, O'Rourke, and Dermot himself, the Leinster chieftain found his armies defeated, his principal rath in flames, and his fortunes tied to those of strangers from across the sea whose customs he could not fathom nor their language speak.

Dermot MacMurrough

The substance and chronology of this alliance between Dermot and Strongbow is well known in Ireland. Three contemporary sources describe it, two in some detail. A Norman *chanson de geste*, or "song of acts," was composed after Strongbow's death in 1176 on the commission, perhaps, of his widow, and this quite naturally made much of de Clare's abilities and successes. A history of the invasion was also written by a Welsh/Norman cleric, cousin to FitzStephen, which tended to feature (again not surprisingly) the exploits of his relations who had preceded the arrival of Strongbow, the Geraldines. Irish annals, though at first rather meager, fill in some information from the native perspective. From these came the rest, all in general agreement, from

Holinshed in 1578 to the poet Tom Moore's *History of Ireland*, published in 1835. They relate the advance of Norman arms into Wexford and Waterford, on through secret mountain passes known only to Dermot for a sudden descent on Dublin and its capture, to the scattering of Rory O'Connor's multitudinous levy before that city's gates in 1171. The catalogue of fighting is lengthy and impressive. Under certain circumstances, in fact any that involved novelty in tactics or formation, the Irish fled precipitously. The Normans, in these first forays, can be seen delighting in their advantage—"Our foes are naked," as one said deliriously, "Strike, barons, strike!" But the Irish, while primitive, could be pesky. Though often lured into traps whereby they were caught in open fields and run down by the heavy Norman cavalry, they proved a different foe when encountered in marshy woods or undergrowth where horsemen could not venture. The Norman on foot was a cumbersome warrior, surrounded, harried, prodded, and nicked by scampering kerns (lightly armed foot soldiers) darting in and out of cover. Powerful knights found themselves unhorsed by slingshots, then attacked by swarming scavengers eager to hack off their limbs with a few chops of an ax. The Normans continued to pursue wild charges out into the open, no matter the odds, but they came to dread their passages through the dark woods.

The traditional Norman usage of terror is also amply recorded. After one early battle, a rout of the Irish where the Normans used a herd of cattle to spearhead their charge, the barons debated what to do with their prisoners. Hervey de Montmorency, who retired to a monastery at the end of his martial career, urged brutal calculation on his comrades, and he carried the argument. Seventy captives had their limbs broken with sledges and hammers before they were thrown over cliffs to the beach and sea below. Even Dermot MacMurrough, a thorough rogue, sensed at times that matters were out of control. He arrived at Waterford town just as Strongbow breached the walls. The slaughter was so excessive he implored the Normans to stop, and with some difficulty he persuaded them.

Dermot, long vilified in Irish histories as a traitor to his country and culture, in fact had little idea as to the long-range impact of his association with Strongbow and the other barons. He regarded it as a temporary and expedient maneuver, no different from hiring Vikings from the Hebrides or Isle of Man, certainly a traditional feature in Irish warfare. Dermot had an immediate goal in mind, to seize back what he held before. The promises he made to the Normans, symbolized by the marriage between Strongbow and his daughter, meant nothing to him. Promises were there to be broken, and whatever meanings Strongbow gave to the marriage (which were feudal and thus significant to him) Dermot paid little heed. His vainglorious personality pursued typically Celtic goals: revenge and kingship. He took great pleasure in seeing the Normans slaughter his enemies. In one pile of heads taken in battle, and arranged on the field by his no doubt bemused Norman allies, Dermot recognized one of a particularly hated foe. Shrieking in delight, he grabbed the head and bit off the lips, ears, and nose. And as the Normans advanced, Dermot's ambitions kept pace. He now dreamed of becoming high king, that peculiarly evaporative title so vainly desired by countless Irish warlords. When he died "of an insufferable and unknown disease," according to the Irish annals, whereby "he became putrid while living," the dream was appropriated by Strongbow. For perhaps the first time since the invasion began, the Irish were appalled.

The true intent of the Normans became clear only after Dermot's death. The Irish expected the foreigners either to leave or to content themselves with the Viking towns they had stormed, which were valueless to the natives, who preferred open living. Dermot's designation of Strongbow as his heir, sealed by marriage, was nonsense as far as Irish custom was concerned. An Irish king did not own his territories, as William the Conqueror owned Normandy and then England. He could not physically pass them along to whomever he chose, and by no means through a woman. Dermot, in Irish law, was custodian of the land in the name of his tribe, which held it in common. When Strongbow claimed Leinster and thought to take the entire island, the Irish gagged. When Strongbow "enfeoffed," or planted the territories his men had occupied, starting first with the ubiquitous mottes and baileys, then with manors and fortified farmsteads, the Irish who were thrown off the land could not contain their rage. As the Geraldines and other Norman families pushed into Meath and Munster, the Irish fought back with more determination. In the end, ironically, they prevailed.

The Normans proved too few in number. In defeating the high king and occupying all the major towns, they had expected to see the island fall. They were in the habit of thinking that one climactic battle would win them the campaign, as Hastings had done for the Conqueror. But Rory O'Connor was not Harold of England. Rory stood

Motte and bailey

for himself and the empty title he so craved. He was by no means the king of a nation united. After Rory, as the Normans were to discover, some other king could appear, claiming an equally outrageous sovereignty, and should the Normans topple him, another would take his place. Ireland was so decentralized, so riven by tribal and dynastic dispute, that Norman victories over individual chieftains were more often than not celebrated as loudly by the Celts themselves. A vacancy in kingship gave the opportunity for succession, gleefully pursued by as many individual claimants as possible. The Irish had time on their side, and women. Strongbow's precedent in marrying an Irish princess was a custom followed up on the local scene by many a Norman knight. What the Irish could not win on the battlefield they won in bed.

Strongbow, no doubt, misunderstood this at first. Perhaps by the end of his life he no longer felt that all of Ireland could ever be his. But Leinster he had won. His henchmen began a pattern of settlement that proved stolid and enduring, however galling the interference from England, for Henry II was now worried. Strongbow had succeeded too well. Henry had heard rumors that de Clare planned to crown himself king of Ireland.

A MESSAGE IS DELIVERED

I probably know what little I know about the bloody struggle for Northern Ireland more from reading newspapers back home in Boston than from what I may have picked up in Moyode demesne during my episodic stays there since the 1970s. From Bernadette Devlin to Bobby Sands to the commotion over the "permanent" cease-fire of the Irish Republican Army (IRA) in the late 1990s, the ripples of current affairs have made but scant impression along the cow paths and overgrown lanes of this formerly great estate. Local gossip or the occasional—very occasional—outburst of violent crime certainly make my neighbors take notice. A triple murder on the slopes of nearby Slieve Aughty—a young mother, her child, and a village priest, all shot in the head by an as yet unapprehended killer—shocked the collective psyche for miles around. Yet generally speaking the greater world of Irish politics, other than taxation and farm subsidies, barely earns a mention.

This may sound like heresy to more committed observers of the Irish scene, especially those who frequent the pubs of Dublin and Cork or those near any of the national universities, where the patriotic desire for a united Ireland still flourishes. But I have rarely seen any reaction at all from my country friends here as they've witnessed, vicariously, to be sure, via their televisions, the various provocations served up by the likes of British prime minister Margaret Thatcher in the 1980s or Ian Paisley ("Fuck the pope!" as I've heard a few times over the airwaves from some of that man's cantankerous followers). "That's far removed from this little crossroads," one old friend said to me, and in an astonishing remark he continued, "You know, it would probably have been better for us farmers if Ireland had never gone independent for good and all."

It's the price of cattle and pigs, fertilizer and sheep dip that gain a rise out of this politically dispirited assemblage of families. "I had an agricultural man out here a few months ago," Alphonsus Harty related to me recently, "and he said I needn't worry about educating all three of my boys. 'The older two,' he said, 'you'll have to send them to university for the good jobs. But the third one, don't spend a shilling on him. He can be the farmer of the family.'"

Alphonsus, one of the few full-time farmers left in the neighborhood, is aghast at the agricultural prospects facing his operation, grown now to 250 acres. "You need more and more land, which is very dear, to support more and more cattle, which are even dearer, to return less real profit in the end. With dairy farmers you could make a living having forty cows in 1980. Today you'd need six times that number." This reminds me of some economics Thomas Uniacke once outlined for me. In 1969, the year I purchased Moyode, Thomas would buy a steer for £100. A decade later a three-year-old cost £450, and Thomas would hope to turn a £100 profit on the beast after fattening it for a year. A 1994 price would be £600, the hoped-for profit in a season's time being around £200. "When I was a boy," Thomas had told me, "my father could buy a bullock for 10 shillings, sell it later for a whole pound."

In the light of these provincial concerns, what locals term an economic disaster, what the IRA does in the Bogside of Belfast's Catholic slums doesn't amount to much. "We have the freedom of our religion," one old buck said to me. "One Ireland, two Irelands, three or six, I don't much care."

This is not to say the IRA and issues surrounding it are ever scoffed at, derided, or boisterously criticized. "It's best not to talk about it," is the usual advice. But late one evening in 1973, their presence was remarked upon in Moyode demesne.

Driving through the mists of a soggy rainfall, I returned to my campsite at the castle to find it a shambles. Admittedly my vision, affected by Guinness, was not the sharpest, but I was convinced after close examination that my tent lines had been cut. What was the message being conveyed here? "Yank, go home"? "Yank, don't think you 'own' our national heritage"? "Yank, be off with your lucre and leave Ireland to the Irish"? Who else but the IRA?

"You be daft, Jim," said the late Gerald Harty to me when I conveyed my suspicions. "No one has any idea you're back in here—ye came unknown to me, for example—and the IRA have other things on their minds."

"Look at these lines. Cut with a knife or I'm a paranoiac madman."

"They could be, but likely not."

"Then who's at fault?"

"I don't know, Jim. We're an awfully mixed cargo of humanity here in Moyode, to be sure it's God's truth, but I doubt very much if anyone has a grudge in it for you. Why would they?"

"Maybe they don't want national treasures gobbled up by foreigners. No one seems to like Germans in this country, buying up trout streams and locking gates."

"Jim, Jim! This old tower has no value to the likes of us. That's but a memory of bad old days. You be welcome to it a thousand times over. Relax. You're on holiday. And by the way, you ran over one of my chickens last night when you came in."

"My heartfelt apologies. I'll pay you for it."

"Oh, God be praised, it's no bother, one spoonful of the porridge. But if you didn't see that old tired bird, what makes you think you saw a knife cut in those lines?"

The next evening I caught the culprit in the midst of his rampage through my tent, a bull so startled by my approach that he "left a trail of ballast," in Gerald's genteel phraseology. Mrs. Harty washed out the tent for me, but the faint odor of manure lingered in the fabric for years to come.

STRONGBOW CURBED

Though the present appearance of Athenry dates mainly from the early decades of the twentieth century, when progress brought sewers, running water, paved streets, electricity, and the railroad, little imagination is required to recreate its grimy origin as the frontier outpost of a few enterprising, though often desperate, Norman warlords. Athenry exudes an aura of force and hard will, and nothing of the elegance that long-established power generally bestows on its surroundings over time. The old streets and alleys, often clogged with lorries and farm carts, seem hardly to have changed since medieval times, dedicated as they are solely to agricultural trade. Manifestations of baronial might in the crumbling town walls, the castle (known as Bermingham's Court), the Dominican abbey, and the Collegiate Church of St. Mary's—all more or less in ruins—testify to an original planting that never outgrew the danger of its first creation. Even in sunlight Athenry seems a roughhewn place, and during rainfall its masonry buildings and stony, slate gray colorings make it positively depressing.

The Irish Tourist Board, it is rumored, has spent well over £1 million restoring the castle, a work in progress for as long as I've been coming here. Word is about that a tea pavilion is planned for inside the courtyard and that busloads of foreign tourists are projected as the key to Athenry's revival, spending their deutsche marks and, yes, even yen in the city's shops.

This is all madness. What will they buy? Blood pudding from the seven or eight butchers in town? A metal feed bucket at the hardware store, some carrots from a peddler at the market cross, a milking machine at the co-op, perhaps a permanent at the Athenry Beauty Shoppe? This is not Switzerland, I tell my friends here. Where are the flower boxes, where are the lovely cheeses or fine local wines or gourmet picnic shops, to say nothing of boutiques and high-fashion gift stores? Where are the industrious entrepreneurs and civic boosters sweeping up debris and manure in the streets, painting store fronts, disguising petrol stations, burying power lines, curbing traffic chaos? One look out from my friend Tom Ruane's place of business near the old Brittin Gate is a testament to an irretrievably downtrodden Athenry, an atmosphere that I would judge as more or less historical and not to be tampered with. Yeats called Athenry a forlorn place. It dampened his spirits. In many ways this is just the impact that barons of the de Burgo family initially desired. Whatever tourists are hauled into Athenry will inevitably wonder why they picked a bus tour that included such a stop on its itinerary. They will, of course, be missing the point entirely, as most tourists usually do. Athenry is for purists. I cannot think of a place in all of Ireland that tells its ancient and chilling tale quite as well.

Bermingham's Court and the utterly insignificant town that surrounds it are the tangible results of policies first put in motion by the great Angevin monarch Henry II. It would be difficult to overstate the fascination that historians have had with his career and those of his two surviving sons, Richard and John. Wars in France, the Becket affair, the Third Crusade, triumph in Jerusalem, the Magna Carta, and so on are more than enough for several volumes of books. Ireland has a place in some of this, though, again, not of a central nature.

And yet there is no reason to doubt that Henry's expedition to this island in 1171 was anything short of a formidable and single-minded exercise. It is true the king was delighted at the opportunity to put himself as far away from the reach of Rome and its bulls of excommunication as possible. Becket was dead, the pope was clamoring for Henry's public confession: What better excuse to hie away to Ireland? But Henry's warlike preparations, massive in scale, betray a purpose

The view from Tom Ruane's petrol station

more malignant than just avoiding the vexatious complaints of an Italian primate. Five-hundred knights, 4,000 archers, a siege train with towers and all the necessary implements to reduce whatever forts he might find—Henry was ready to take the country. The Celtic rabble he would scatter; his Norman barons (traitors) he would crush. He came to awe the narrow little Irish world, and he did.

Strongbow understood the rules of feudalism. He was high enough on the social scale to see how much he stood to lose should he defy his king, a man noted for shortness of temper and vindictive personality. Strongbow's penniless retinue—FitzStephen, the Geraldines, and all the rest—saw little to lose other than life in fighting Henry, but the earl did. He had claims, valid claims, to vast holdings in Normandy, England, and Wales that by rights Henry should one day restore. If he claimed Ireland, he would lose those territories, more settled and valuable, to gain at best a kingdom that had to be won and quartered by force. Irish resurgence in the countryside warned him of dangers ahead. Ever "prudent," in the words of his *chanson*, he submitted all that he had won to the king. Henry helped himself to generous portions, regranted others back to Strongbow, belted him earl of Leinster, but left behind a viceroy of his own to govern the colony. Thus began the royal policy of sowing discord among the earliest adventurers. Favorites of the court like Hugh de Lacy found themselves the recipients of enormous grants to enfeoff as they saw fit, much to the anger and jealousy of the Geraldine faction, many of whom reaped little reward for all the hard fighting they had so far expended.

As for the Irish, they flocked to Henry's tent pledging fealty and honeyed obeisance, little realizing the significance of these submissions in the mind of the king. Once an Irish chieftain returned to his own *tuath*, whatever promises he might have given simply evaporated in a mental haze. Such a lapse from the Norman point of view, however, was always welcome, an invitation to declare the chieftain a villain and his *tuath* forfeit. At first Henry seems to have encouraged restraint among the colonists. Over time he did not care enough to bother.

Henry's impetuous nature failed him but once. Over wine he again unleashed one of his aggressive barons, John de Courci, with the remark that Ulster was his if he could win it. The results of yet another of his jokes (as Strongbow's *chanson de geste* characterized it) would torment the Crown in years to come. No one expected de Courci to head off into the wilderness with fewer than 300 men, still less that when next they heard any news it would tell only of one improbable victory after another, leaving yet another vainglorious Norman "at the summit of power." More royal armies would then have to be assembled and put in the field, again to overawe an overly ambitious vassal, an expensive and irksome process whether blows were struck or not.

Henry at least understood his finances; his son Prince John (John Lackland, or "John who had no land") initially did not. Henry gradually came to see in Ireland the perfect legacy for his youngest son, the only one of his five he seemed to love. When Strongbow died in 1176, leaving but a minor daughter who was sent for safekeeping to the Tower of London (where she lived for thirteen lonely years before a marriage was finally arranged), his entire fief of Leinster reverted to the Crown. This was the price Strongbow paid for submitting to the king and his failure to sire a son. Many of these revenues were steered toward John, created lord of Ireland in 1177 when a boy of ten and given an army of 3,000 men upon coming of age eight years later for a royal progress through the island—the king was often a generous man. To Henry's disgust, however, the trip proved a fiasco. Eight months later, having squandered the monies given him, frittered away his soldiers, alienated both Normans and Irish alike, John returned to court with little to show. Left behind in Ireland, however, was William de Burgo.

OTHER VISITORS, MORE FAMOUS THAN I

The Irish have a charming trait of accepting people on pretty much their own terms. If you come laden with gold and buy every round of an evening, you're a grand lad indeed. Likewise if you're without a tuppence in your pocket and just hang around the neighborhood drinking everyone's tea and eating their brown bread, still the word "champion" follows you out the door.

As I grew older and the reek of prosperity and a future seemed more and more the statement of things past, I was greeted nonetheless with undeniable warmth of feeling. To my discredit, I also found that people had hoarded their old blankets and pillows, even unwanted canned goods, to pass along to their American "itinerant." "You always look cold," Mrs. Uniacke once said to me as she pushed an old bed cover into my Citroën. "What would your mother say if she knew we had neglected ye?" At the time I was over forty.

This is not to say I was ever considered a tramp or, far from it, dirty. Every morning I could be found at one or another of the wayside water pumps that used to be in the countryside (most everyone has indoor plumbing now), scrubbing myself up and down or brushing my teeth. No, what they felt about their visitor was that he was, well, odd. Such as the year I decided to economize, both financially and dietetically: no expensive restaurants and no beef or pork. I had Mrs. Harty boil me up two dozen eggs, and I lived off them and Guinness for ten days, until I developed a dreadful case of the hives. Thereafter I resumed my Viking affection for meat. Or the time I came upon a used flagpole in Athenry and put it up on the roof of Moyode with wet socks and underwear pinned all along the shaft, a makeshift laundry line. "That is not the coat of arms we expect from your lordship," I was told. Or my famous Citroën, an old rust bucket I had fixed up as a camper, usually surrounded in the morning by ten or so cows who would slather the windscreen with drool and rock the old thing back and forth scratching their neck and flanks, breaking side mirrors and door handles, much to my annoyance and frequent public tirades. Word got around pretty quickly, "The king of the castle has a fearsome temper!" To say nothing of my visit to the local doctor when I discovered a tick well imbedded in my penis. "Not to worry," he consoled me; "like the gout, a common ailment of the local aristocracy."

I did find out, however, that other visitors to Ireland could generate more press than I. Cassius Clay (when he was so called) made a stir when he said, "Ireland would be all right if they put a goddamned roof over it." And the pope's trip in 1979 truly convulsed the nation in a frenzy unknown either before or since. "The greatest event in our history since the coming of St. Patrick," wrote one ecstatic priest to the *Irish Times*. (Since then the pope's hardened position on various social issues has diminished his popularity, as references to the "dour Slav" in our local paper attest.) But far and away the most interesting comet to come and go was Ronald Reagan in 1984. "He went down the treat," one admirer from Loughrea opined, but in fact the U.S. president's reception proved far more complex and indeed might well be viewed as a watershed in Ireland's emergence as at least a pseudomodern country.

When Reagan arrived in Ireland that June, I watched some of the festivities on local TV. The president's penchant for cliché was amply fulfilled in remarks that made my stomach churn, such as "the tug I felt in my heart when I saw the Emerald Isle from Air Force One" or "the joyous feeling [of] coming home after a long journey" or "the new contentment [in his] soul" and so on. This emotive pap, so generously served up whenever an American celebrity arrives here, is glibly swallowed by all the locals as they "paddy wag" before the cameras, a theatrical production as time-honored as standing for a round of drinks and, in the end, just as hollow. Even the Irish know this, although Reagan's speechwriters and indeed the old film star himself did not quite grasp it. To them the truly heroic verbal excesses from the past, the mother lode of imagery from the Sarsfields, Robert Emmets, Wolf Tone, and other martyrs, were there to be plundered, mined, transformed into the fool's gold common to all politicians no matter where they come from, in the certain knowledge that the Irish would never know the difference. "But we have changed," as the *Irish Times* noted. "We have come a long way since we welcomed JFK."

Undeniably, it was different for John Kennedy in 1963. He at least was Catholic and could prove where he came from. Reagan's "coming home" to the utterly obscure village of Ballyporeen in County Tipperary was less convincing. There were press reports, hardly trumped about at the time, that a church registry recording the baptism of the president's great-grandfather in 1829 read "Ryan" not "Reagan." And what about the villagers? One person was said to be selling tourists bags of mud from the suspected field where the alleged ancestor had reportedly lived in a farmhouse that no longer existed. This was too much even for the Moyode crowd, who hooted me derisively, to the point where even I felt defensive. One gets tired after a while of people "barking in your face," as St. Patrick said of a druid who proved too contentious.

This is not what we expect of the Irish. It is natural for them to be generous hosts, and certainly Reagan was for the most part kindly received. (A demonstrator who threw an egg at the passing entourage was "severely admonished" by the police.) But in effect the Irish were embarrassed and, more to the point, knew it. They recognized in their own souls that well-traveled highways of loose talk no longer took them very far. They recognized that their old heroes no longer had much to say to them, and this was both disturbing and a cause for shame.

Tragic heroes from the past, and more particularly the causes for which they fought and died, seemed provincial in the European scheme of things as the millennium dawned. What Emmet said as he stood at the gibbet has little relation to VCRs and new automobiles. The dim reaches of the past are bulldozed to the side as Irish people march relentlessly forward. During his visit President Reagan may have believed (as did his handlers as they indulged his penchant for nostalgia) that he was addressing a people different from his own, people from the faerie land of the old sod. In fact, he faced his mirror image, a nation more American in its desires for material goods than ever he saw in his own home state of California.

I recall at the time a very apt picture of this real transformation taking place in Irish society. Automatic bank tellers were the rage in Ireland back in 1984. They constituted the latest toy, a symbol of the new age dawning in Ireland. At the little bank in Galway City that I frequent, I saw a queue develop in front of this newly installed gadget that consisted of thirty-two people, all lined up in the drizzle out on the sidewalk. Through the doors of the bank itself, I noted five human beings in starched green uniforms, what some of us might call "real" tellers, standing at their counters doing nothing. I thought then of the famous prophecy of the druid Lochru, who foresaw the coming of Christianity and the death it augured for his own pagan order. It would be "brought from afar over the seas," he claimed; "it would be honored by all, would overthrow kingdoms, kill the kings who offered resistance, seduce the crowds, destroy all their gods, banish all of their crafts, and reign forever." And the people would only say, "Be it thus, be it thus."

SELECT CHRONOLOGY

1177	Prince John decreed Lord of Ireland.
c. 1185	William de Burgo, "the Conqueror," empowered, granted lands in Tipperary.
1208	Death of William the Conqueror.
1209	John, having become king, lands in Ireland for a stay of eight months.
1226	Richard de Burgo granted Connaught.
1235	De Burgo launches major invasion into Connaught.
1238	Myler de Bermingham begins work on Athenry Castle.
1242 or 1243	De Burgo dies.
1250–1270	Career of Walter, third de Burgo Lord of Connaught.
1295–1326	Career of Richard, "the Red Earl."
1315	Edward Bruce lands in Ulster with Scottish army. Dies in battle three years later.
1316	De Burgo faction shatters O'Connors in battle before Athenry.
1329–1333	Irish career of the Brown Earl, murdered in Ulster.
	Minor de Burgos split Connaught into private kingdoms.
1350–1500	"The Conquest Limpeth": Crown control diminishes throughout Ireland. Gaelic "revival." De Burgos hibernicized into Burkes.
1459–1534	Earls of Kildare rule the Pale. The "Great Earl" in power 1478–1513.
1504	Battle of Knockdoe outside Galway. Ulick Burke defeated by the Great Earl.
1534	Revolt of "Silken Thomas," who is executed.
1537	Henry VIII of England breaks with Rome. Monasteries suppressed.
1540	Policy of "surrender and regrant" officially begins.

De Burgo and Burke

1185–1540

His voice had become hoarse by constantly shouting and raising his war cry in battle. His hand was against every man, and the hand of every man against him.

William de Burgo Empowered, 1185

The interesting thing about words is the way they grow. Once they've been given their initial meanings—often direct, to the point, in close association with basic facts—they tend to collect many layers of additional nuance that open a wide gap between the original, single-minded definition and something far broader and more encompassing. Chivalry derives from the Latin word *caballus*, or "nag," from which came the old French *cheval*, or "horse," whence *chevalier*, "horseman," then "knight." The historical interconnection between the warrior and his steed was thus straightforward, but over time ramifications emerged to alter what had been a simple categorization. Courtly love, romance, manners, and etiquette, all developing within the confines of royal society, and at first among the circle of Queen Eleanore, Henry's wife, added a softening, refined touch to what was otherwise the rather crude and boorish reality of life in those bellicose times. A knightly code began to develop, embodied in the word "chivalry," or the manners of a *chevalier*. By the time several centuries later when novelists like Sir Walter Scott came to use the term, the list of prerequisites had become quite expansive: valor, nobility, fairness, honesty, courtesy, respect for women, protection of the poor. Rarely in medieval history had these attributes customarily prevailed.

In Prince John's time a knight most certainly needed valor. Without that he might as well join the Church. Honoring the poor, no matter the Gospels, was another matter. Villeins and serfs were no better than dogs and treated so. The knightly virtues of courtesy, fairness, and noble bearing were restricted primarily to relations between a vassal and his overlord or king. Between vassal and vassal, treachery was the more likely code of behavior. Respect for women did not exist. Marriages were important as vital instruments of policy, but the women were not. Land and estates—in other words, power—came with the matrimonial sacrament, usually at the desire of a king who could order any match he wished, as was the case with Strongbow's daughter.

When Richard the Lion Heart granted her to William Marshal, a hitherto valiant though utterly penniless knight found himself transformed into one of the mightiest barons of the Angevin kingdom. Marshal knew that. Within seconds of Richard's bequest, he had mounted his horse and rode off in breathless haste to the coast of France. In the surge to board his vessel, he and his now dazzled companions overtaxed the gangplank, spilling the entire melange onto the ground, breaking arms and legs. Injured though he was, Marshal sailed to England, rushed to the Tower, demanded his bride, and announced his intention to carry the heiress to Leinster for an immediate and, most important, public marriage. A councilor advised against delay. Marry her now! And so a nineteen-year-old woman, without a moment's notice, found herself before the altar and then in bed with a middle-aged knight she had never met. No one asked her what she thought or wished, and, indeed, depending on the advice of her friends, perhaps her valuation of marriage was slight to begin with. Romantic love, at least in Queen Eleanore's court, was actually the celebration of illicit love, where the heart could play its part along with passion. The idea that love could exist within marriage was deemed farcical.

The knightly virtue that truly counted, alongside valor, was generosity, and the affairs of women and what to do with them really belonged to that category. As a rite of passage, emerging peers like Prince John usually held small courts of their own with retinues of young, arrogant, and usually poor gentlemen of not altogether high lineage in attendance. Until some source of income or inheritance was passed their way, these gangs of young bucks idled their days through tournaments and the chase, gratified and relieved when John's father might come through with allowances or gifts to support their sloth. The lordship of Ireland was an opportunity they all could recognize. They now had a prince who could grant lands or help arrange profitable marriages. It was their task to remind their patron that chivalry demanded he reward his followers, both for their loyalty and their patience.

John, whose reputation is beyond salvage, was certainly a venal, suspicious, grasping, and paranoid young man. He did develop into a competent monarch with a decent grasp of administration and familiarity with the ruthless usages of power, but these abilities are usually obscured by the dreadful accounts of his personality and the seemingly immense calamities that afflicted his reign. Certainly his early career in Ireland proved inauspicious, though we should keep in mind, as certain Irish chieftains did, that at the time he was "a mere boy."

By 1185, however, the situation in Ireland had changed. Just twenty or so years after the initial landings, the first wave of barons was dying off, many of them without issue. Settlements (called plantations) and manors were empty, unsecured, or threatened by the Irish; new waves of settlers seemed of less caliber—"cut throats, murderers, and lewd fellows," in the opinion of one Geraldine—and some powerful barons were clearly disaffected from the king. Within this volatile mix, John could not keep pace. His young crew of followers had little respect for the elder Normans, none for the few Celtic kings who came to do homage. "They rudely pulled them by the beards which the Irish wear full and long according to the custom of their country" and generally treated them "with contempt and derision." To one of these yapping sycophants, William de Burgo, Prince John granted large tracts in County Tipperary.

In the *chanson de geste* of William Marshal, we see the emergence of a great baron—his forcefulness, his assumption of real political power as opposed to simple mastery of an opponent in combat, the development of a courtier's skill—from the moment he assumes the patrimony of his wife. In William de Burgo's career, far less intimately portrayed for us by contemporary witnesses, we see it in the broad outlines of his behavior. Much is murky, much is guesswork, but the feeling one has is the same as that from Marshal's *chanson*, a sense of

Grave and effigy of William Marshal, the Temple of London

relief. William de Burgo, primogenitor of the greatest Norman family in Connaught and perhaps in the entire island, had finally, in feudal terms, achieved his freedom through this simple charter. Through the generosity of his patron and lord, he had been granted land, without which he would forever be an appendage to the court. The fact that he had to conquer what his prince had given him meant nothing, merely a challenge any valorous Norman would rise to. He had wheedled and connived, schemed and flattered, and this so-called parchment grant was his reward.

Ireland proved a perfect venue for de Burgo, who apparently had little or no superior bloodline from which he could boast or profit.

His brother Hubert, who had served John well when he finally reached the throne in 1199 and would later be justiciar of England during Henry III's minority, was resented as a parvenu and later slandered by Shakespeare in *King John* for his alleged desire to gouge the eyes of Arthur of Brittany with a hot poker. "Out, dunghill," the earl of Norfolk warns Hubert before a fight; "dars't thou beard a nobleman?" But competence and bravery served both brothers well. Hubert defended Dover Castle against the French in 1216 and even won a naval engagement the next year in that same war, while to William came the epithet "the Conqueror."

For twenty years, William de Burgo marched, planted, and intrigued his way through the fertile plains of Tipperary and Limerick, on into Connaught. In about 1193 he took as second wife the daughter of O'Brien, the Irish king of Thomond. Children of de Burgo's marriage, and that of the other barons, unwittingly promoted the trend of assimilation, for the first language any baby learned was undoubtedly that of the nurse and the kitchen. Even William probably learned some Irish and certainly came to understand something of Celtic mores through exposure to the councils of his father-in-law and O'Brien relations. In the Irish annals we see mention of his engagement in alliances with various Irish septs in their pursuit of tribal vendettas and his leading expeditions all over the west of Ireland. Usually flame and death followed in his wake, and not a shred of anything we might in our modern sense label patriotism ever reared its head in any of these maneuverings. Every Norman and every Celt looked out for his own best interests, suffering the suspicions of friend and foe alike. On more than one occasion, King John himself commanded his vassal to relinquish property or prisoners; in his next breath he could grant him all of Connaught.

When William died in the winter of 1206, he left behind a reputation for ruthlessness and insatiable greed. The monks who wrote the Irish chronicles in their scattered monastic scriptoria developed a code to signify their displeasure with various personages of history, usually in the form of a hideous final illness or a death without sacrament. William's obituary is the model of supreme disapproval:

> William de Burgo took the spoyles of all the Churches of Connaught, but God and the patrons of these Churches shewed their miracles upon him, that his entrails and fundament fell from his privie place, and it trailed after him even to the very earth, whereof he died impenitently

> without Shrive or Extreme Unction, or good buryall in any Church in the kingdom, but in a waste town.

From William's issue came the great de Burgo barons of Ireland, who, more than any others, shaped the destinies of Connaught. Their primary battleground was here, the rolling fields of central Galway, the "plain of great assemblies, no small kingship," as the Gaelic poets called it, outstretched in view for miles from the top of Moyode Castle. From this vantage, on any given day of the thirteenth century, one could probably see the crude and single-minded de Burgo strategy at work: kill, slash, burn, then fortify, settle, and farm. This simplicity of intent gives no illumination, however, to the tortured and at times unrelievedly complicated maneuvering that lay beneath their attainment.

William, our first de Burgo and a quintessential Norman, had not been content with his significant, though hardly regal, grants in Tipperary. He had enfeoffed this property to some degree of return, sufficient to allow the establishment of Athassel Priory on his demesne, where his body was eventually interred. But speculative grants in Connaught impelled him to move on. His career was never concerned with past achievement, only with riches and fame that lay in the future. William's master, King John, both unleashed and curbed him. This was every monarch's standard approach to marcher lords, or palatine barons, as they were also known. John, like his father, delighted in confusion. He thought nothing of issuing multiple titles of settlement to a single piece of territory and letting the unfettered dogs blood one another to exhaustion. John granted Connaught to the Irish O'Connors, who had held it for as long as any *filid* could remember, but he also gave it to de Burgo. This allowed the king at any given moment to judge whomever he wished in Connaught as guilty of treason. This appears to us today as grossly counterproductive at best, but to John it made sense. He wished never to see a man like de Burgo secure, particularly in a palatine lordship.

The word "palatine" explains in many ways the king's dilemma. From the Latin *palatium*, its meaning is "palace," and in the medieval sense fairly specific to the Romans, Caesar, and royal prerogative. A baron such as de Burgo, entering the wilds of an uncolonized Connaught, was recognized as a palatine lord to compensate for the risk and expense that such speculative grants entailed. As such, he was allowed, by royal leave, to operate as a king himself. He settled all matters of law, dispute, and justice; he dealt with any matter of policy

Athassel Priory, County Tipperary

himself without interference, consultation, or permission from any royal justiciar or official; he was entitled to any profit derived from settlement. Invasion of marcher territories required such freedom of action. But the sword was double-edged. *Palatium* also referred to Caesar's personal guard, the Praetorian legions—"of the palace"—and the old Roman histories were certainly full of instances where these same soldiers, compromised by rumor and hysteria or swayed by disgruntled officers, had turned on emperors and murdered them. Palatine lords were necessary evils.

William de Burgo embroiled himself in the politics of the O'Connors, always seeking some opening or angle whereby he might implement his charter from John. His experiences ranging back and forth through Connaught taught him much about the countryside itself and the various feuds of the clans. His son Richard inherited this obsession.

DEALING WITH LOCAL CUSTOM

"Put Jim's name in the kettle," a neighbor called to his wife as I came in one evening through the door, uninvited and unannounced, for the inevitable cup of tea. When I first began coming to Ireland, the notion of barging in on people was alien to me, but as the Irish showed little hesitancy themselves in poking about my tent or car unannounced—"Are ye up then, Jim? 'Tis a grand morning"—I saw no reason to restrain my often hungry self from doing the same.

Visiting your friends for a cup is probably the most durable social convention in all the country, irrespective of religious creed or sectional background. From a cultural perspective, moreover, this is certainly the pleasantest way of all to meet the Irish and witness firsthand what they do best: talk. There are times in the best of these circumstances when the clock seems pushed back by a century or two, as it did whenever I chatted up the Uniackes in their kitchen or any number of the older farm families who live around here. Nowadays, as many others besides me have noted, television and, of all things, the telephone have served to staunch much of the flow. "Since people got the phone," Frank Broderick told me, "they've stopped talking altogether," by which he meant that the loneliness Irish people feel so keenly is now easily relieved and the visit is becoming a relic of the past. "No one's bored anymore, Jim. They've too many easy things to do."

However pleasant the social dimensions of Irish talk, its more formal applications can be deadly. Most political rhetoric is a dreadful mash of oozing insincerity with the usual dollop of blatant untruths, all served up in a syrupy presentation that, again, seems a nineteenth-century caricature. Televised debates of the Dáil, Ireland's parliament, are stupendous bores no matter the topic. Sermons are not much better, but at least they dispense with the note of evasion that characterizes political chitchat. Though fire and brimstone is for the most part a thing of the past, Catholic stands on various issues are still pretty straightforward and presented directly, with little gloss. In the sphere of the law, bureaucracy, and business, however, the gift of the gab is downright poison, and a person on the receiving end usually has no choice but to swallow the fatal draught.

For years, I will admit, I drove my old Citroën around the countryside without the benefit of legal plates or insurance. The original French tags were painted right on the car, and though good for only the initial six months of my ownership, they were not dated and thus at a glance could possibly be accepted as current. But as the ancient hulk began to disintegrate, so too did the tags.

To compensate, I made it a point whenever I traveled to other European countries to pick up as many foreign-looking stickers as I could for the Citroën. A couple of years I had a nice "P" for Portugal and lots of soccer slogans and provincial flags stuck to the bumper. But the weather is so damp in Ireland that none of these lasted very long. Portugal gave way to "I" and a very fine sticker of the pope in his miter showering the crowd with a blessing in Italian. My last set was racing decals from the Circuit du Mans in France.

Occasionally, however, I would be stopped in Ireland for running a traffic light or some other minor infraction. As a rule, the policeman in charge might spend a few moments walking around the vehicle, noting (I hoped) the left-hand drive and thinking (I hoped), "Another stranger to our land." At the opportune time, I would then begin speaking a garbled sort of French in as heavy a Gallic accent as could be faked, pretending that as far as English went I was deaf, dumb, and blind. An officer in Galway, I remember clearly, was not up to the task of dealing with me. "Ah, you bloody foreigners," he said right to my blankest of faces. "Did God never tell you that He only speaks English? Ah, be off with ye!" and he waved me along. I never once got a ticket, but after I had kids of my own, I decided to obey the law.

One fine day I reported to the local police station. "I'm here to register my car," I announced.

"And why would you want to do that, Jim?" the officer replied, "Ye've been fine all these years without one."

"Well, responsibility, and maybe a commitment to law and order."

"That's highly admirable indeed. How many years is that old car?"

"1972."

"Have you the old registration?"

"The weather destroyed it."

"Bill of sale?"

"Some mice got into the car one year. They shredded it."

"Have you any proof it's yours?"

"I have the owner's manual and some repair bills with my name on them, in French."

"Well now, Jim, no way can you register this car. I don't know it's yours, for example."

"Well, Tom, you've seen me driving it here these past eighteen years."

"Aye, I have, Jim, but nevertheless you might have stolen it in France. No, the best thing for you to do is buy a new car."

"Are you crazy? This one runs fine."

"Nonetheless, Jim, I don't want to see that Citroën ever again. And by the way, could you drop off Mrs. Murray here down the road? Her motor expired outside the butcher's, that's a good lad."

Later I explored the possibility of buying insurance at a local agent, who doubled as a barkeep at the Abbey. "You've come to just the place, Jim."

"It's the Citroën, Seamus, I need some coverage."

"Fine, Jim, fine indeed. No problem at all. Can I see the registration?"

"Haven't got one."

"Not to worry, Jim, not to worry, a worthless scrap of paper, you know it yourself. You bought that in France?"

"Yes, I did."

"Right-hand drive?"

"No, left."

"A problem, Jim, I cannot insure you."

"That's crazy!"

"I know, Jim, I know, but I can't do it. Now, go to three other agencies. Tell them it's a left-hand drive. Get rejected, come back with a letter from each, and I'll insure you."

"Is this a joke?"

"No," he said waving me away, "only Ireland."

A week later I returned with the three rejections. "Fine now, Jim, we'll sign you up—left-hand drive, is it? Not a problem. We'll put you down as right-hand."

"How can you do that? If I had an accident everyone would see what side of the car my steering wheel was on, and they'd automatically blame me and sue. You know the Irish."

"Quite so. In that case your insurance would be worthless, quite worthless. Now your first installment, Jim, will be £300."

"Wait a minute . . . "

"Jim, it's this or nothing. Insurance or no insurance. It's your choice."

"But you're telling me the insurance I buy will do me no good."

"It's inexpensive, though, Jim, a grand bargain, and it will look as though you were trying to do the right thing. Appearances are important, you know. But if you like, you could buy a new car. I have a wonderful Kadette, only 120,000 miles, for £3,000. No problems there!"

The Ancient Town of Athenry, 1238

To William de Burgo's son, Richard, known as the Great Lord, goes major credit for taking Connaught. His uncle Hubert, justiciar of England after King John's death, facilitated the legalisms of Richard's predatory dealings with the O'Connors, and though the de Burgo grant was successfully challenged when Hubert fell from power in 1231, Richard redeemed it with a fine of 3,000 marks, an "enormous" sum in the opinion of an esteemed Irish historian but rather paltry when compared with King Richard the Lion Heart's ransom from an Austrian dungeon in 1193, which totaled 100,000 marks. The degree of monetary difference reflects, I think, the relative poverty of a so far uncivilized Ireland when compared to the rest of Europe as well as the huge challenges that authorities in London recognized a man like Richard de Burgo faced.

For ten years, Richard continued the pattern of playing the various O'Connor factions against each other. He chose kings and pretenders as he wished, gaining footholds here and there through the countryside, such as the present site of Galway City, where he erected a castle in 1230. We have few records of pitched battles or hostings beyond the usual. Most bloodletting was probably in the form of ambuscades, skirmishing, cattle thieving, and border raids. Alliances, treaties, and oaths were all taken and violated with great celerity. Hostages were exchanged and often sacrificed. A recorded instance of an Irish attack in Sligo may well be typical of the times. The bailey was taken by Irish raiders, who then could not breach the motte. During the stalemate, Norman knights took hostages in their keeping and strung them by the neck over the wooden wall, their bodies a gruesome challenge to the Irish, who knew the victims by name and blood. We can only imagine the curses and taunting that must have flown between these two small groups of soldiers in an encounter as savage as it was insignificant.

In 1235 Richard de Burgo altered the entire frame of reference for the province of Connaught. At the head of the complete feudal levy of Ireland, some 500 mounted Normans and many hundreds more archers and footmen, Richard stormed across the Shannon at Athlone and devastated the O'Connor patrimony. In Moyode itself "they committed great depradations." Using siege machines and taking to the sea in ships, plundering cattle and burning all before them, the "English," as the Celtic annals called them, "left the country without peace or tranquility." In their wake Gaelic renegades swooped in to steal whatever was left. The barbarities of Germanic invaders, so feared by the Romans as their empire collapsed, seem little different from these happenings of eight centuries later.

During the next campaigning season, Richard again harried Connaught. The countryside degenerated into chaos, the O'Connors becoming utterly fragmented. Annals record the desperate surrender of petty chieftains to de Burgo. "Dermot, son of Manus, went into the house of the English, that they might spare such part of his people and cattle as were then remaining with him." In 1236 de Burgo built his major castle at Loughrea. Two years later Myler de Bermingham, one of Richard's principal vassals, began work on Athenry. The Berminghams would in time style themselves the first barons of Ireland.

The purpose of these castles was no mystery. They were to resemble points of a spider web connecting all the outlying posts of de Burgo power to the center and to one another "in order to harass his enemies," as Strongbow's *chanson de geste* put it. "In such manner, know ye all, was the country planted with castles and with cities, with keeps and with strongholds. Thus well rooted were the noble, renowned vassals."

The strategic position of Athenry guaranteed a Norman presence. It lay halfway between Loughrea and Galway, commanding the "ford of kings," where, in a land with neither roads nor bridges, the River Clareen could be crossed. On a small outcropping of rock, Myler de Bermingham built his keep, later surrounded by a wall with towers and fortified gateway called the bawn. In 1241, moving steadily along, he invited the Dominicans to Athenry. These were not "inferior clergy" of the native Irish, whose lives the Normans frequently stamped out and whose churches and sanctuaries they stripped for stone and timber, but French-speaking monks from abroad. Berming-

Rathgorgin Castle (Oldcastle motte, left background)

ham purposely wanted friars who specialized in urban ministries, for Athenry was meant to become a city. Indeed, tentatively spreading southwest of the castle, small groupings of settlement began to appear, surrounded by ditches and moats often flooded by waters from the river. Alongside these, and only 300 yards from Bermingham's Court, the Abbey of SS. Peter and Paul was commenced. Three years after its foundation stone had been laid, the baron received further grants for the charging of tolls and a market fair within city limits. His agents spread word in England, Wales, perhaps as far as Normandy, that Athenry was ready for settlers.

Out on this frontier, the Laws of Breteuil, so called after a town in Normandy, prevailed. Terms of rent and commerce were so generous that farmers and small merchants may well have put aside their understandable fears of Celtic ferocity for the chance of a cheaply acquired prosperity. Interconnecting the major towns, mottes and baileys like Rathgorgin were thrown up, superseded as time and finances allowed by stone castles, usually within sight of the older earthworks. In such ways was the solitude of the countryside reduced. From the top of any single castle, garrisoned with "brave knights of great worth," another could most likely be seen. Either through bonfires or short bursts of horse speed, alarms could be spread. Development was the goal—working farms and manors where teams of oxen would plow the communal fields to produce wheat and other grains, traditional mainstays of Norman agriculture, generating the food and rent that could free a great lord to leave peace behind as he set off to scourge then settle new kingdoms. To the Irish these objectives were pedestrian and absurd. In the words of a medieval historian, progress was a notion unheard of in Ireland. The past, present, and future of Celtic life were all of one spinning.

This does not mean that the Irish were necessarily backward. A look or two at de Bermingham's castle in Athenry would not remind any reader of Camelot. In its first manifestation, the keep was a crude two-story building of approximately 35 by 60 feet. Entrance was at the second level, reached by a moveable ladder pulled up each night. There were no windows and no chimneys. An open fire for light, warmth, and cooking was probably built up each night on a central stone hearth and smoke allowed to escape through a hole in the most likely thatched, then timbered roof. Sanitation was crude. A chute extruded from the second floor through which all waste was thrown, both human and animal. A drainage ditch from this privy to the river was deemed a waste of time and never dug, which at the very least has allowed archaeologists to examine trash.

De Bermingham and his people used straw for toilet paper. They were formidable meat eaters, enjoying above all beef, small and tough cattle that hardly resemble the chemically enhanced beasts that Thomas Uniacke raised. Pig's head was a great delicacy; sheep were slaughtered young; deer were still plentiful. They ate considerable quantities of eel, not that much chicken, quite a variety of game birds, as much wild fruit as they could find, some eggs, some gruel, porridge, and bread. Vermin and rat bones prove very common, a reminder that the Anglo-Normans were ravaged by the Black Death of the fourteenth century, which concentrated its dreadful effects on the colonial towns and villages far more than the scattered raths of the Irish.

Rory O'Connor, high king of Ireland, was caught nude, bathing in the Liffey, by Strongbow's knights when they broke out of Dublin during the siege of 1171. We will never know if the earl of Leinster, or

The Norman ideal: plowing and seeding the land, Bayeux Tapestry

in this case Myler de Bermingham, ever took a bath in his life. There was no running water in this place, nor a well.

The filth, gloom, smoke, and din of these castles, especially at night, must have been considerable as a lord's dependents and family gathered together in their sealed citadels to warm themselves by the fire, eat their dinners, and worry about the deceitful machinations of Irish enemies prowling about in the night outside. Medieval man detested being alone, and modern notions of privacy were certainly alien to de Bermingham and his friends. He felt secure in the central hall only when surrounded by people—his wife and children, his various counselors, loyal henchmen and knights, his bard and harpist, one or two monks from the priory, perhaps his overlord de Burgo and some of his retinue. These rather mangy gatherings, for want of a better word, were the society of the times. Royal courts such as Henry II's or King John's, passing from castle to castle, town to town, with their merriment and festivities, lavish food and gifts, were events of extraordinary rarity for Ireland and nonexistent in Connaught. Games and knightly tournaments, the rage of William Marshal's youth in France, were known in Irish circles only through the songs of troubadours. What passed for entertainment in a town like Athenry might be cap-

Bermingham's Court, Athenry

tives dragged to death through the streets or torn apart by horses whipped in different directions.

The progress of a de Burgo from one of his strongholds to another provided the high point of the yearly calendar in Norman Connaught, and in his wake various soldiers of fortune, importunate vassals, quarreling Celts, or refugees seeking asylum would filter in from the countryside, their oaths of loyalty or pathetic requests for favor silencing the domestic bickering of his retinue. "I put myself under your safeguard, O Champion, graceful, bright and fierce," cried the famous Gaelic poet Muireadhach O Dalaigh to Richard de Burgo as he fled the wrath of O'Donnell in the north after murdering his steward ("I killed the serf. O God, is this a ground for anger?"):

There is no chessboard without a king,
There is no brood without a leader.

Abandon me not to O'Donnel of Derry and Drumcliff, O Richard,
The northern prince does not abandon one who is bold against thee.
Little thou knowest who I am of the men of Ireland,
Thou art bound to give my verses heed, for I am O'Daly of Meath!

O Richard of the bright land, forsake not the men of art,
Whatever exploits one may do, no one is famous without generosity.

Be not gentle toward thine enemy, O prince of the foreigners,
Be not humble towards a High King.

Be not timid towards a warrior, be not strong against a poet,
O prince of the Connacht race.

It was nothing strange one day, O knightly Richard, that I should hold as my own a swift steed bestowed by a foreigner, or a smooth and lidded goblet.

History records that de Burgo refused the request. Perhaps he threw the man out, down the privy chute for all we know of Richard's rough humor. At night the lord would sleep, surrounded on the floor by his followers.

Men such as de Burgo had two fears: a summons from the king and a minor heir. De Burgo suffered both in 1242. Henry III, in standard Plantagenet fashion, embarked on a continental war in the winter of that year, ordering all his vassals to appear in person to assist him. Such news was never welcome to the Norman barons of Ireland. De Burgo had been making great progress in Connaught, and even the O'Connors seemed resigned. Their king, confused and dumbfounded by developments—solaced at Henry's court in Windsor yet harried unmercifully by de Burgo's men at home—had finally acquiesced in the transfer of nearly all Connaught to the colonists, reserving for himself the five *cantreds* of Roscommon. It did not take long for him, or the mutinous young men who contentiously roiled the O'Connor cauldron, to see that even this was not enough to satisfy the foreigners, who built a castle in Roscommon town in 1278. Though burned repeatedly by the O'Connors, this edifice gradually evolved into one of the largest castles ever erected in either England or Ireland.

De Burgo resented the royal summons at such a juncture, as did his family, especially when they learned of his death in faraway Poitou late that winter, and no grown son to take their lord's place. For the absence of a strong master allowed the resentful Irish to peck away at Norman advances. For eight years, the absentee Crown held de Burgo's lands, taking its revenues, complicating its title, leaving its direction slack. Men like de Bermingham held on as best they could, relieved and delighted at the congenital inability of the Irish to adapt. In 1249 a renegade army of O'Connor bucks appeared before Athenry, full of brave self-regard and bluster. The Normans, in battle gear and mail, rode out from the town and arrayed themselves in formation, another thundering Norman charge in the offing, the kind of battering ram that Anna Comnena said "might make a hole in the walls of Babylon." "Fear and dismay" at this apparition coursed through the Irish ranks, say the annals, and a great rout ensued. But in smaller terms, in lonely woods or muddy tracks, at moments of seeming calm, individual Norman knights could be attacked and slain, farmsteads put to the torch.

WALLOWING WITH THE GAEL

There is in all of this de Burgo narrative a sense of ebb and flow, the conflict between order (as the Normans conceived of it) and something close to chaos that would seesaw through decades of bloody strife. There is also the sense of hopelessness, the desire of men to enforce their will on a landscape that in the end renders all such efforts meaningless. I noticed this characteristic myself over the years of coming and going to Moyode, "the green plain of the grassy sod," as the poets called it, watching various farmers and landowners in their projects of improvement. One year a house or farm or shed would show the results of industry and money; three or four trips later all would be engulfed in a tide of weeds or rot, blamed on circumstances as varied as human nature. In the end, relentless Irish weather seems to get the better of everything, a virus of despair to afflict all who come here with dreams or hope in their pockets.

Walter de Burgo, the third of his line to test his fortunes in Ireland, claimed the family lands when he came of age in 1250, and with his ascension the struggle again became focused in very narrow de Burgo terms. Subtle changes, however, can be picked out from the often dry monastic chronicles. The Irish began to see themselves no longer as kings but as chiefs or barons, seeking whatever rights they could under the new terms of Norman law, Walter and other foreign knights for their part began adapting Irish usage and custom when convenient. One moment de Burgo is the Norman lord of Connaught, soon to be the single most powerful vassal in Ireland with additional grants in the north, along with the new title "earl of Ulster"; in another he is described carousing with Hugh O'Connor in the manner of a tribal chieftain, "in one bed, cheerfully and happily," to cement a treaty—"wallowing upon the skins of wild animals," a Roman reported of the mainland Celts in about 21 B.C., "with bedfellows on each side. Although their wives are beautiful, they pay them little attention."

One century after Strongbow's landing, the Dolphins of Moyode receive their first mention in the annals of Ireland, in 1270 A.D., "the Age of Christ." John Dolphin, vassal, knight, and tenant of Walter de Burgo was murdered, along with his son, by Hugh O'Connor, chief of that clan, in a sequence of events most significant to the fortunes of Connaught.

De Burgo had known Hugh O'Connor for years—they had even "wallowed" in bed together. But no matter the sugary words, their ambitions brought them repeatedly into conflict with such a degree of bitterness that monks record no English or Irish could separate the two nor "keep them from annoying each other." The earl gathered his feudal levy (John Dolphin among his knights) and set off to confront the O'Connor. After skirmishes, less enthusiastic parties arranged a truce. Dolphin accompanied the earl's brother to O'Connor's camp as a hostage to keep the peace, but the treacherous Irish seized the minor de Burgo and killed his escort. Seeking revenge, the earl was murderous in the next morning's affray, but in crossing the ford of Connell's weir, his Normans were struck down in a frenzied attack that caught them by surprise, unable to reach open ground. A new element was introduced to the battlefield: the gallowglass, a helmeted foot soldier of Scots-Norse heritage, dressed in mail, carrying a battle-ax, and available for hire, in this case by the O'Connors. "These sort of men," as a minister of Henry VIII was to report in 1543, "be those that do not lightly abandon the field, but byde the brunt to the death." Nine knights, milling about in the water, were cut down in minutes, and the attack carried through the Norman column right to its van. De Burgo escaped only through flight. His brother was butchered at the same ford later that day during the victory orgy. For the first time, records make mention of bodies being stripped for their coats of mail. Crushed and depressed by this signal defeat, de Burgo died the next

Gallowglasses, Dominican Priory, Roscommon

year in 1271, again leaving a minor for his heir. His estates reverted to the Crown.

SEARCHING FOR DOLPHINS

"The people drain here in Connaught is a nightmare. You'd think with the twenty-first century approaching that Irish people would not be contemplating the same dire courses of action that their great-great-great-great-great-grandparents did over the cottage hearth in the 1840s—'What shall I do? Where shall I go? I can't stay here.'" So said a local antiquarian in nearby Loughrea whom I searched out for any information she might have had on the Dolphin clan, whose association with Moyode Castle intrigued me. "The Dolphins have disappeared from the face of the earth," she continued, "and if there were any left here now, they'd all be on the next plane to America, green card or no. If I wasn't so well along in years myself, I'd be going with them. No, you won't find any Dolphins here, nor the mention of them either."

Years before, I remembered, there had been a shop on Loughrea's main street called Dolphin's, but its old sign has disappeared, so too the establishment. There are no Dolphins in the local telephone directory, none in the parish register, and no glint of recognition when I mention the name to any of the locals. An 1850 evaluation had listed twenty-seven landowners in Galway of that name, all Catholic and all paying the mandatory tithes to the Protestant Church of Ireland. "They didn't die out," my antiquarian source informed me; "they were thrown out or just left."

One of only a few monks still in residence at the Carmelite Abbey hauled out his old ring of keys to unlock the gate at the ruined friary next door, founded in 1300 by Richard de Burgo, the Great Lord. Near the spot where the high altar used to stand is a weather-beaten crypt with delicate, sinewy dolphins carved along its four sides, looking more like eels than fish. "The mortal remains of this fine family," said the monk. "Not a mark or trace of them to be had around, whereas before in the days of earls and grandees they stood a place of honor in their retinue. And many's the time I'm sure they drew a sword in defense of their land and religion. The last of them here, I think, held Turoe House outside of town, where the old cultic stone from the Iron Age stands—you must have heard of it, and well worth the visit. The owner there now has done a grand job." We walked back to the gates. "I'll be saying a prayer for you tonight."

"Well, thank you, Father. When might I notice the results?"

"Tomorrow morning to be sure, and why wouldn't you?"

That afternoon I drove to Turoe House and had a cup of tea with the farmer who owned the place, the proud developer of a petting zoo, just completed, to complement the Iron Age La Tène pillar stone. "Do you think archaeologists or historians are going to think this sort of thing appropriate?" I asked him as he showed me the tame lambs and turkeys.

"They'll be mad for the place. It gives the stone a little lift, if you take my meaning."

"Well, I sort of don't."

"Do ye think the Turoe Stone should be some special preserve for the educated elite? Why can't the common people of this country enjoy some of our own history?"

"No reason at all. But you don't need a little zoo here to drag them in."

"Ah, they'd never come without it."

Later I asked about the Dolphins, who had owned this property a hundred years before. He'd never heard of them.

Edward MacLysaght, the dean of Irish genealogy, had offices for years in one of Dublin's crumbling Georgian mansions on Merrion Square. Paying a visit to his shabby conference room during one of my stops in Dublin did not contribute much to my store of knowledge on the Dolphins. Pulling out a tattered folder, the aged MacLysaght looked through his scribbled notes. "Pretty much a blank slate," he informed me genially. "The name is Norse in origin, and they undoubtedly came over from England with the first invaders. Given their association with Loughrea and the territories around it, they must certainly have been in league with the de Burgos, and we have scattered references to them in the annals and such as Connaught was overrun by the Normans. We also have notations as they in turn were pushed aside by the Elizabethans. Let me see now—here we have Dolphins in the Spanish army during the 1500s; here we have some pardons issued by Queen Elizabeth to various, shall we say recalcitrant, Dolphins in the 1580s. Thorough rogues, all of them, I'm sure. In 1586 I have a note showing a Dolphin trying to dun the Queen's government for money owed—he was probably a victualer of some sort to the Crown forces. Here we are for 1656: eight Dolphins transported to Barbados." MacLysaght leaned back in his chair and stared at the ceiling for well over a minute.

"I was in Japan as a young man," he finally said.

"Is that so?"

"Yes, took a bath there once—in public, if you can imagine. No one wore any clothes. Quite extraordinary."

"Is there a connection here with the Dolphins?"

"Well, in the West Indies I heard they were involved in tea plantations. You might find some of them there."

"Is that so?"

"Yes. Quite extraordinary really."

The Red Earl, 1316

In the shadow of Athenry's castle is a small blacksmith shop run by its proprietor at irregular hours of the day and night. I often stop by on my way into town of an evening, if I see lights on, to watch him clang away at his rusty shards of metal or to shoe a recalcitrant pony or hunter. Tonight the word is out that I am a celebrity, booked on a local radio program to discuss what foreigners think of the complexities of Irish history. "I'll be sure to listen," says the smithy, "so that I can correct ye in the morning."

Customers here are a varied lot. Many are Ascendancy types whose views on the Irish past border at times on the ludicrous; others can be local windbags who claim St. Patrick is skewering Cromwell's soul with a crosier as we speak. Surprises, however, do crop up. A local farmer having a wagon rim repaired starts to chat about the de Burgos when he hears I have an interest in them. "A mighty family," he says, and then for the next several minutes he recites with extraordinary detail their entire pedigree down to the duke of Clarence in the 1360s.

"Where did you learn all that?" I ask.

"Oh, from my father," he says. "It was a hobby of his, like fishing was. He'd stand in the stream casting line and go through all the de Burgos start to finish. That man had a grand memory for fact. I heard it so many times I couldn't forget if I wanted to, and that's what I call the de Burgo curse. He had a favorite one too. He said all the de Burgos were evil men, but the Red Earl, he topped the list."

The Red Earl—Richard II de Burgo—spoke Gaelic and was no stranger to the raths and open haunts of the Irish, but he was not crowned here in the style of a native chieftain. The de Burgos had not as yet abandoned themselves to Irish custom, though those days were shortly to come. The earl remained an Anglo-Norman magnate, familiar with England and the London court, cognizant of the diplomatic forms required to do business with the ever-increasing floods of justiciars, envoys, and officials being dispatched to Dublin. His remarkable career saw great triumphs commingled with humiliating defeats. He witnessed the final days of Norman supremacy and, rare for those tumultuous times, even had an old age in which

The de Burgos in Ireland, Simplified Genealogy

William de Burgo
"The Conquerer"
In Ireland @ 1185
d. 1206

Brother to

Hubert de Burgo
earl of Kent
Justiciar of England
d.1243

m. Isabel, natural dau.
Ricahrd I, the Lion Heart

m. (2nd) dau. of O'Brien,
King of Thomond

Richard
"The Great Lord"
In Ireland @ 1224
d. 1243

Walter
"Earl of Ulster"
In Ireland @ 1250
d. 1271

Richard
"The Red Earl"
In Ireland @ 1286
d. 1326

John m.
Eliz de Clare

Eliz m.
Robert Bruce

Edmund
d. 1338
Killed by cousin
Edmund "Albanach"

First cousin

William
"The Grey"
d. 1324

William
"The Brown Earl"
In Ireland @1328
Murdered 1333

m. Maltida of Lancaster

David II
King of Scotland

Elizabeth m. Lionel of Clarence
3rd son, Edward III
King of England

Walter–murdered by The Brown Earl
William–"Uachtarach"–assumed chieftainship of lower Connaught
Edmund–"Albanach"–assumed chieftainship of upper Connaught, after killing Edmund, son of Red Earl

to consider for himself the merits of a system he had done so much to build.

It was not until fifteen years after his father's death that Richard came to Connaught in pursuit of his legal inheritance, but he did so in the usual fashion, at the head of an army: "Richard, the Red Earl, son of Walter Earl of Ulster, son of Richard, son of William the Conqueror, obtained sway in every place through which he passed, and took the hostages of all of Connaught." He made kings, and he dethroned kings, again in the usual manner, and feuded with fellow Normans, particularly the Geraldines in Sligo, who at one point unhorsed the earl and imprisoned him for several months. But de Burgo persevered. He was the palatine lord nonpareil, effectively the uncrowned king of almost half the island, whose daughter Elizabeth helped perpetuate the royal line of Scotland, giving birth to the son of Robert Bruce who later became David II. When Edward I of England demanded de Burgo's presence for the feudal levy against his Scottish enemies in 1301, he simply refused to go.

The ruin of de Burgo, and indeed for the colony of foreigners, was the disastrous interference in Irish affairs by the Scots, who in a way were merely returning the favor. Edward's army, punished at Bannockburn (where the de Clare family of Strongbow, in its major line, was extinguished) had been heavily supplied, financed, and manned by resources from Ireland. At the worst possible moment, Robert Bruce shipped his thoroughly ruthless brother Edward over the Channel with an army of 6,000 mail-clad warriors and a single piece of advice: If he wanted Ireland, if he wished to be a king, overrun the place. From 1315 to 1318, Edward did. At one point Robert joined him.

The devastation of the land was a shock to all who witnessed it, and dark memories of these evil times lingered for generations, encouraging monkish chroniclers to write at new levels of hyperbolic gloom, whereby "men ate each other in Ireland."

Richard de Burgo was a prominent sufferer. He had reluctantly poured much treasure into the king's expeditions to Scotland, and from 1302 to 1304 he was in attendance himself. But English barons distrusted him, especially when Bruce landed in Ireland. De Burgo, after all, was being asked to defend the realm against his daughter's family, and in every engagement his performance seemed lackluster. No matter the battles, no matter the earl's hard sword, no matter his breathtaking retreats from pursuing enemies, he was now suspect. The citizens of Dublin, who burned their own suburbs to the ground as Bruce approached the city rather than see their enemy comforted with shelter and spoils, refused to fight under de Burgo's command. Instead, they threw the earl into prison. Treachery was in the air.

No finer example presents itself than the behavior of Felim O'Connor, a young warrior of only twenty years' age who claimed the hereditary title "king of Connaught." Felim was a chieftain "with opposition," meaning that rival claimants from the considerable pool of legitimate aspirants for leadership of the clan disputed his power, in particular one Rory O'Connor, whose brother (murdered by bodyguards for a bribe) had been the previous king. De Burgo, for whatever reason, backed Felim, who accompanied the earl on his march north to face Edward Bruce.

We will never know the details of how Edward the Scot broached treason to Felim. Perhaps no other history of a European country, with the possible exception of Italy, is so ridden with lurid tales of conspiracy, betrayal, and couriers in the night, but in some such form a turncoat reached the ear of Felim from the enemy camp. If he deserted the earl, Bruce would guarantee his position in Connaught and restore the ancient patrimony of the O'Connor sept. Unknown to Felim, Bruce gave the same assurances to his hated rival, Rory, who immediately went on rampage throughout Connaught, burning its towns and ravaging farmsteads devoid of protection. Felim abandoned de Burgo, seriously weakening the earl's forces, and clawed his way back to Connaught. There, to his undoubted horror, Rory crushed him in a great confused melee. De Burgo, his forces depleted, was in his turn routed in Ulster.

An acquaintance of mine drew all these complicated interminglings of blood and alliance on a blackboard for me one afternoon at his office at University College in Galway. By the end of our session, he had the genealogical equivalent of a Pythagorean theorem scribbled all over the classroom, and I had to wonder if I understood a tenth of it. "This is the essence of Irish history," he told me. "Perhaps a bit more complicated than what we're now used to in these modern times of democratic elections, where heirs and blood ties no longer count for anything, but our intellectual heritage all the same. No race has ever been so aware of family and kin than the Irish, though I fear this awareness has dimmed considerably over just the last few years. Television, as I'm sure you know, decreases the power of memory. I think Caesar first pointed that out, even though he was referring specifically to reading and writing as the villain.

"Anyway, the dynamic of Celtic Ireland was driven by considerations just like these, the commingling of family trees, divided loyalties, thwarted ambition, so on and so forth—the usual human stew of good intention versus bad, the evil in a man's soul overwhelming what might be good. What was Rory O'Connor's position vis-à-vis Felim O'Connor? you might inquire. How did their second, third, and fourth removed cousins interact and arrange themselves within the context of this premier rivalry within the O'Connor clan? What deeds of foul play—murders, blindings, kidnappings—either sealed or destroyed various allegiances within the blood group? And how much or how little did the Scotsman Bruce and the Norman de Burgo understand the roots or tentacles of the family intrigue? Undoubtedly, de Burgo had most of the angles pretty clearly before him, and as a master strategist himself had chosen which of the strong men to back with an equal portion of common sense and just plain emotion. Being a grand betrayer himself, he probably wasn't surprised when Felim betrayed him. It was just another check mark to put in his book, something to be remembered some future day.

"There's a marvelous entry in the annals somewhere that describes one of de Burgo's Irish tenants looking for his master in Loughrea Castle in the wake of these disastrous engagements—sort of going in, wringing his hands, saying, 'What are you going to do now?' And instead of finding a confident de Burgo there, issuing orders and all to retrieve the day, he finds the Red Earl nowhere at all, the castle headquarters full of all the principal Irish chieftains of Connaught—O'Kelly, O'Brien, MacDermot—outnumbered only by mobs of lesser Normans, all refugees, all men who had backed the wrong O'Connor, just as de Burgo had. The annals described this tenant in a very literary way—he was 'abashed.' Next thing you know the little man was out in the bogs searching for Rory O'Connor, the man of the hour, to whom he gave hostages."

The great plain of Moyode "was wasted and destroyed," cries of lamentation and death filling the air as "great routes of gallowglasses" raised havoc in the countryside. De Burgo's wealth evaporated; he "was without force or power in any of the parts of Ireland." Plundered herds of cattle bogged down in the muck of sodden moors, and pitched battles were fought in the mud as pursuers caught up with the pursued. Churches were stripped of their jewels and chalices to pay the wages of mercenaries.

William de Burgo, "the Grey"

In the next year, Felim O'Connor had the audacity to beg de Burgo for help, and the earl mustered what strength he still claimed, including forces from his principal tenant, Richard de Bermingham. Rory was brought to battle in Mayo and finally dispatched, Felim thus becoming undisputed head of the clan. But with haste unseemly even by Irish standards, Felim then betrayed the Normans again. Gathering perhaps the greatest tribal levy ever seen in Connaught, among them many of the chiefs last seen in de Burgo's great hall broken and suppliant, Felim headed for Athenry.

This was certainly not the rabble of seventy years before that the Normans had easily dispersed. Felim's force included gallowglass contingents, mounted men, many warriors with mail and helmets, along with the usual assortment of pesky kerns. On the feast day of St. Lawrence in 1316, they did not run or scatter when the Normans sallied out from behind the town's moat, and many fought to the very end. But crushed they were. Led by de Burgo's able cousin William "the Grey" and Richard de Bermingham, the Normans in a "fierce and spirited engagement" finally shattered the O'Connors forever. This clan would never reform to threaten the province again. The list of principal chiefs who died appalled the annalists:

> *Many sons of Kings, whom I name not,*
> *were slain in the great defeat, around the great plain.*

When King Edward heard the news in England, he made Bermingham baron of Athenry. With spoils collected from dead bodies and the Irish camp, walls of the town were built. A town seal was designed showing the heads of Irishmen impaled on pikes. Ironically for Athenry, this stunning victory marked the beginning of its decline.

As the generations passed, Athenry, and later Galway and Loughrea, became solitary outstations for the Englishry of the province. Only on the few narrow, muddy streets of these marcher towns was English ever spoken or respect for the Crown maintained. The countryside, and the de Burgos in particular, degenerated to the level of mere Irish. As such, Athenry became booty, a symbol of foreign wealth, an object to be threatened, taken, burned, and ravaged whenever the opportunity arose. Far from becoming the great city that the de Berminghams envisioned, Athenry remained an imperiled frontier town. Bermingham's Court never emerged as a Windsor Castle, its old keep the nucleus to a fortification expanded over time into an enormously complicated feudal seat. A third story was added and then a set of roof gables, but the castle stands today in much the same condition as when built, a rough-and-ready medieval barracks that could neither shed its colonial function nor evolve into roles less warlike and more mercantile. Everywhere were Irish spies, like the infamous Donald O'Gillapatrick, "the third greatest plunderer of the English," who liked to drift into town on market days in disguise to reconnoiter the terrain:

Spiked heads,
old town seal of Athenry

He is a carpenter, he is a turner,
My nursling is a bookman;
He is selling wine and hides,
Whenever he sees a gathering.

Upon Richard de Burgo's death in 1326, his grandson the Brown Earl inherited the great legacies of Connaught and Ulster. This young man had an English mother and was married to Maud of Lancaster. When he crossed from England in 1329, he was shocked, and perhaps frightened, at what he found. His cousins, progeny of the Red Earl's great ally of Athenry, William the Grey, could hardly be recognized as worthy knights of the realm, so degenerate had they become through marriage and alliance with the Gael. But in their hands on the local level great power was being appropriated at the Brown Earl's expense. He promptly threw one of these into the dungeons of Carrickfergus Castle in Antrim and starved him to death, inciting his kinsmen to their usual disgust with absentee lords. The Brown Earl, only twenty-one years of age, was slashed to death by his own retinue while crossing a ford. His wife immediately fled back to England with their daughter, whose marriage as an infant to Lionel, duke of Clarence (a son of Edward III), produced over a century later, in a tangled family tree of considerable complexity, the English monarch Edward IV, who naturally claimed for the Crown his rights by English law to the de Burgo earldoms, yet another in that long line of futilities that litter Irish history. The de Burgo inheritance had long since been carved apart.

The original Anglo-Norman families, having in some cases invested over 150 years of bloody effort in their Irish estates, were no longer willing to abide by the rules of feudal primogeniture, whereby the profits of great landed fortunes could go beyond their control into the coffers of even greater families in faraway England. The fortunes of the de Burgos are a fine example. Minor septs, or junior branches, of the family blanched at the idea of paying homage and rent to an absentee such as Clarence, whose only right to that wealth came from his marriage.

In many a hall of a grim Irish castle, Gaelic women—wives to de Burgo warriors—berated their men to accept Irish ways of succession that, albeit bloody and treacherous, at least kept control on their own level. If a lord died childless or with a minor heir or daughter, cousins were available to keep the patrimony distinctly local. Such was the case in 1333, as William the Grey's ablest sons divided Connaught between them. Edmund Albanach (or "the Scot") arrived in the province from exile speaking Irish and with gallowglasses in his train, not mounted Norman knights, along with a court of Irish lawyers, Irish harpists, Irish bards, and Irish monks. He immediately married an Irish princess and threw off his Anglo-Norman title to assume an Irish dignity. Cornering his chief rival in battle, he took the man prisoner, tied a great stone around his neck, and dropped him in Lough Mask. Regardless of the duke of Clarence's claims, he took the northern half of Connaught, mostly County Mayo. His brother William, no longer styling himself FitzWilliam but rather, after the Irish fashion, MacWilliam Uachtarach, took Galway and the plains of Moyode—again, Clarence be damned. The de Burgos became Burkes, and Connaught came to be known by the Gaelic bards and *filid* as Clanricard, or the Kingdom of Richard's Clan. The original French-speaking de Burgo warlords were gradually canonized into saga figures, a pantheon of ancestral patriarchs for countless Celtic septs who now looked on that family as their overlords.

RUMORS OF WAR, 1994

Bright new signs promising a welcome to both industry and tourists have been erected on all the major approaches to Athenry, an indication of the town authorities' confusion about development as they view a worrisome future. If only they saw some trend or glimpse of prosperity, any reed promising salvation, they would grab it immediately, no matter the consequence. Should some multinational corporation pull into Athenry offering jobs and a cash flow, it could pretty well do whatever filthy job it wished. Likewise the allure of tourism, constantly promised but never the plunder that national statistics indicate it should be. Why can't some theme park operator see the potential here just waiting to be harnessed?

"No one knows what they want to do," a souvenir shop owner said to me, "but as far as tourists go, we hardly notice them. A few Yanks, and we like them because they spend no matter what; a few English, but they never spend anything; and a mixed lot of Dutch, Germans, French, usually on bicycles, and what can you buy that fits on one of them? Most visitors we get are Irish, and they buy drink and candy bars, that's about it."

Without a clear idea of what's happening in any of these complicated areas, the townspeople allow industry to mar the landscape pretty much irrevocably. An unsightly collection of grain silos was erected on the major approach into town, butt up to the medieval walls and drum towers, and a major impediment to what is, I believe, the most universally inclusive view of a medieval complex in Ireland. Permission has just been granted from Dublin for this truck-inviting blight to engorge a few additional acres as well. The old country road feeding this complex was bulldozed and widened just enough to ruin the Old World flavor of its predecessor.

Over on the other side of Athenry, word has it that the farmers' co-op also wants a simpler truck route and that the euro will soon come to do away with all the twisting, turning lanes of old, including a lovely arched bridge, in favor of a highway straight to the cash register that will inevitably eat up the perhaps archaeologically rich site of the medieval fairgrounds. When all of these improvements are undertaken, a few people will note that what little there was attractive about Athenry no longer exists, and a hue and cry of surprised citizens will argue, yet again, over what to do about tourism.

Some indication of the Disney-style possibilities that exist here presented itself to the collective consciousness of Athenry in the summer of 1998, when townspeople organized a reenactment of the de Burgo–O'Connor bloodbath of 1316. People dressed up in reasonably authentic medieval gear (or as they imagined it to be), though eyeglasses, hearing aids, and Walkmans proved detrimental to a completely realistic recreation of era. Jousting took place and certainly seemed dangerous enough, as the wild horses with knights astride veered back and forth in tourneys. Open fires and boiling broth, bands of musicians and colleens with harps, all amused the throngs who certifiably poured into town, the climax for whom was the mock battle. Papier-mâché rocks and water balloons rained from the parapets of Birmingham's Court, a fake battering ram and catapult were hauled out to do their grimy work, and about 300 people surged back and forth in the mud clubbing each other with fake weapons. In the middle of this affray, an ambulance wound its way through the crowd, which initiated the deliciously gruesome rumor that someone had actually been flung from Athenry Castle, suffering a broken back in the fall. By evening the rumor had specified the "victim" as a young woman who, amid the mayhem was mistaken for one of the many dummies that were thrown over the side. Word had it, as a matter of fact, that she was dead. By nightfall all the pubs were full of it.

"One way to put Athenry on the map!" one of my friends exulted. "Tourists would come here by the droves if we could provide them as decent a spectacle, and what could be better than flinging locals over the castle walls, especially the ones I owes money to!"

Uproar over this tragedy (which was, of course, unfounded, the dramatic entrance by medics occasioned solely to treat a foot injury) obscured the fact that organizers of the event could not decide on an outcome for the ersatz battle. "Justice would seem to call for a Norman triumph," someone on the committee told me. "After all, they won in 1316. But popular sentiment was all on the side of the Celts. Why couldn't we win just for once, and get some pleasure out of it?" In the end the battle was declared a draw.

GALWAY AND KILDARE, 1504

Over the many years of my coming to Moyode, I gradually tired of camping outside the building, where cattle, sheep, and the despicable weather proved destructive to the fabric and lines of my tents. In the mid-1980s I knocked together a crude ladder to reach a small chamber on the second floor, directly over the entryway to the tower, and decided to build a plywood platform there for my sleeping bag. Athenry, of course, had nothing to offer, so I drove the twenty minutes or so to Galway City, one of my favorite places in the county.

Galway, a bigger, gloomier, noisier version of Athenry, was and is a predominately gray and stony city that has for centuries owed whatever good fortune it had to a marvelous location on the sea. Encastled by the de Burgos in 1232, it followed a different course from those of Athenry and Loughrea, their other important bases of power. An English observer, Sir Oliver St. John, noted the contrast in 1614. The de Burgos's inland borough towns were built "whiles they had their swords in their hands and kept themselves close in garrison." When the barons' men spread out to the countryside and settled the land with smaller fortresses of their own, dependence on the castles of Loughrea and Athenry diminished. As a matter of fact, the towns became in and of themselves targets for plunder, especially as over generations they came to epitomize a more English, mercantile aura to the by now Hibernicized petty warlords. The two were burned and looted repeatedly. In 1601 Lord Carew characterized Athenry as a mere "waste town." St. John wrote thirteen years later that it was "all ruined save the walls."

Galway, in contrast, enjoyed varying periods of prosperity through its maritime trade. A significant moneyed class emerged, its success clearly manifest in the various counting houses and fortified townhouses that survive today as banks or shop fronts, in the Collegiate Church of St. Nicholas, and in a residue of later wharves and warehouses that mark the waterfront. Galway merchants exported fish by the ton in medieval times, much of it to the Iberian Peninsula, and served the surrounding countryside as the solitary outlet for its agrarian surplus of tallow, wool, and, most important, cattle hides. In return, Galway imported enormous quantities of wine, significant supplies of salt, iron, munitions, and contraband of various sorts, along with inexhaustible quantities of discomfort to the Crown during unsettled times in the form of rumors, accusations, gossip, spies, papal nuncios, émigré soldiers of fortune, cash, and treasonable plots of assorted hues. Galway, more than any port in Ireland, was home to Spanish ships of commerce.* But what had been an asset for Galway City in its medieval period proved less so by Elizabeth I's reign in the latter half of the sixteenth century, when the religious question poisoned every aspect of Ireland's civic and commercial life. Spain came to represent all that was most degenerate in "ye papist carrion." Galway began a lengthy decline, a slide of over four centuries' duration.

My foray into the world of available building supplies in 1991 confirmed, to my mind anyway, the continuing status of Galway as a commercial backwater. I might as well have been in Nigeria or Madagascar. Simple fittings, a few odds and ends, any variety in lumber, plumbing gadgetry, a couple of tools, all were nonexistent. One needed to be flexible, to grab what might work before another customer got it, and expect to pay an outrageous price for the privilege of doing so. Another prerequisite: avoid looking too surprised or contemptuous at the motley supply of goods. I was tempted to inquire why my sheet of plywood came from Indonesia of all places but resisted the impulse.

Since then Galway has spruced up its downtown. Some of the renovated warehouses and commercial buildings are stunning. But these changes seem oriented toward tourism, and aside from jobs in the construction trades, no long-term bolster to the local economy seems evident to me. The wharf area in particular remains underutilized, vast terminals for a collection of rust buckets and small coasters, interspersed with the frantic comings and goings of ferries to the Aran Islands, whose day-tripping passengers are inevitably speedily ruining the largest of these, Inishmore.

But at least this old town has survived. It is busy; people live here and bustle about while suburban sprawl, largely achieved through credit, disfigures the surrounding hillsides. There is just no questioning Galway's status as the premier city of western Ireland. It achieved this position largely by cleverly maintaining independence from the de Burgo family that first built its castle here in the thirteenth century. As often as the people of Galway supplied the MacWilliam Burkes,

---

*Christopher Columbus visited the city around 1477, looking for gossip and nautical chitchat relating to Western sea-lanes. Irish sailors for centuries had explored the open Atlantic, reaching the Faeroe Islands and Iceland well before the Vikings, and perhaps Greenland and even the Americas later.

those of Galway and Mayo alike, with all their needs, so too did they slam city gates in their faces or lead thieves of that clan to the gallows. Unlike Loughrea and Athenry, they had alternative means of support—overseas trade—which freed their dependence on the local lordship. In fact, they often had the Burkes at their mercy. More than one earl of Clanricard pawned his jewels and plate for ready cash from a Galway merchant.

By 1450 the city of Galway was undoubtedly one of the few places in all of Ireland about which the English Crown knew anything, yet such was the state of information at that time that the king would have been hard-pressed to explain exactly where the town was, what its current economic condition happened to be, or the state of its relationship with clans from the surrounding countryside. English consciousness was now largely confined to the Pale, a very small expanse of fertile countryside on the eastern coastline of the island, stretching from Drogheda at the mouth of the River Boyne down to the foothills of Wicklow. Its western borders sometimes reached as far as Athlone on the Shannon but at times of severe unrest ran barely 30 miles inland from Dublin, its principal fortress.

Whatever ministries of government the English devised to rule here originated from the stone keep of Dublin Castle. Heads of traitors, whether Gaelic or Anglo-Norman, were traditionally spiked on the gatehouse ramparts. Such was the weakness of the Crown's hold, however, that few of these trophies were supplied by English commanders. They did not rule beyond the Pale, having neither resources nor the will to venture far from Dublin. Heads of villains were secured by money or provided by Irish allies seeking help in their usual feuds. The Norman conquest of Ireland had been totally reversed. English kings claimed earldoms like those of the old de Burgos that hadn't seen a soldier of his majesty's forces, to say nothing of an army, for a century or more. A commander of royal blood occasionally came over to try his hand. Lionel, duke of Clarence, husband to the Brown Earl's only daughter, Elizabeth, arrived in 1361 with a royal commission to recover his patrimony in Connaught and Ulster. The great Anglo-Norman lords ignored him and offered no assistance. Clarence, soon bored by a task that was generating neither riches nor honor, decamped to more glorious battlefields on the Continent, where he quickly died. His only real achievement in Ireland was promulgation of the Statutes of Kilkenny, a parliamentary decree of thirty-five prohibitions that he engineered in 1366 and that have long been studied in Ireland. Written in French, the statutes were a recognition of the "degenerative" status that many of the Old English lords had fallen prey to, but their condemnation of various cultural interactions with native Irish—marriage, tanistry, dress, speech, transfer of lands and titles, even the mode of riding horseback—were universally disdained and ignored.

Richard II's expeditions at the end of that century were generally reminiscent of Henry II's some 200 years before: obsequious submissions, pledges, and oaths from his loyal subjects, all tossed aside as the king's ships returned to England. No British monarch set foot in Ireland again for another two centuries.

The Pale surrounding Dublin continued to shrink. Galway City, inaccessible from Dublin, developed as it saw fit, maintaining for all practical purposes the status of an independent city-state. As a point of pride, it cherished an aura of Englishness, a sense of superiority to the rabble who skulked about in the dark woods and watery bogs that lay outside its walls. Unlike the MacWilliam Burkes of Clanricard, the intelligentsia of Galway did not embrace the Irish tongue as their primary language. Nearly all important merchants were bilingual, those who knew and wrote Latin trilingual. The place was indeed the Crown's solitary outpost in faraway Connaught.

The Gaels and Anglo-Irish, of course, knew where Galway was, and indifferent or frustrated English monarchs began to put their faith in local warlords to keep Ireland in some sort of order for the Crown. The exploits of three earls of Kildare—the seventh, eighth, and ninth—inject ingredients of such ripe character to the already histrionic Irish story as to defy the reaches of fiction. Their colorful and in the last analysis tragic stories have kept many historians preoccupied for entire careers.

The earls were FitzGeralds, direct descendants of the Geraldines from Wales who had formed the vanguard of the original Norman invasion. By the latter half of the 1400s, they were powerfully settled in the rich farming lands around Maynooth and Kildare, their principal fortresses some 14 and 30 miles from Dublin, respectively. These castles were neither more nor less imposing than others in Ireland, and their lords neither more nor less rapacious than the Butlers and Desmonds to the south, Burkes to the west, and O'Donnells and O'Neills in the north. Simply by virtue of geography, however, the FitzGeralds became supreme in the Pale.

Through judicious intermarriage, wary diplomacy in both Dublin and London, and a very canny balancing act within their own personalities of the contrasting racial strains each carried—an impossibly tangled mixture of Norman, Welsh, English, and Celtic bloodlines—they managed to influence all elements of the Irish scene to their own, and sometimes the Crown's, advantage. This was a complicated and often perilous task that few of us today could imagine, yet it was carried off with great level-headedness and usually cool restraint by the Kildares.

Beginning with the seventh earl, Thomas, through the "Great Earl," Gerald, and then his son Gerald Og, this regal house in effect governed the Pale for nearly seventy-five years, between 1459 and 1534. English monarchs often despaired of the arrangement. The earls ruled as palatine lords. Their proximity overawed Dublin Castle. English administrators found Dublin's bureaucracy totally infiltrated by men loyal to Kildare and the interests of other Anglo-Norman magnates. English military men discovered that their standing "army" numbered a puny 120 men. At any given moment—aside from Kildare's private force, which boasted artillery and many hundreds of his tenantry—the earl could muster thousands to his standard, both Anglo-Norman and Gaelic, whose loyalty to the Crown was recognized as derived solely from the earl's importunings, threats, and promises of reward.

What made the Kildares unique, however, was their studied caution. At no point in their lengthy run with power did they ever take that final, ruinous step and yield to the seductive words of the bard, who "made men of the country to believe they be descended of Alexander the Great, or of Darius, or a Caesar." They never reached for the crown of Ireland, which on various occasions they certainly could have taken. The Great Earl in particular resisted the urge to go too far. In an age and culture where circumspection was unheard of, the earl seemed content to rule as a king without trappings or title. He was sublime enough to be satisfied with the power.

Henry VII and his son and successor, Henry VIII, recognized the temptations set before this family and, being as conspiratorial as all the Tudors, were prone to believe whatever reports spies and enemies of Kildare sent along. Each of the earls was accordingly accused of treason at one time or another. Some were recalled to London to answer charges (Gerald Og on three occasions) or be confined to the

Tower. All were challenged to prove their loyalty whenever their monarch became either nervous or angry, the usual occurrence when matters of finance were raised.

What revenues the Pale generated were all allocated to the earl's accounts for the support of military expenditures "in his majesty's interests." What constituted official business as opposed to private feud, however, tended to be a matter of blurred lines. Executions and enforcements of the king's justice often seemed arbitrarily applied by the earls, with properties destined for the Crown's revenues sometimes mysteriously transferred to favorites of the Kildares. Instructions of English envoys could be obliquely ignored. In such cases their stock might drop in London, their office of lord deputy transferred to another, but resulting explosions of lawlessness and threats to the Pale usually convinced the English king of the moment that there was no alternative to the House of Kildare.

Only the foolish and exceedingly immature behavior of "Silken Thomas," the tenth earl, goaded the Tudors to behavior they had always, in their most inebriated condition, wished to pursue. The impetuous rebellion initiated by that excitable young man in 1534 led to his execution and that of five uncles in London. The castle at Maynooth was taken by artillery, and all within it were slaughtered.

At the turn of the sixteenth century, however, the House of Kildare stood paramount in the king's affection. The Great Earl was lord deputy and, in his official capacity as Henry VII's lieutenant, about to embark on an ambitious expedition to parts rarely visited by representatives of the Crown, the environs of Galway. His objective was to destroy his son-in-law, the MacWilliam Burke of Clanricard.

Of all the degenerate Old English, the Burkes were universally regarded in Dublin Castle as among the worst. Indeed, since their conscious rejection of English law and custom more than a century before, they had adopted the mannerisms of Irish warlords with complete abandon. Bards reminded them now and again of their noble English blood, which reinforced a penchant for self-glorification and allowed them to posture as grandees before their Gaelic followers, but in fact they were utterly mongrelized by 1500. Intermarriage and fosterage of children in Irish households had produced a Burke totally Celtic. The history of my small plot at Moyode became that of "intestine commotion," in the words of an English lord deputy, the passage back and forth of armed bands seeking either cattle or the chieftainship of clan. As far as the Tudors were concerned, these were the Dark Ages.

We will never know anything about the intimate personality of Ulick (or William) MacWilliam of Clanricard. His principal castle remained at Loughrea. The Dolphins, still loyal men to his standard, were probably settled in Moyode, though the castle I purchased from Thomas Uniacke had not yet been built. They answered the call for hosting whenever Ulick issued it. His feuds would likely be with one of three parties: those within his own family desirous of his position; the MacWilliam Burkes of Mayo, his cousins; and the Gaelic O'Kellys, whose lands lay to the east of his.

In all likelihood Ulick was no polished courtier but a man of the sword who oppressed friend and foe alike. He kept a few dozen Scottish gallowglasses permanently on hand as the core of his private army, supplemented by a slightly larger number of kerns, wild foot soldiers who "think no man dead until his head be off." These forces were quartered on Ulick's tenants, a form of taxation (or oppression, depending on your point of view) known as coyne and livery, a source of continual irregularity and complaint. During times of general warfare, Ulick would call out his tenants (men like the Dolphins) and his more dependable allies (usually the O'Briens, to the south near Limerick). In his confrontation with the Great Earl, his muster is believed to have been around 3,000 men.

Ulick had a rough genealogical sense about him, and he understood the dark ways of intrigue and alliance, blood pact and social cachet. His marriage to Kildare's daughter was certainly advantageous for him, in about the reverse proportion as his subsequent abuse of her turned out to be.

The status of women as political components had not much improved since the days of William de Burgo in 1185, though it would be a mistake, I think, to regard them as chattel. Irish women were outspoken, expressive, opinionated, jealous, and dominating individuals who in many proven instances goaded or restrained their men in the intrigues of the day. The fact that Kildare used one of his children to secure a connection with the lord of Clanricard seems cold-blooded and Machiavellian, which in a way it was. But Kildare reacted as a father when word came to him that his daughter was being mistreated.

Undoubtedly, in his diplomatic way, he managed to send a warning to Ulick, but (as is usually the case) a lord far from the center of power generally feels safe in his obscurity. Ulick Burke continued to behave as he wished, first attacking the O'Kellys, allies of Kildare ("no wilder men of Ireland be than they"), and then forcing open the gates of the hitherto independent Galway City, clearly an affront to English interests. But rumor had it these were but Kildare's formal excuses. Lord deputies and armies from the Pale rarely chose to venture deep into the extremities of Ireland. Kildare had no uncommonly villainous or treasonable provocation that might require such an effort. It was, as an Elizabethan put it, "a private grudge" that motivated the earl.

His force of about 5,000 men was considered immense by contemporary accounts, and the battle he fought with Ulick on a summer's day in 1504 on the hill of Knockdoe outside of Galway City was "such as had not been known in latter times." In many ways this sanguinary encounter was the last purely medieval battle in Irish history, fought largely between ax-wielding gallowglass mercenaries from each side, with kern milling about the edges, hurling spears and hacking at fallen men, and archers letting arrows fly into masses of foot soldiers. For the first time in Ireland, the use of a handgun is mentioned, though significantly the owner did not fire the weapon but used it instead to beat in the head of a fallen horseman. Those who fell at Knockdoe met a largely personal death. They saw who it was who dealt them the final blow, face to face.

Ulick's host, outnumbered by the earl's forces, were shattered after a long day of indeterminate struggle, one vast melee of pushing, shoving, hacking, stabbing men. Nine brave companies of Clanricard's gallowglasses were reduced to but "one broken battalion." As they left the field they were harried by the earl's army. Numerous stands were made and broken, until finally Ulick's men disintegrated and fled along byways best known to them that might finally lead home. In their ritualized fashion, when faced with the task of describing the resulting carrion, Irish annalists turned hyperbolic: "The field became rough from the heaps of carnage, from the number of the spears, the swords, the battle shields, the bodies wounded, mangled, and of young men stretched in heaps, of beardless boys, loathsome, unsightly."

The Viscount Gormanston, ancestor to my old friend Penelope Preston, was alleged to have suggested to Kildare that he complete the good day's work by killing off their Irish allies, the O'Donnells and O'Neills. The earl declined. Among his prisoners were four of Ulick's children (whether by Kildare's daughter or some other woman we do

A Burke gallowglass, Glinsk, County Mayo

not know). Ulick himself escaped. The next day Kildare marched into Galway and reestablished its freedom from Clanricard's control, and did likewise for Athenry on his march home. The Great Earl informed King Henry that a great victory had been won. Henry took his word for that, having no idea who MacWilliam Burke was and wondering all the while at the alleged benefit to his coffers. Kildare was made a knight of the garter as reward.

Eight separate MacWilliam Burkes of Clanricard held control of the sept for the next two decades, generally unmolested in their martial intrigues by any interference from Dublin, to say nothing of London. Knockdoe had not crippled or diminished their natural resiliency. Irish politics became the despair of England, particularly as the Kildares engaged in a more or less open vendetta with their principal enemies, the Butlers of Kilkenney, earls of Ormond. The execution of Silken Thomas in 1537, with its virtual extinction of FitzGerald power in the Pale, resolved that particular dispute but confronted the Tudors with their usual dilemma: What were they to do with Ireland?

Select Chronology

1543	Ulick Burke, "the Beheader," created first Earl of Clanricard.
c. 1550	Moyode Castle built, presumably by Dolphin family.
	Elizabeth I ascends the throne of England.
	Lord Henry Sidney created Lord Deputy of Ireland.
1567	First wooden bridge thrown over the Shannon into Connaught.
1588	England defeats the Spanish Armada.
1594–1603	Rebellion by the Great O'Neill.
1599	Battle of Curlew Mountains. O'Donnell routs Crown forces, among them Richard, future fourth Earl of Clanricard.
1600	Battle of Kinsale. O'Neill and rebels are crushed.
1607	Flight of the Earls. O'Neill flees to Rome. Old Gaelic society declines.
1626	Charles I offers first "Graces" to Old English nobility of Ireland (mostly Catholics).
1633–1640	Wentworth's tenure as Lord Deputy of Ireland. Initiates plan for plantation of Connaught.
1641	Execution of Wentworth. Rebellion in Ireland; many Protestant New English, such as Reverend Robert Persse, flee their homes.
1642	Civil war in England: Charles I versus Parliament.
1649	Charles I executed.
1649–1650	Cromwell invades Ireland, takes Drogheda and Wexford with attendant massacres. Clanricard attempts to

	defend Connaught from Parliamentarians.
1652	War ends in defeat of Crown and Catholic forces
1658	Death of Cromwell.
1660	Monarchy restored with Charles II.
1685	Death of Charles; his brother James II ascends throne.
	Anne, daughter of James II, and her husband, William of Orange, lead rebellion.
1690	Battle of the Boyne. James II flees to France.
1691	Battle of Aughrim. As Jacobite cause unravels, "Wild Geese" (Catholic soldiers) flee to France.

DOLPHIN AND CLANRICARD

1540–1700

The wars here is most painful.

THE ONLY NOOK IN ATHENRY

In Ireland I am a daily drinker. I don't know if it's the dank or chill that I need protection from or the company and chatter I want, but at the hour of seven or eight o'clock I am usually on my way to some pub or another. It's the same with one of my neighbors, old Frank Broderick, who lives in the former milking parlor of Moyode House. I often pass him on the road, whether rainy or cold it makes no difference, bicycling along into Athenry for three or four pints of Guinness. He is usually embarrassed when I stop and pile his antique Raleigh into the back and then drive him in. He likes to be dropped off right outside of town.

There are fifteen pubs in Athenry and two hotel bars. The Abbey is a favored spot for Athenry's more genteel set, people like the Ruane brothers or priests from Esker in for a quiet evening of drink. Tom Ruane is one of my favorite Athenry characters. His father is a legend in town, an entrepreneurial man who lit up the entire village back in the 1930s with an enormous generator that he brought from England. He set up a mineral water works as well, his drivers hauling flavored drinks all over Galway, along with a tractor dealership that his two sons inherited and ran until the general economic collapse of the 1980s overtook them. "In the twenty-six counties during the boom, there'd be sales of anywhere between 11,000 and 12,000 new tractors a year. When we closed up, those figures were down to around 1,200 a year. We couldn't compete in that climate." Tom and his brother still own the large showroom and service workshops, now deserted, and earn their primary livelihood by running a petrol station out front. The other day, stopping for gas, I caught him catching up on his reading, plowing through a 1798 issue of *Walker's Magazine, a Compendium of Entertaining Information*.

Once or twice a week, Tom visits the Abbey "to demolish an evening," as he puts it. This hotel bar used to be a rather pleasant haunt until the owner became obsessed with his television, keeping the volume permanently stuck on high. Tom never seemed to mind. "I can't stand that TV," I'd say to him over the din.

"Yes, the color is very bad," he'd reply.

The Abbey recently changed hands. We are fearful that its elegant decor of old prints and Georgian accoutrements will be altered, thereby "throwing all of us into the street," in Tom's words, because for this set there is no alternative. All the other bars are pretty dreadful and beneath the dignity of a gentleman to frequent.

As I am not a gentleman, I have over the years inspected each and every pub in the town. One would think, given the sheer number of establishments here, there would be several to choose from depending on one's mood of an evening, but such is not the case. Some are lounge bars with faded plush and torn seat covers, some are concrete sheds of indescribable gloom, still more are newly decorated in a style I can only describe as Celtic suburban. All are dominated by television. To the best of my knowledge, only one pub in Athenry lacks a TV, and that is generally where I go.

Maura Burke, the publican of Keane's, has been in this business for thirty-five years, a statistic more telling of longevity than wealth, as she readily admits. Keane's is the sort of antique bar and goods store that once was common to Ireland but is disappearing as grocery chains and roadside lounge bars with entertainment proliferate. Her inventory, for instance, is delightfully idiosyncratic. A recent customer I observed purchased the following off her shelves: one package of shoelaces, two pairs of socks, a can of salmon, one packet of dry soup, one candy bar, one nip of gin, and a box of matches. "God bless all here," he said on leaving.

Maura Burke, publican

The decor is 1930s: counter and shelves painted a high-gloss green, frosted glass panels separating the grocery from the bar, a nook big enough for four stools, on the walls framed pictures of hunt scenes and Galway hurlers, the floor poured concrete with an electric heater ready to plug in on cold nights. The door, hard to squeeze through, rings an old bell as you enter, which brings Maura from her kitchen. If it's me, she will hastily change the radio station to Irish music. "It's not Michael Jackson ye want to hear, I know it!" she says. "Your man here must be served," is her response to anyone there before me who might object to a different station. She enjoys the fact that I love her place.

Keane's has a limited clientele these days. Only old-timers locked to habit frequent this pub, and they generally never show up until an hour or so before closing. "Drink is so dear now, they come in late so they won't spend as much." Before the cattle mart moved out of town to a modern co-op building, business had been steady and fairly good. "We'd have the street mart on the first Friday of every month, and, oh, the lanes would be jammed with cattle and carts. I'd be open at four in the morning to receive the farmers, who often had been on the

Street market, Athenry, c. 1940s

road all night walking their stock in. We'd serve 'shorts' first to take the chill off them—rum, whiskey, gin. After breakfast they'd turn to beer and stout and visit all morning. Nowadays it's all business. They ride to the mart in their tractors and Land Rovers, then straight on home. They've no time at all." Maura stays open more out of habit than anything else, pouring her pints of Guinness slowly and with care, as they should be. A winter's evening here is a return to an old Ireland that will cease to exist in my lifetime.

Surrender and Regrant, 1541

The Dolphin and his petty kingdom—a few hundred acres in the middle of "Clanricard's great plain"—violated just about every precept of good order and governance that Henry VIII and his Privy Council desired. Most obnoxious and galling was that a little man like the Dolphin and, by extension, a greater one like MacWilliam Burke, enjoyed "imperial jurisdiction in their rooms," unfettered by any obligation to the king or his treasury. Henry had considerable loathing for landowning magnates who held estates not through grants or by leave of the English Crown but rather by age-old rights of conquest. Irish custom of devolving these parcels on the death of a chief through "barbarous" tanistry or selection of the fittest sowed disaffection, feud, bloodshed, and ruined economies, yielding no benefit to the Crown in rents and duties, merely crippling military expenditures in a field of operations that produced no glory, no honor, no fame.

English policy (on paper, anyway) had one primary goal from which all else proceeded: to "enclose and husband" the Irish countryside. English law regarding primogeniture ensured the orderly transfer of property that would in turn encourage a commitment to settled agriculture as opposed to seasonal herding, "a very idle life and a fit nursery for a thief" according to the poet Edmund Spenser. Settled agriculture meant a secure population, never troubled or abused whenever a major landlord happened to die.

The Tudors wished a radical transformation of Irish society. English tradition would replace the *brehon* code of ancient Irish legal usage, English farming practices would supplant those of the more primitive Irish, the English language would be spoken by all, English currency would be favored over simple barter, an English tax system would be universally imposed and accepted, and the Irish would conform to a new state religion. In England some argued that only through complete military conquest could such an agenda be accomplished. But Henry, like all English monarchs before and after, cared more for France and continental affairs. He was uninterested in pledging the kind of funds his generals demanded, much to the relief of his Anglo-Norman subjects in the Pale. They approved of all the king's goals (save that of taxes and the new Protestant religion Henry was introducing in his feud with the papacy), but a military solution meant a standing army, one that would be quartered on Anglo-Norman lands and largely paid for by them. With the House of Kildare in ruins, however, the Pale was vulnerable on its borders. Although conversion of the wild Irish into king's subjects was the only solution to their growing misery and ruin, the Anglo-Normans encouraged a more diplomatic approach to "allure the Irish to obedience," in effect a bribery scheme aimed at seducing the incredulous Gael. It would be a cheaper way out, the king agreed. The Palesmen then proclaimed Henry "king of Ireland," and another conquest of Ireland was put to motion.

"Conquest" is, of course, a pretentious word, and certainly the initial stirrings of English lord deputies were modest in scope. In cinematic terms this was not a cast of thousands. An aerial view of Lord Leonard Grey—trekking into Galway with a ragged band of foot soldiers, dragging along a train of one or two cannon and assorted munitions—would not remind anyone of a climactic struggle such as Hastings. No roads, only marsh and bog, dense scrub woods, surly and filthy natives, dreadful wet weather, chieftains "who would not be ordered"—these were the mundane and depressing realities of Irish service. The only vivid color Grey ever saw was crimson in the robes of the mayor and his council, who stood on the walls of Galway City watching him approach. Once inside, Grey complained, townsmen treated him saucily.

His objective was to find or create malleable subjects. Who among the wild clans could be approached? Who could be made to ally themselves with the Crown? What rivalries and feuds could Grey exploit? For an Englishman like the lord deputy, a blunt fighting man of little subtlety, the quandary must have seemed insurmountable.

He first decided, after conferring with the mayor, that the current MacWilliam Burke, "who did much hurt to the town of Galway," was not a man he could deal with. Leaving the city, Grey lumbered from castle to castle, "braking" some with cannon, taking others by stealth or a sudden rush to the main gate, and these he turned over to one Ulick Burke, some "for money" (which Grey pocketed) and others on pledges of fealty. He gradually came to see in this Ulick a man who was "sure to the King," and without consulting anyone else in Clanricard, he knighted him the new MacWilliam Burke and took additional castles to solidify this installment.

Ulick was no puppet, however. Known as "the Beheader," he more than held his own in the bloody strife that was commonplace in "Bourken Country." The lord deputy's support simply turned the balance more decisively in his favor, and he was as grateful as any devious, cunning, and amoral Irish chieftain could be. "Small gifts and honest persuasion," he told Grey, would ensure his loyalty, upon which the lord deputy whispered more enticements.

King Henry's policy, known as "surrender and regrant," was offered to Ulick. The king, with his artillery, would support Ulick as the new

Clanricard. Ulick would surrender all his lands to Henry, who in turn would regrant them to Ulick by royal patent and English law. Ulick would hold this domain with a royal honor or title to be chosen by London, and upon his death both the appointments and the land would pass to his eldest son and heir. Additional burdens would be required: Ulick would endeavor to introduce English customs and language to Clanricard, put the lands into cultivation, disband his private army, obey instructions from the lord deputy, destroy all rebels, join lawful expeditions, and eventually pay a rent in return for the Crown's protection. To each and all of these provisions, Ulick agreed, though in fact he considered them a comedy. As Grey continued his progress south into Limerick, humiliated that the O'Brien had sent as an official escort but a single gallowglass—"to the King's greatest dishonor that ever was seen in Ireland!"—Ulick no doubt relished his gains. He was the new MacWilliam Burke of Clanricard, thanks to the guns of the foreigner whom he would never, surely, see again.

As to the particular fate of Leonard Grey, Ulick was quite on target. Henry recalled his deputy and executed him, for reasons still unclear today. But after Grey came more and better men. There would be no future lord deputies of Anglo-Norman blood under the Tudors, just a succession of capable, aggressive, often ruthless Englishmen who, as the Irish quagmire threatened their careers, became more resolute and demanding of those men like Ulick who had blithely cast their lot with the Crown.

Ulick's bargain, as he came to see it, had not been as shrewd as he originally thought. Some of the provisions were ludicrous. Ulick could not speak English himself; how was he to see it spread through Connaught? Give up his gallowglass? He would be dead within a week, traveling along "up and down the country, like a priest." Pay taxes with what, cattle? He had no money. Worse than that, as his lawyers the *brehons* told him, English title to the land (the clan's land, as they would have informed him, not his own) contained the heavy curse of possible attainder and escheatage, whereby the domain could revert to the king almost by whim should Ulick displease him, a foregone and happy conclusion to the Crown's advisers. The English knew that men like the Beheader could not fail but slip into treason, "so apt to offend, as it is very likely that by justice they will make your highness in small time the owner of all." And as for his eldest son and heir, who might that be? Which of his sons was even legitimate? Yet cast off his association with the English he could not. Ulick's position was too precarious. Henry's power had put him where he was, so at some lucid point in his deliberations Ulick MacWilliam Burke of Clanricard decided that his fortunes lay with the ultimate persuader, the king's artillery.

When the new lord deputy required Ulick's presence in Dublin, the lord of Clanricard obeyed, dismal and dangerous though such a journey through hostile territories was. His reward, a gilded cup, evoked such a response of obsequious gratitude that even the lord deputy was taken aback. The scene calls to mind that of colonists giving trinkets to American Indians.

On the whole, Henry's policy of surrender and regrants produced varied results. It was completely ineffective in the north with native dynasties such as the O'Neills and O'Donnells, though more favorably received by the O'Briens in Limerick. Ulick Burke was its outstanding success, the lord deputy praising him for "improving the savage quarters under his rule." But Ulick decided that he wanted more than a heavy cup; he wished to be "a grand captaine of his country as the Earls of Ormond and Butler be in theirs." He began prodding to find out which "grand honor" the king would give him and suggested "earl of Connaught."

Ulick's design, quite clearly, was to benefit his own grand ambitions, not those of Henry VIII. He sought English aid to expand his rule through all of Connaught at the expense of Burkes in Mayo and the native O'Connors and O'Kellys to his north and east. He dreamt of becoming the reincarnation of Richard de Burgo, the Great Lord of legend. But though the English sought to rule the wild Irish through the instrument of Ulick Burke and men like him, they had no wish to create a monster, another Kildare. On Ulick's petition the duke of Norfolk wrote an emphatic no.

Ulick Burke, sitting in Loughrea Castle, then composed what is to me a remarkable document, no matter that more seasoned historians might find it mundane. It is true that in the annals of English history as preserved in the voluminous calendars of state papers and official documents that were assiduously collected and annotated in the nineteenth century, portraits of many famous statesmen shine forth in their own words. The letters of a Surrey, Sidney, Essex, Wolsley, More, and Cromwell all contribute to an at times fulsome insight into personality and motive. Such is usually not the case in Irish history. Ulick Burke left no diary or letter book behind, nor printed records of hardly any sort. His sword strokes and piles of decapitated bodies were glorified by bards and poets who sang their verse from memory to an audience that could neither read nor write. To examine Ulick's petition to the king, composed by or dictated to a secretary, is to glimpse a rare moment in the history of Moyode and its "fair champaign country," the actual words of its principal lord.

> To your most Excellent Highness I, William de Burgo, otherwise called mac William or Lord fitz William, your true and faithful subject, most humbly submit me, my life, and goods, and desire your most gracious pardon.
>
> Please it your most Excellent Majesty to be advertised that I and my ancestors, being brought up in a rude country, without order or good civility, and not knowing Your most Excellent Majesty, hath of long time by ignorance, neglected our duty of allegiance. And now, hearing of Your most Excellent Majesty's famous renown, have submitted me to your Deputy and Council in your land of Ireland. And yet therewith not being satisfied, am desirous of seeing Your most Excellent Majesty, to resort to see the same, whereunto nature did procure me, remembering that I and mine ancestors were descended on English blood, and in time past a Baron of the Parliament.
>
> Therefore lamenting the decay and misorder of me and my ancestors, which have been brought to Irish and disobedient rule by reason of marriage and nursing with those Irish, sometimes rebels, near adjoining to me, wherefore now, most dread Sovereign Lord, I willingly submit myself, acknowledging my ignorance, and put lands, body, and goods in your gracious mercy, giving up all that I have in your hands, willing nor desiring anything but that shall please Your most Excellent Majesty to give me, of your mere gift. I so utterly do refuse all contrary laws, submitting me only to your law, according my most bounden duty, and prostrating myself before the feet of Your Majesty, most humbly desire and ask your gracious and merciful pardon of all mine offenses, disobedience, and transgressions.

The king replied in a gracious manner. While regretting the "wild and savage life he and his ancestors have lived," which "might justly move the King to proceed against him," Henry was disposed to accept Clanricard as his loyal man, for surely a knight such as he, with the noble ancestry of his lineage, would be horrified to live an existence offensive to God and king and all that "smell anything of dishonesty." The king would be pleased to create him a viscount or baron by letters patent. Should he come to London, however, he would dub him an earl.

To the American reader, and indeed to many English or Irish, talk of titles and their relative merit on a power scale, from knight to baronet, baronet to baron, on to viscount, earl, marquis, duke, and prince seems all so much empty chatter, and nowadays it largely is. But in medieval times a title meant land, and land, as we saw in the Norman saga, translated into authority and wealth, though definitions of prosperity are certainly variable. Henry VIII's estates were translated into coin and jewels. The dowry of Ulick's granddaughters consisted of cattle.

Ulick MacWilliam Clanricard stood dazzled by the prospect of an earldom. Though he was the "chieftest man in Connaught, who domine all the land," he was in fact a ragged freebooter if compared to the magnates of England or even some of his own contemporaries in Ireland. That he was aware and jealous of the Butlers of Ormond we know. His ambition required that he be their equal.

Ulick's immediate desire was a proper wife, someone more refined than the strident prima donnas of the Irish countryside who knew more about hens and milking cows than they did of etiquette at the court. Sensing the need for someone who spoke correct language, he repaired to Galway City, there to court and marry a widow, Dame Marie Lynch, who "was of a civil and English order of education and manners." The fact that Ulick had two wives, both alive and undivorced from him at the time, seemed no impediment to proceeding. Dame Marie, according to reports, "civilized" the soon-to-be earl. Coming from a prosperous merchant family, she also provided cash, 100 marks, along with plate and jewelry suitable for pawning—a gold chain with cross (£36), a silver cup with cover (£10), and another cup, called "a nutte," worth £17. In 1541 Ulick took ship to London.

This must have been an overwhelming experience for the Beheader. Indeed, perhaps more than any event, these few days in Henry's capital sealed the allegiance of Clanricard to the English Crown forever, no matter all the follies and intrigues and treasons that followed. More sophisticated Irishmen like the Great O'Neill or Ormond could absorb the dazzle of court and keep their wits about them; more "barbaric" Celts like Grace O'Malley or Shane O'Neill could glorify their sense of independence by scorning the heretical hand of England as shallow and decadent. Ulick, though a defiant and spirited man, was perhaps more easily seduced by greed, vainglory, and maybe a touch of reality. Clanricard was a substantial holding, later estimated by Elizabethan commissioners as comprising well over 200,000 acres. English power had given him its control and promised the even greater honor of a continuing patrimony to remain within his family forever. The Irish were keen genealogists, and the notion of originating a dynasty would certainly have appealed to Ulick. There was also the question of accessibility. O'Neill, O'Donnell, and Desmond could all hide away in their truly remote and isolated domains. Ulick's completed travel to London may have convinced him that Connaught was more easily penetrated than any of the Irish provinces and thus more vulnerable to a king's wrath.

On July 1, 1543, Ulick and the O'Brien were rowed downriver to the palace at Greenwich. Entering the Queen's Closet, richly hung with tapestries and strewn with rushes, the two men heard high mass with the king and his principal ministers. They were then dressed in robes of state, for which one John Malte, tailor, presented a bill for £59, 3 shillings, 10 pence ("19 yds crimson velvet for a robe and hood, 12 yds for kirtle and tabards, 20s for making as well as delivering 3 yds crimson velvet to the cutler for girdles and scabbards for swords"). The men proceeded to a state chamber, and in the presence of the court Ulick's letters patent were delivered to the lord chamberlain, who handed them to the great chamberlain, who handed them to the king's majesty, who handed them to the secretary "to read openly." The king next buckled a presentation sword around Ulick's waist, whereupon the Irishman knelt to receive a chain and cross of gold around his neck. Henry knighted five of his followers. The entire assembly, preceded by trumpeters, then retired to a great feast to celebrate Ulick's investiture as first earl of Clanricard.*

Irish annalists recorded the event laconically. They were most impressed that Ulick "came home safe," but in fact he did not. Having caught an infection in London or perhaps during his trip back to Ireland, he became ill and died. Dame Marie, allegedly regretful at mar-

---

*Depending on the context, the word "Clanricard" now signified (oftentimes interchangeably) either the person of the earl himself or the territory he controlled. Thus contemporaries, when referring to Connaught, often simply wrote "Clanricard," that is, the countryside over which the earl had lordship. Likewise, when speaking of whichever earl happened to be in power, chroniclers often identified him as "Clanricard" or "the Clanricard."

rying such an uncouth man ("An ape will be an ape, though he were clad in cloth of gold," as an Englishman later wrote), took as her third husband a more proper citizen of Galway City and appealed for possession of the late earl's "ale cup, chalice, and other ecclesiastical jeweles and plate, partly broken," that were currently in pawn.

The policy of surrender and regrant was now grievously exposed, depending as it did on the orderly observance of English law and custom, which had nothing whatever in common with the late earl's matrimonial misadventures. By the time a royal commission headed by the earl of Ormond had entered Clanricard to assess the inheritance, open warfare and rebellion had broken out. An election to the chieftainship along the proscribed Gaelic lines had produced a candidate who busied himself marching up and down the countryside imposing his order, settling grudges, exacting tribute, stealing cattle, and generally creating havoc. At the gates of Athenry, Ormond himself lost five horsemen and fifteen kern in a bloody demonstration of parochial contempt for the Crown's interference.

Part of Ormond's dilemma was his inability to determine just who Clanricard's heir really was. Primogeniture was a fine concept for an ordered society, but here in Galway the Burkes lived "diabolically, without marriage," with bastards everywhere pressing claims (along with various mothers) to their rightful possession of the earldom. Ormond confessed to complete bewilderment.

Ulick had clearly been a bigamist, and so too his first wife, who, apparently already married, exchanged vows with the earl in a ceremony attended by numerous witnesses. That alone, in the view of his other wives, invalidated the union, thereby bastardizing their son, Richard, and legitimizing their own claims as the earl's genuine wife. There were also the usual concubines, with issue, to deal with and, most bedeviling, all the progeny were minors. Ormond temporized.

His final rather labored decision, which bred more disorder and bloodshed, had a rough English logic to it. He simply chose the eldest son available from whatever marriage could even approximately be deemed legal, thereby selecting the aforementioned Richard, who would be known throughout his life as the Sassanagh, or Englishman. The new Clanricard being yet a boy, Ormond selected a strongman from among the Burkes to rule in his stead. When Richard came of age, to no one's surprise, this man would not relinquish power, and "between them both the whole country was wasted." Richard appealed to the lord deputy, who "within one fortnight, having put certain gentlemen to execution, by terror thereof I placed the Earl quietly."

It would take some sixty years, spanning the careers of the first three earls of Clanricard, for the transition of power and title to run as smoothly as English authorities had intended. Richard Sassanagh proved even more degenerate than his father, running through six wives, innumerable farm girls, and uncounted concubines, all the while fathering the usual brood of half brothers and bastards who would spend their lives in fratricidal mischief. The earl's amatory inclinations "recall those of the poultry yard," in the view of one Englishman. His first wife, whom he alleged practiced witchcraft on him, was dispatched with the aid of an ecclesiastical court. The second, from whom "he had got thre sons, and by God's grace, do entend to get anor," conveniently died. The third was simply retired. The fourth, fifth, and sixth were disposed as whim and convenience dictated. By the finish of Richard's run, which ended for all intents and purposes in the Tower of London, English authorities had despaired of Connaught, a place "that was not worthy to be called a commonwealth." The practical effects of their policy had been to breed confusion, not only here in the western province but equally so in Ulster and Munster. The conciliatory, barely financed efforts of Henry had not pacified the island. "Poor Ireland, worse to worse."

Moyode Castle, 1550

In many ways it was fortunate that I never began work on Moyode back in the 1970s. As the years passed, I gained some experience on my own, restoring the various homes I had lived in during my young and middle adulthood. There's something about smacking your own thumb now and again, shedding blood on your own roof, that gives you perspective and shapes a desire for perfection. Doing for yourself

Moyode Castle, 1982

also arms you for encounters with other builders less careful or scrupulous. In Ireland if you don't watch it, you can be skinned alive.

One of my biyearly trials was to have people come over to Moyode to discuss the job. The hurricanes of talk I endured! The mountains of pledges, promissory notes, drawings, and quotations that never materialized! The baits and traps strewn in conversation! In over twenty years, I never met a builder I thought I could trust.

Yet all these conferences and the many years of hiatus between them gave me plenty of time to familiarize myself with both the building and other peoples' ideas about it. To me there was not much room to maneuver conceptually. Moyode was a piece of rock, and any grandiose schemes to render it a modern chalet would involve structural changes of enormous complexity and cost. I was not about to reconfigure walls, open up the inside, or install a Jacuzzi for the medieval toilet. This disappointed many a contractor, one of whom suggested a glass roof to let in more light. I finally determined that I would live in Moyode much as those who built it had, with few if any frills.

The tower lent itself to simplicity anyway, though its manner of construction and layout were ingenious and complicated. Moyode was never intended as a medieval fortress. Its walls, for a start, are only 4 feet thick at the base, and no elaborate defensive mechanisms such as a moat, outer barbican, portcullis, or web of underground dungeons were ever considered. Moyode mirrored the era in which it was built, about the mid-1500s, when warriors realized that no wall could withstand artillery, no matter how primitive that new weapon happened to be. The times being manifestly perilous, however, no man of position or property could function without some base of protection, some defense against the petty raids and midnight madness of his neighbors. Moyode Castle was, in modern parlance, a minimum-security building, sufficient to resist the quick and duplicitous warfare of the day but an acknowledgment nonetheless that any sustained attack by forces armed with a cannon or two would certainly, over time, breach its walls.

There is also no way of knowing with any exactitude who commissioned, paid for, oversaw the construction, and literally owned Moyode. Unlike England, where records remain in some abundance for these corresponding years of the sixteenth century, the reverse is true in Ireland. Warfare, pillage, and fire, the discord of several murderous eras both then and later, have destroyed our ability to find any of the small details of life here. The architectural record is telling in this respect. Barons in England were by that time finally yielding to their wives' desires for homes more commodious, light filled, and gracious, with resulting floor plans that spread out their buildings laterally with large windows and welcoming doorways. Nighttimes of alarm and unexpected slaughter were no longer everyday concerns. But in Ireland the times still demanded strongholds and citadels; local knights still piled up their narrow towers, featuring window slits and holes for guns.

One or two castle lists drawn up by English officials in 1574 do list the Dolphins as holding Moyode along with several other towers in the immediate vicinity of Loughrea and stretching outward toward this great field, a modest assemblage of territory known as the Dolphinage. It seems clear from their long tenure as important vassals to the old de Burgos that Dolphin chieftains held these lands under feudal, then tribal contract with their traditional overlords. How they behaved and fared in the internecine struggles of the various Burke pretenders that marched back and forth over their lands we will never really know.

As to the tower itself, the doorway was quite clearly of great importance to the scheme of its defense. A great oak door blocked the way. In the entry chamber, slots still exist for a thick wooden bar or wedge that would have been dropped in place at night when the lock was thrown. Anyone trying to batter his way in would likely be at that job for some time, deterred in some measure by the door's great natural strength; by the *bartizan*, an enclosed projection situated on the ramparts 50 feet above, down which rocks, missiles, and heavy debris could be dropped on attackers; and by a small hole chiseled through the wall to the right of the entry, presumably for a handgun.

Should the gate be breached, the intruder would immediately enter a small foyer, hemmed in and blocked by two more heavy doors, one to the ground-floor chamber, used to store food or livestock at night, with the other leading off to the right for a circular stone stairway upstairs. While attempting to break through these obstructions, the attacker would find himself speared or doused with boiling water from a rectangular opening in the ceiling called, melodramatically, the "murder hole."

In some instances on record, attackers avoided the heavily defended front gate and tried the walls instead, using a contraption as old as time called a "hog." Area churches or monasteries would be looted of their heavy framing timber and a shack thrown together on rollers or wheels, which could then be pushed to the base of a castle. There men with bars and picks would pull apart the fabric of rubble and stone, seeking to create a gap. Wet hides would protect the hog's roof from fire, and, the attackers hoped, engineers could do their work at a faster pace than defenders, who all this time would be dropping heavy stones from above, attempting to crush the housing and all inside of it. When the hole was wide enough, the attackers would attempt to force their way in.

The Dolphin who built Moyode was left-handed. Should the door to the circular stairwell be successfully forced or his walls breached, he would have defended each and every step up the tower, aided in large measure by its counterclockwise design, which ensured him a free, unimpeded swing with his sword arm. But at this point he would have had ample cause for alarm. His chief defenses had failed. Room-to-room fighting would inevitably favor the more numerous attackers, now surging, hacking, and thrusting forward. By this late stage in the fight, moreover, surrender would gain little. Tempers being hot and blood having been shed, little mercy would be offered or shown. Last stands on the roof would likely end with mutilated bodies being thrown over the top.

None of this makes for particularly cheerful contemplation. Movies have hopelessly romanticized medieval warfare by depicting, in all their color and heart-pounding adventure, the great confrontations of mounted knights in armor and heraldic gear. In Moyode there was certainly no glamour. The shoving match between two or three sweating men on each side in a dank and gloomy stairwell, punctuated by cries of pain as a sword or ax or dagger bit the flesh of leg or arm, hardly presents a scene in which Errol Flynn is going to shine. Movies demand speed and action. Here in Moyode the fight would be grubby and full of stalemate, six stairs won, six lost, a withdrawal to eat lunch or get an extra breath, then back up those stairs for more of the same. Our silly fantasies, as Yeats said, feed the heart but then recoil from the awful stench of this entirely brutal business. Certainly, in my own case, I do not dwell too heavily on the rivers of gore that may well have splashed the walls of Moyode. Who could ever cook a steak here thinking about any of that?

A more pleasant exercise is to follow the narrative of one Luke Gernon, who wrote of his visit to a tower house in 1620. What he saw was a tall and rather graceful building 50 to 60 feet high, built of rough and undressed limestone set off by an often finely carved great doorway and attractive window mullions. "The lady of the house meets you with her train. Salutations past, you shall be presented with all the drinks of the house, first the ordinary beer, then aqua vitae, then sack, then old ale. The lady tastes it, you must not refuse." You enter, as in Moyode, and proceed upstairs to the great hall, a word I use advisedly. Moyode's is only 20 by 18, but the great arch is 25 feet high at its apex. Here a roaring fire in a splendidly carved fireplace greets the visitor, "where you may solace yourself till suppertime." The small chamber off this hall, where the Dolphin used to pour scalding water through its murder hole down to the foyer below, I will use as a kitchen.

In the great hall, Gernon feasted the evening of his sojourn, the table being "spread and plentifully furnished with variety of meats, but ill cooked, uncleanly dressed, and without sauce." He did enjoy

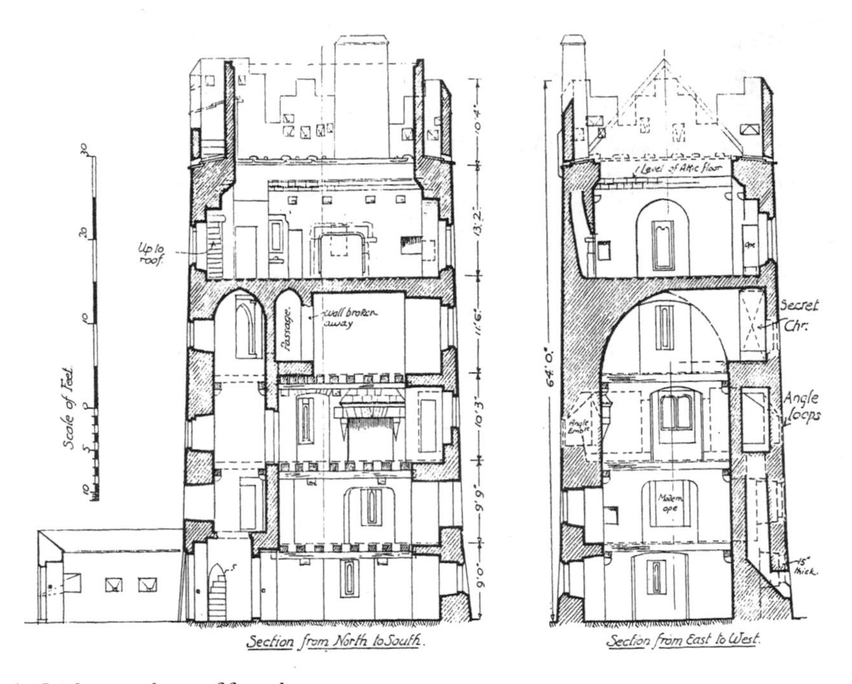

An Irish tower house, fifteenth century

the mutton, however, and "a pasty or two of red deer." The Irish "feast together with great jollity and healths around. Toward the middle of supper the harper begins to tune and singeth Irish rhymes of ancient making. If he be a good rhymer he will make one song to the present occasion. Supper being ended, it is your liberty to sit up or depart to your lodging."

Choosing bed, Gernon would return to the stairwell and climb up. In Moyode, between the great hall and the top floor, two side chambers run off, one a long gallery that ends at a toilet chute, called a *guarderobe*, that runs down the inside castle walls to a refuse pile outside, the other a small bedchamber. Continuing up the stairs, he would reach the top floor, what I will use as the main bedroom. This is a delightful space with five tall windows that, because the enclosures are splayed inward to give a bowman room to maneuver, allow considerable light to enter. Here Gernon found rushes or hay on which to sleep, much of it crawling with lice. "Do not expect canopy and curtains." From this room a separate and very narrow stairway leads to the roof, and a gallery between the outer parapet and the gables allows for extensive views over all the surrounding country. From here the enemy's movements could be noted and appraised, negotiations shouted back and forth. In one such recorded exchange a defender asked his attacker where he meant to train his cannon: "I satisfied his curiosity, and asked him what he meant by this question. 'Because,' he said, swearing with some warmth, 'I will cover that part, or any other your lordship shoots at, by hanging out both my daughters in chairs.' 'Tis true the place was not of much importance. However, this conceit saved it."

In the morning Luke Gernon was awakened to a cup of aqua vitae. "Breakfast is but a repetition of supper. When you are disposing of yourself to depart, they call for a stirrup-cup and you are presented again with all the drinks in the house, as at your first entrance. Smack them over and let us depart."

HIDDEN TREASURE

I must say that as the years passed I despaired of ever emulating Luke Gernon's experience. For a time, I considered the idea of bringing over some American friends to start the job, which would have been a disastrous cultural decision. But in the spring of 1987 the National Monument people steered me to one Paddy McCarthy, and he came over one day, reluctantly, to see the castle.

Paddy seemed to me to have a more northern disposition—unenthusiastic, somewhat dour, pessimistic, not given to idle chatter. I was impressed even more when he clearly stated that this job was not for him. "Too much danger here of losing money," he said. "I've three near-relations on this crew, so I know I wouldn't be making a profit." This sort of clarity was something I had never encountered in Ireland. We met again a few days later, and he gave me a figure that, to my amazement, I could live with. I started tearing down ivy the next day, proof positive both that we were beginning and that I may have finally grown up.

Moyode's ivy-clad appearance, of course, had been one of its initial lures. Who can resist the spirals of deeply green vegetation curling picturesquely up a castle's walls? What use was an ancient building that did not have this romantic cloth of *Hedera hibernica*? "You know what this stuff is really doing, don't you?" an old friend of mine once told me. "It's sucking the life right out of the place, turning the mortar into gravel, worming its way into the joints, destroying its integrity, and inevitably pulling the building apart." I refused to believe him.

My opinion changed one year when I leaned against a window enclosure and nearly went out the ensuing hole in a shower of masonry, a drop of some 30 feet. Then I borrowed a neighbor's ax, never sharpened in its long life, to batter and sever a primary taproot 8 inches in diameter at the castle's base, which took me over an hour. Satisfied with my avenging deed, I waited for the ivy to die. Three years later, when I next saw Moyode, it was as thick as ever, sustained by satellite roots that had entrenched themselves in the fine night soil that covered the great arch on the third floor. Hacking everywhere that year, I was shocked to see on my next visit that I had killed only a third of it. Paddy now told me it all had to go, and quickly. He could not repoint the walls until it was gone. Thoughts of King Arthur, Tennyson, and picture postcards went out of my mind as I went over to Seamus Taylor and got his tractor.

With lines tied to the ivy's largest creepers, the tractor heaved and hauled to no effect. "I can't believe this," I remember saying. Running up with hatchets and pole saws, Seamus and I cut as many tentacles as we could reach. Eventually the upper quarter of Moyode's coat began peeling back, and when next the tractor was applied, a great avalanche of ivy crashed to the ground in about a 12-foot heap. "Now that made a grand impression!" Seamus yelled in triumph.

For six weeks, Paddy and his men repointed the castle walls. In another three he rebuilt the gables, set the foundation for a roof, put up a new chimney for the fireplace in the great hall, and inserted four new window assemblies. When I returned in the fall, we heaved up the 14-inch-square support beams and installed the new flooring and timber roof.

By now I knew all the lads in his crew, a predictably cheerful and witty group who had little if any appreciation or respect for the building they were restoring. "You must be mad, Jim," was the usual rejoinder. When I explained the heating arrangement (two coal stoves, one in the great hall and another for the upper bedroom), they couldn't believe it—"You'll be perished!" When I said no to electricity, they were dumbfounded—"How are you going to write about us? With candles?" When I talked aloud about using an outhouse, they were aghast—"You know, your highness, we don't live with our pigs anymore over here." On the last point alone did I eventually concede, making plans to put in a toilet, but only because the old medieval waste chute conveniently hid the necessary pipes.

That fall, as the job progressed, there was more grumbling than usual, especially so as most of our work now revolved around the top of the building, where the assembly of materials had become a truly tedious chore. Workmen employed by the Irish government on restoration of national monuments have the cream of machinery to assist them, the likes of cranes, elevators, electric mixers, and so on. Not so the noble crew working on Moyode. "Did it ever occur to you, Jim, that we're no bloody better than the stupid yokes who put this thing up in the first place?"

As we sat in the van for a tea break one windy day, I had to agree. Not a single power tool was to be seen; the equipment box contained but a raw assemblage of beat-up saws, rusting screwdrivers, nicked old hammers, and scores of buckets for hauling concrete. An American carpenter, jealous of his privately owned, top-of-the-line tools, would be horrified at the common pool of assorted equipment with which his Irish counterpart is forced to deal. And as for grunt work, no worker in the States would put up with any of this. All concrete was mixed below, then hauled to the top with an ancient rope winch set up on the battlement. Every heavy beam and slate and stone went up the same way. If anything slipped or fell, the men below scattered for their lives.

Frequently, if the load was a big one, there would be four or five of us heaving and hauling on that old frayed line, up to our knees in mud, just for the fun of having Paddy or his cousin, struggling at the top with whatever it was, slip the knot and let everything fall to ground. "Oh, the faggots," one old bull would yell. "Those weak-kneed old women! For Christ's sake, we be drowning down here, our ankles pulled off us, and they can't untie their little booties!"

The only rise I ever got out of this assemblage was over lunch one day up on the third floor over the great arch. As usual, the peasants were mocking me. "By God, will you look at that, the king of the castle spreading mustard with a screwdriver! And look at that again, he's peeling an orange!"

"If you eat one of these a day, my toothless friend, you may keep the four or five teeth you have left," I replied. "Ever heard of scurvy?"

"Ah, that's an American disease altogether, like ulcers and AIDS. All you Yanks ever think about is money and sex."

"You don't think about money and sex?"

"Sex we take for granted. It's a gift from God. And as for money, if you had a lot of it, it would damage your health altogether. Spend it while you have it, boy, and then forget about it."

"Well, then, you wouldn't be interested in the buried treasure. I guess I'll look for it on my own." This took everyone aback.

"And what baloney are you serving today, then?" one asked.

"Well, I think there'd be a chance for treasure up here in the secret chamber."

"Secret chamber? Where?" All eyes were now on alert. I explained that whoever built this tower excavated a small hidden chamber from the fill spread out between the peak of the great hall and the tower walls. Over in a nearby castle, this little room was under the hearth of a fireplace, but in Moyode it lay over by the south wall under a window. "What would it be for, then?" they asked.

"A place of hiding for women and children, maybe a dungeon where they'd put some poor fellow and let him starve to death. Or more likely, I think, a place to keep their jewels and gold coins, Spanish doubloons or plate—whatever had value."

"How do you know it's over there?"

"Because if you look at the castle from the south, there's a small window in the wall between two floors. It has to ventilate something now, doesn't it?"

Bedlam erupted, shovels flew through the air, and before I could even taste my ridiculed orange, the boys were hard at it, digging up the secret chamber. Never had I seen such speed and interest in any other job involving Moyode.

"Pay dirt!" one cried as his spade broke through, and some of the excitement even took me over. Would we find a skeleton or some old manuscript? A chalice studded with precious jewels? A coin horde or an old sword? One of the lads squeezed through the breach. "This is a virgin fit," he groaned, disappearing below. The silence was tantalizing. What had he found? His head finally popped out. "Nothing, your highness. Nothing but dead crows and bird shit. A fine treasure, a fine treasure indeed." A couple of them were definitely angry. This had been the one chance in their entire lives to win a great, unexpected windfall.

"Money's not important, right lads?"

"It is when it falls in your lap," one replied.

Of course, money is very important. With unemployment at a staggering 20 percent, emigration continues to drain Ireland of its enterprising youth. The countryside has never seemed so forlorn of people over the time I've been coming here. Paddy, I began to learn, was one of those who had left. To his eternal regret, he was dumb enough to return.

"I couldn't have come back at a worse time," he told me; "1979, when everything began going sour. When I think of the ten years I could have still been in Britain with my crew here, who all came home with me, I almost get sick. I had property there, rental units, lots of work. I guess it cost me £120,000 or so in lost wages. My house here depreciates yearly, and my English places are worth five times what I sold them for. Four weeks down the road, that's all the money I have in the world."

But what really gets Paddy angry is government, a resentment toward the capital city of Dublin that is more or less historical from the twelfth century on. "There are three parties to blame, actually: the banks, the unions, and, worst of all, the politicians. Between them they've ruined Ireland for good and all, stripped the nation of its values, purpose, and sense of nationalism. They penalize me, who hires people and gives out wages, by taxing me to death and making the dole attractive. It's absolutely true and absolutely crazy.

"The government has created this huge social welfare state, mostly in Dublin, and funds it by making me pay ruinous wages to my men, most of which I deduct from their checks and mail to bureaucrats for health insurance and so on. Those are wages I can't afford to pay and which turn out to be less in my lads' pockets than if I was paying cash. So for a while I didn't do it. I paid cash, kept the lads in work, but then I got caught. The government lads, they could have cared less about my crew. All they wanted was to screw me down for the money I was supposed to take out of their pay that goes to people being on the dole. I says to them, 'If you do this to me, I'll go out of business, and these six lads go on the dole themselves. Which do you want?' 'They can go on the dole,' was what they said. If that isn't immoral, I don't know what is."

The revenue people threatened to take Paddy's house and some other property of his, so he settled with them, a fine. "I guess you'd rather be in England, then," I said.

"I'd rather be dead."

"Well look on the bright side, Paddy. Moyode is keeping you busy."

"Do you think I'm making money here? Of all the Americans who could own a castle and be rich, I get hired by a pauper. Down there in Headford, outside Galway, some rich American woman spent £250,000 on her tower, and here I am hauling up concrete in little buckets by hand. You should be ashamed of yourself, having so little money. I tell you, Jim, I begin to understand what the famine times were all about working on this job."

QUEEN ELIZABETH'S DILEMMA, 1558

Earl Richard Sassanagh was a martial man. Annals record his victories and defeats with the usual enemies, O'Neills and O'Donnells from the north, the Burkes of Mayo, roving bands of gallowglasses from Scotland whose only objectives were plunder and "rendering their names famous." When required, he dutifully obeyed the lord deputy and accompanied him on hostings. What he could not do, however, was control his sons or temper in them at least a semblance of loyalty to the Crown, an art that he himself, like his father, was prepared to play. Unfortunately for the earl, English tempers had by that time worn thin.

The 1560s saw tremendous changes in the attitude of England toward its ungovernable possession. There was by no means a consensus about what to do, and specific policy agreed to one day could entirely change the next, to the exasperation, annoyance, and treasonable oaths of many a lord deputy, but a definitive hardening is all too apparent.

Two primarily different elements had come into play. The first was a new monarch, Elizabeth I; the second, religion. Elizabeth was mercurial and demanding, prone to persuasion by her various favorites and advisers, and exceedingly stingy. She was also destined for a long career on the throne, which did, despite her mood swings, offer some general consistency of purpose, if only because treasury expenditures in Ireland kept increasing and royal anger maintained the pressure that something must be done.

Elizabeth had the same three options as her father. She could let Ireland go and be done with it, as it brought her no income, only grief—"I could wish it sunk in the sea," as one counselor put it. Or she could continue her father's policy of surrender and regrant, hoping that through modest expense perhaps this unhappy country might balance its books until some better day arrived. Or she could do something no English monarch had yet succeeded in accomplishing, that is, conquer Ireland.

The first alternative, although emotionally appealing, had become impossible because of the religious controversies that divided English society—Henry VIII's "new error and heresy" that Irish monks attributed to "pride, vainglory, avarice, and lust." In Henry's day monasteries were certainly despoiled and appropriated by the Crown, who in turn parceled many large grants to loyal subjects, including the Catholic Clanricards, but freedom of religious conscience was usually respected. By Elizabeth's reign that sense of tolerance was fast disappearing, as attitudes grew militant and bureaucracies united to advance the practice of Protestantism. Catholic Ireland came to be seen as a potential gateway to England, whereby French and later Spanish papists could enter and topple the queen. Ireland would not be jettisoned.

Nor could the current state of affairs continue. Her father's calculations had largely failed. "There is no order, nor justice in the country," the queen was advised. "Everyone does which is right in his own eyes." The only real solution was the last.

The queen initially agreed to stricter measures. In particular, the schemes of Lord Henry Sidney, who was to serve as lord deputy for three terms, received her sanction. Sidney was an able, visionary man, extremely ambitious and progressive, who saw in Ireland great opportunities for commercial profit. He advocated various plantations that would benefit the Crown financially and bring English adventurers and soldiers to invest, settle, farm, and defend the countryside. He proposed as well to undermine the power of palatine lords, men like Richard Sassanagh, whose arbitrary exercises of authority "fare well for his friends and followers, while the rest go to wreck." Sidney advocated a tremendous reorganization of Ireland's financial basis whereby all landowners, great and small, would no longer pay their primary rents and dues to the lords but rather to the Crown, which in return assumed responsibility for the military protection traditionally provided by Clanricard. The new revenues would support provisional presidencies, armed military governors, for the most part, with permanent small armies to enforce the peace. Such a presence, naturally enough, was a mortal threat to the independence of local magnates.

On paper all of these proposals were appealing, and Sidney proceeded energetically to carry them out. The usual problems stymied him, however. Elizabeth wanted results, not more bills. She never seemed to realize how the two went together. And she proved susceptible to the conflicting reams of advice and reports, praise and vilification, that flooded the corridors of her court. The earl of Ormond, for instance, mercilessly intrigued against Sidney. The Anglo-Normans of the Pale for whom he spoke resented the new string of Protestant lord deputies who seemed as interested in despoiling them as the native Irish. As much as the Anglo-Normans craved peace in Ireland, the notion of a diminished status under heretics hardly seemed appealing.

Two great cataclysms shook the island during Elizabeth's reign, the first being Desmond's rebellion in Munster, the second and far more serious the general rebellion of 1595, when the Great O'Neill and Red Hugh O'Donnell, with Spanish aid, nearly won control of Ireland. Overlapping this span, Connaught degenerated into total chaos.

AN ENVIRONMENT IN TROUBLE

The three major baronies of Clanricard were those of Athenry, Loughrea, and Dunkellin. Dunkellin lies only 3 miles to the east of Moyode, straddling a major drainage basin that wends from Galway's interior down to the sea in a series of streams, rivulets, and something the Irish call *turloughs*, or winter lakes. It is by no means particularly scenic countryside, being low, wet, and marshy, but to area sportsmen it was once a paradise of fish and fowl, and historically the landscape abounded in ruins of various sorts, though many have been allowed to decay and disappear, as I was to discover.

Over time the eldest son of the reigning Clanricard of any particular moment was generally appeased with the title "baron of Dunkellin" as he waited, often impatiently, for his father's death and the subsequent assumption of a grander title and fortune. A great tower, the Castle of Dunkellin, stood by the river of that name that flows through the barony, more of a stream really, being only 30 or so feet wide. Great flocks of wild birds live here, from the enormous swans known as whoopers to widgen, teal, geese, and other migratory waders who throng to this watershed each winter from mainland Europe.

Dunkellin Castle disappeared long ago, though its substantial mound, capped by a single and incongruous telephone pole, gives a fine view of the river channel below. Taking in an early winter sunset there one evening, I was startled by a great sweep of onrushing commotion. Turning about, I saw a pair of magisterial whoopers slowly beat their way to the Atlantic just over my shoulder, flapping in rhythmical, steady bursts, their wing span a prodigious 5 feet. Being a city person and generally unacquainted with nature's more grandiose displays, I was overwhelmed with the elegance of their flight.

For centuries, a coronation mound stood opposite the castle on the northern bank of Dunkellin River. Known as Caher na Earle, or the Earl's Chair, it marked the spot where successive earls of Clanricard (along with the usual assortment of traitors, usurpers, wayward sons and cousins, impostors, and would-be Clanricards of various temper, ambition, and sanity) were hailed and anointed by vassals and clansmen alike. Inconspicuous remnants of the past, be they pillar stones, mass rocks, mounds of dirt, or mangled, scarred irregularities in some corner of a meadow, for some reason appeal to me if they were once, in some age far removed from our own, sites of sanctity, power, or great events. Unfortunately for a modern Ireland that is fast forgetting its history, even relatively innocuous sites such as these can no longer exist unmolested. No one in this immediate assemblage of cottages and farms seems to have a notion where the Caher na Earle can be located. Even with maps I cannot pinpoint it. "Do you know where the Earl's Chair is?" I ask a young man in his twenties whom I meet on the road.

"Furniture, is it? You might try Galway City."

"No, no, the earl's coronation mound. It should be in that field over there."

"Well, now, I haven't a clue. He never told me."

"Who never told you?"

"The earl. He never said where it was."

Finally an old woman gives the answer. "You'll never find that. The man below was tired of people asking for it, trampling his corn and all, so he broke the old stone that the kings stood on down to pieces and dragged it to the river and dumped it below the waters. Then he bulldozed the mound so flat that no one will ever know where it was, and good riddance, he said. When people don't like something here, they get rid of it. That wasn't the way it was long ago, but people suffer from impatience now and do things their parents would never have allowed before."

My friend Tom Ruane agrees with this melancholy assessment but thinks the implications are far more sinister than just losing one or two mounds. "You look at Ireland now, Jim, it's so green and pastoral and seemingly unchanged, and you think all's right with the world, but it's not. The old country's being ruined right in front of our eyes, mostly through greed and ignorance, those two old devils of human nature." Tom used to be an avid fisherman and hunter, but he rarely goes out these days either shooting or fishing his beat on the old Dunkellin, a few hundred yards seaward from the Earl's Chair. "I haven't killed a salmon in years. Last summer now, I went out for two or three hours. Not only did I not get a single bite, but I saw no trace at all of any fish, and it's been that bad for ages. Just ten years ago I could stand in the Dunkellin and lose count of all the great Atlantic salmon running up to spawn. There'd be literally pools and pools of fish. But today, not a one.

"They breed salmon now in fish farms—10,000 tons of it just last year—so they look at the whole thing as a business deal and forget about the consequences for people who live here. Look at the government. They give out licenses to big offshore commercial fishermen who wall off Galway Bay with enormous drift nets and simply haul in these salmon trying to come back to their spawning grounds up the Dunkellin and dozens of other little streams in Galway and Clare. With monofilament nets, which are so thin the fish don't know they've been caught, they can clean out the bay in a few afternoons. Who's hurt? Families in the estuaries who've been fishing out of dories with draft nets for generations, sportsmen, and of course all the old hotels that used to brag about their salmon-choked fishing beats.

"Look at these statistics. As far back as twenty years ago, the government has known there was trouble here with the stocks. In 1963 draft-net fishermen caught 4,000 salmon. Ten years later, only 230.

The big boys took 150 in '63 when they started their drift-netting offshore. By 1974 they were pulling in 21,000! Look at the fish counter at the sluice in Galway City, marking salmon running up to Lough Corrib, which used to be the grandest sight in the world. In '74, 2,533 salmon counted, down from 20,400 in 1967, only seven years before. Add to that lice infestation from salmon farms that have made the ocean trout virtually extinct here in the west, and you have a catastrophic environmental alteration going on."

In October 1992 an even graver threat confronted the old barony of Dunkellin. Tired of losing hundreds of acres each winter to *turlough* flooding, a phenomenon unique to the limestone lands of Connaught, when whole fields are suddenly submerged under several feet of water for weeks at a time, area farmers independently financed an enormous drainage canal through eighty of their holdings along the course of the river. An unsightly ditch of nearly 2 miles' length, in places 60 feet wide, the funnel has already freed 1,000 acres to year-round pasturage, as intended. Environmental consequences, however, were barely given a thought. "All this talk of bird life drying up is madness," said one of the entrepreneurs. "You can't tell me Dunkellin is an Irish version of the rain forest," said another. "The birds will come along as usual." Speculation that this new canal will dump tons of silt into Galway Bay and ruin its famous oyster beds is ridiculed, as is the notion that *turlough* fields, once naturally enriched by lime sludge during flood season, must now be fertilized with poisonous chemicals instead.

"If anyone unilaterally did that to a wetlands in the United States," I told Tom, "he'd be jailed for the rest of his life."

"This is a world gone mad," says Tom, "and really, Jim, isn't it a pity?"

CONNAUGHT IN FLAMES, 1580

The old Dominican abbey of SS. Peter and Paul is, aside from Bermingham's Court, the major archaeological sight of Athenry, "a noble ruin" in the words of an enthusiastic antiquarian at the turn of this century, but in the cold light of day not anywhere near the caliber of a dozen other friaries scattered about here in the west. This is certainly not the Dominicans' fault. Between 1271 and 1574, they lavished care, attention, and treasure on what must have been a beautiful church and cloister, endowed in no small measure by all the warrior families of the region, both Norman and Gael. An accidental fire in 1423 gave the monks an excuse to refurbish the entire complex, their most signal addition being the graceful, gently tapered belfry that so distinguished Irish church buildings in the fifteenth and sixteenth centuries. But the ravages of history have guaranteed that little of this is left. The fabric of the abbey, aside from one or two windows, is entirely nondescript. A few tomb slabs in the chancel and nave are of some interest, and for local historians the family vaults of de Burgos, Berminghams, and Burkes merit scrutiny. But the cloisters have long since disappeared (demolished to provide stone for barracks when English troops were quartered here in the 1700s), the belfry collapsed in 1850, and vandals pretty much obliterated everything else that Cromwell's soldiers had not previously mutilated.

Archivally, nothing else much remains either. One or two sets of monastic records lie preserved with Dominicans in Dublin; a chalice from penal times dated 1725 can be seen with the Dominicans in Galway; and an old relic known as the Tooth Shrine of Athenry—a small satchel inlaid with jewels by Meyler de Bermingham in the 1270s and meant to carry the abbey's chief relic, a tooth of St. Patrick—sits in anesthetic isolation at the National Museum, also in Dublin. Until relatively modern times, the tooth shrine was hawked about the countryside as a cure for humans and animals alike. Just as the *Book of Durrow*, a manuscript from the eighth century, was soaked in water and then hung around the neck of ailing cattle, so too was this ancient leather bag. All else from the abbey has literally been cast to the winds or reduced to ash through fire and plunder. It comes as some surprise that most of these calamities did not begin with Henry VIII's disaffection with Rome, which had produced no telling effects in far-off Connaught. The 1560s, however, saw all that change.

"I gave order for the making of a bridge at Athlone, which I finished," wrote Lord Henry Sidney in 1567. "I am sure durable it is, and I think memorable." Sidney had a keen eye for terrain and knew from the tales of old soldiers how many crossings had been built and burned over the Shannon at Athlone, "the only key that opens and defends passage from the Pale into Connaught." Leaving a garrison

Site of the cloisters, the abbey, Athenry

there, he dispatched to Galway City Sir Edward Fitton, the new president of Connaught. The mercantile elite of that town welcomed his appointment, but no matter their loathing for the disruptive Burkes, even they may have questioned whether Fitton's tactics were not perhaps too extreme.

Ranging about from Galway's gates, Fitton ignored the advice of William Cecil in London to "stir no sleeping dogs" and relentlessly harried the countryside, noose and sword in hand, writing dispatches back to Sidney that Clanricard seemed to him a reluctant ally at best.

Small castles and towers, over seventeen in one of his sweeps, were battered and taken, their small households of twenty or so inhabitants routinely butchered whether promised quarter or not. On a visitation to Athenry, he threw all the friars out in the street and turned over abbey buildings and 1,500 acres of farmland to the town council, at all times a politically correct, and by then correctly Protestant, municipal body, for a yearly rent of 26 shillings, 6 pence. Sensing insurrection, he undertook the most impolitic step of all, the arrest of Clanricard,

The Athenry chalice, made in 1725

whom he trundled off to Dublin Castle. The earl's sons, "those graceless imps," according to Fitton, then raised the entire province into revolt.

It would be an excruciating endeavor to detail all the twists and turns of the ensuing several years, but the principal actors were Ulick, John, and William, all sons of Richard Sassanagh though by different mothers, a circumstance that overburdened their already fevered emotions by confusing the issue as to whom they hated more, the English or one another. Frequently they acted together, sometimes alone or in tandem, often as enemies across the lines of battle. Their rebellion was of the smoldering variety, capable of intense and prodigious outburst, where hundreds of gallowglasses went on rampage through the province, at other times more manifest in simple robberies and muggings out on the country lanes, followed by a fast retreat into bog or woods.

At all times the level of violence was horrifying. In one fit of rage, Ulick descended on Athenry Abbey and burned it down to a smoking shell, cursing the Protestant harlot from England who had transformed that once holy ground into a den of heresy. Sidney was aghast. "Here was the sepulchre of their fathers," he wrote, "and the mother was also buried there. And Ulick, being besought to spare the burning where his mother's bones lay, blasphemously swore that if she were alive and in it, still he would burn the church and her too rather than any English churl should inhabit or fortify there." With the situation fast deteriorating, Sidney freed Clanricard and sent him home to curb his boys. Richard persuaded them to submit, and they were placed under loose arrest in Dublin. But "younger brothers and bastards scorn all endeavors but liberty and war," and no sooner was Sidney preoccupied with some other crisis than the Burkes had bolted, "stolen across the Shannon, there to cast away their English habit and apparel, and to put on their wonted Irish weede."

Sidney—about whom Irish annalists had many good things to say, even crediting him with a warm and generous heart—went apoplectic with rage, and in speed rare for those times launched an incursion to Connaught, arresting the earl again and this time shipping him directly to the Tower in London, where he was "close confined, and heard not the voice of friend or companion." Sidney garrisoned the earl's principal castle at Loughrea and occupied several more of his major towers as war raged unabated in the countryside. Neither Walter Dolphin of Moyode nor any castle holder in central Connaught could avoid the conflict. "Noisy were the ravens and carrion-crows, and the wolves of the forest, over the bodies" of those slain, wrote annalists from County Donegal, known famously as the Four Masters. Athenry was burned again, "a more woeful spectacle," reported Sidney, "than ever I looked on in any of the Queen's dominions." John Burke attacked Loughrea Castle in the middle of the night, slew every prisoner he took save one, then abandoned the fortress to the anguished lament of his advisers. "Break and raze the house," one wrote to him, otherwise "the English will dwell in them again, and so by that means banish you clean." This prophecy came to be. Sidney regarrisoned Loughrea, which withstood another siege.

By 1581 the exhausted green field of grassy sod was essentially in the control of Crown forces. "These most wicked sons," wrote the

The Earls of Clanricard, simplified genealogy

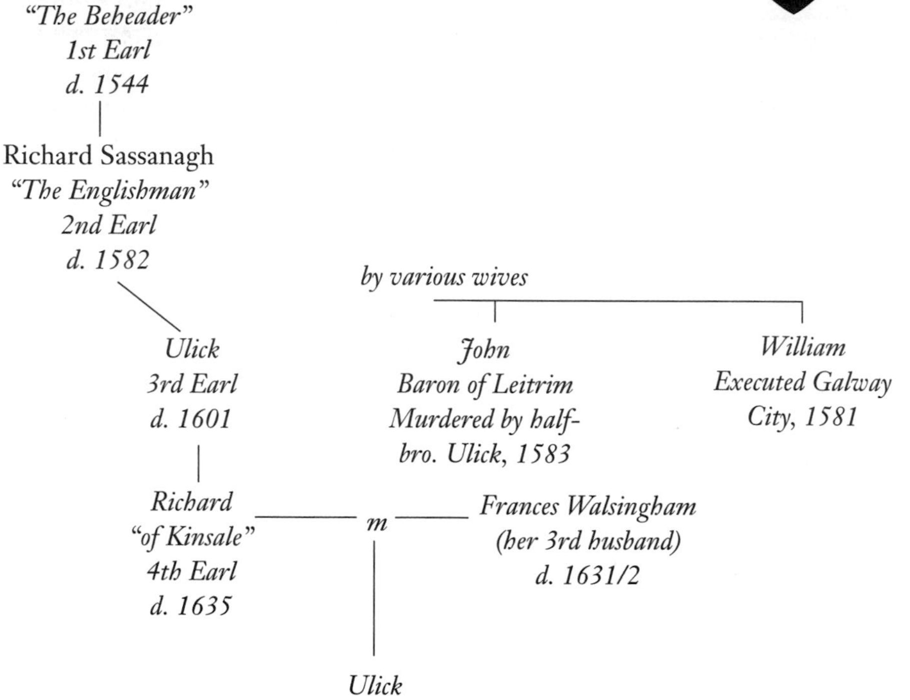

new president of Connaught, Sir Nicholas Malby, "have felt the smart of their follies, for many of their people have been slain, and the rest that took part with them do leave them. They dare not look abroad, but like wild dogs keep the woods and mountains." William (of whom Malby said, "That young man is not well bent") submitted to authorities at Galway City, but notwithstanding a letter of protection he and nine followers were hanged. It is alleged that the merchants of Galway, acting on rumors of a pardon or ransom offer of £1,000 in return for William's release, rushed the scaffold and strung up that unfortunate, thieving Burke as quickly as possible. Richard Sassanagh, hearing of this and other calamities in his prison in London, took ill and began a long waste toward death. Miscalculating the effect that a dying man's plea might have on war-crazed bucks, the queen's council released him with letters of pardon to lure the rebels in. Richard returned home in time to die, leaving in his will "my perpetual curse" on any of his boys who did not submit.

It was not, of course, any sentimental burst of despair, remorse, or affection for their dead father that prompted Ulick and John to "come upon their knees craving the benefit of her Majesty's pardon. They do strive for the title to the earldom, and do mind to try it by the course of the law." This unedifying scramble for spoils confirmed to the Tudors their low estimation of Irish morals. The spectacle of John and Ulick both groveling at the feet of English officials with countless "speeches to our advantage" seemed untoward and hypocritical considering the past decade of lawless misbehavior, yet their subsequent machinations, though appalling, were accepted with a hopeless shrug.

Ulick, as the eldest, was granted the title "earl of Clanricard" and most of his father's great estates. John, however, was made a baron and settled generously in Leitrim. This equitable arrangement, in fact, satisfied neither. Ulick's henchmen cornered John in the bedroom of one of his castles and promised him his life if he would surrender, as worthless a pledge as so many others in Irish history. While Ulick waited by the tower's gate, John was stabbed to death. He would never "disquiet" Connaught again. "It was with difficulty," a shocked monk would later write, "that his body was obtained by those who carried him to Athenry, where the hero was buried."

Ulick's action was universally abominated by the Irish, who, of all people, should have been inured to such base treachery. Philip O'Sullivan Bear, whose famous *History of Catholic Ireland* was published in Lisbon in 1621, called John's murder "odious," and the annals

Clanricard vault, the abbey, Athenry

lamented the death of "that good man—noble, hospitable, renowned." To the English, however, John was one less malefactor to keep reports on. "He had always a treasonable mind," reported an English official investigating the restoration of Athenry, "and did ever thirst after blood. He was a common haunter of women, and men say he had a child by his own sister, and a great maintainer of thieves he was."

Though Ulick's resolution of his private affairs was not what England had in mind as a civilizing example, they viewed the murder as a judicial execution and pardoned the new earl, which consequently earned them as much loyalty as they could expect from such a ruthless man.

Though an Irish-speaking Celtic lord, Clanricard was now universally received as an ally to the English. Haunted though he would be by rumors and gossip, to say nothing of his treasonable past, Ulick in the main "stood fast" for the Crown, especially as events in Ireland careened to a state of general warfare.

This was the practical position for Ulick to take, for in looking about he saw most of his traditional enemies all ranged on the side of rebellion. He was particularly aware of his half brother's progeny, filled with hatred for him as John's murderer and spoiling for the return of their stolen patrimony—"He knows he is not able to bear head against them," an English official gleefully noted. This sort of nervous edge on the part of Clanricard pleased the English, as it should have. On a typically unpleasant foray into the wild interior of northern Mayo during the summer of 1586, an English commander bemoaned his Irish auxiliaries. "They were to me a great trouble and very changeable. During their being in my company, I could keep no enterprise secret, and yet but mean men when they come to action, for at the charge they forsook me." Only the earl of Clanricard and three of his retainers did not abandon the English in battle. Ulick later sent to England as a pledge his eldest son, Richard, as ward of the Crown, to school and later the court.

Yet Ulick remained the quintessential warlord, jealous of his privileges and resentful of unsolicited royal interference. New lord deputies and provincial presidents came with increasing regularity, their dispositions rarely improved by an ambivalent earl, filthy weather, rebellious clansmen, and the general air of hopelessness. They responded with ugly fits of ill temper, public executions over which they presided often numbering a hundred or more at each session in Limerick and Galway, with especially gruesome tortures reserved for serious malefactors like Donald O'Brien, an "arch traitor and demagogue of the plunderers," who was hung from a cart and battered with the flat of an ax, his broken body then strapped to the local church tower, where birds of prey finished the work. But kill and harry as they might, these officials usually despaired and returned to England in either disgrace or ill health, and often penurious as well. "This slimy land," wrote one, "help your friend out of this hell."

Ulick did not object to the English slaughter of his countrymen. So long as those who died were enemies of his, the third earl of Clanricard gladly joined the hunt. But he did resent the new levies of taxation, which sought to drive a wedge between him and what used to be his subjects. English presidents, who depended on these taxes to support their administrative and military positions, spilled much blood setting up the system and extorting revenues. The great landlords fought to establish exemptions for their personal estates (Clanricard was successful, paying rent of only one penny per acre) and to retain the right of collection so as to maintain authority over turbulent neighbors. Ulick attended the Dublin parliament in 1585 to protect his rights, staying on a manor in the Pale, valued at £10, specially purchased for him by the government to board and support his retainers, a tacit recognition that no great lord could travel without his private army.

AN APPARITION

Despite the primitive nature of our little job at Moyode, I have not, to my disappointment, experienced any medieval flashbacks or unduly extravagant fantasies of life as a petty warlord like Walter Dolphin. But one morning, while working on the roof, I did finally catch a glimmer.

On that typically fresh Irish day, the clouds racing in from the Atlantic in gigantic glory, dramatic shafts of sunlight blazing streaks all over the nearby fields and mountainsides of Slieve Aughty, I felt totally in my element hammering away. Without a word being said, I gradually noticed one, then two, then all the crew gradually turn away from their work to stare at the horizon. Following their gaze, I was startled to see a huge contraption slowly rumble into the demesne. "What in Christ's name is that?" said Paddy, and at first I had no idea. "I think it's a siege machine," was my reply.

As we all gathered on a corner of the ramparts to look over the approaching monster, identified after a few minutes as my well driller with his thoroughly homemade and unrecognizable apparatus, I couldn't help thinking of what the owner of this tower might have thought as a lord deputy came into view, hauling in his train some clumsy siege works and crude artillery. Did he say to himself, "Here is death on my doorstep," or was he suffused with anger and defiance, daring the miscreants below to knock their way in if they could? Irish history is many tales of both.

Clanricard Triumphant, 1601

Americans are often told how meager their history is when compared with that of Europe, and by reason of mere longevity such is partially the case. Recorded Irish history, for instance, had a run of some thousand years before English colonists ever set foot in North America, and certainly the reach of saga and myth could extend our familiarity with Irish life at least another thousand back in time. But there are more similarities with the American past than many observers probably realize.

The endless chronicle of Irish warfare during the latter half of the sixteenth century reminds me (and others) of the many American Indian wars fought from New England to the Pacific Coast for a span of over 300 years. The conflicts were sporadic, treacherous, confused, bloody, racial, often exterminating in tone and content. They gave the impression of being continuous, which in terms of petty harassment they could be. In larger measure, however, armies and commanders customarily undertook seasonal campaigns that sputtered back and forth from base camps. The American struggle, because of a lack of written sources on the native side and a sense of cultural superiority on the other, was not as minutely recorded as Ireland's, and indeed was rarely studied with scholarly precision before the 1940s. But in fact the yearly Irish catalogue of strife and contention has all the same characteristics. In both cases, certainly, the English contended they were dealing with barbarians. When Ulick and his men joined the forces of Sir John Norris in 1596, the English all marveled at "the exotic and strange character of their equipment and purpose." I mention these comparisons because a student of Irish history requires, by law of nature, a long memory. The vast rebellion of O'Neill and O'Donnell that truly convulsed Irish society during the last decade of the sixteenth century seems undeniably climactic to anyone who reads through the record. Yet so do all the great Irish wars, with their pivotal battles, from Clontarf in 1014 right up to the Easter Rising of

1916, all surrounded as they were by continual maneuverings, campaigns, preliminaries, sieges, and routings. Were any of these more or less catastrophic, really, than those that came before or after? Was Kinsale a greater disaster than the Boyne? Let historians and propagandists argue about that. My own advice is to look at Irish history as a long genealogy of frantic happenings, with peaks and valleys, low points and high, crescendos and fiascoes, but never reaching the stage where anyone's particular victory ever proved final. Look at Ireland today: The war continues, and in some ways the combatants have not changed. The one enduring element, and the reason for this ramble through cow dung and nettles here at Moyode, is the story of the land. It has always been here, and will remain.

Every year between 1594 and 1601, Red Hugh O'Donnell pushed south from his Donegal highlands and spewed into Clanricard. These maraudings were partly natural feud and hosting and partly an ingredient in what was fast becoming a genuine war with Tudor England, masterminded by his ally Hugh O'Neill, known by either of his titles, in English the earl of Tyrone or in Irish the Great O'Neill.

This war had three distinct phases, the first from roughly 1594 to 1598, often called a "disturbance" by commentators, wherein Tyrone was not yet deemed by Elizabeth as irrevocably in a state of treason; a second that stretched to 1601, which saw a period of uninterrupted warfare that culminated in the Battle of Kinsale; and the last a winding down, entailing the usual dirty war of harrying and mopping up that ended when O'Neill, after admitting defeat and giving submission, fled to the Continent in 1607 with his entire retinue, ending up in Rome as a heavy drinker and a pensioner of the pope. This melancholy end has been called the "flight of the earls," and in fact it did mark the political death of the traditional Gaelic order, if not Gaelic life, and had a profound impact on the great plain of Clanricard.

For Ulick, third earl, these were years of peril and uncertainty. Spies of the Crown despaired of his loyalty, reporting that friars dispatched by O'Neill "to seduce the Earl" were often seen whispering in his ear. But other Elizabethans vouched for him solidly. In these unsettled times, said one, England had need for "men of stomach." What seems clear is that Ulick pandered to both.

In the time-honored tradition of Gaelic chieftains from ages long past, Ulick lied, cheated, and dissembled whenever circumstances demanded, and between 1595 and his death in 1601, these talents for deception were much called upon. His dilemmas were manyfold. Like any great lord, he valued independence and liberty, but the English deemed the earl merely jealous. Ulick's idea of freedom, they believed, was to plunder his tenants at will, a profitable enterprise that lord deputies and presidents of Connaught had sought to eliminate by imposing an orderly structure of taxation, direct to the Crown, that would reduce Earl Ulick's status to that of just another landlord, albeit a sizable one. English presence in Athlone and Galway, Dublin and London, was clearly taking aim at him, and he was shrewd enough and Catholic enough to see it. Still, however much Tyrone tempted him with promises that the old Gaelic order would be restored, Ulick understood that at Tyrone's side stood all his family's enemies. The age-old sport of exploiting small landowners might again be condoned under O'Neill, but would Ulick be in power to enjoy it?

In a bind, the earl delayed and screened his intentions. He sent dutiful letters to the lord deputy telling of rebels slain in all-day chases through wood and marsh. He did not elaborate that killing these dogs improved his estates more than the queen's. Recognizing the desperate straits of hard-pressed English garrisons, he offered 500 head of beef, but "without ready money," complained a commander, "he will deliver not a cow." He wrote Elizabeth that "our daily expectation is to be hurted by O'Donnell's forces," but spies reported that on one of the rebels' incursions, Lady Clanricard arranged for the delivery of two "boardes" of wine to the traitors' camp and that her attendant had a "long talk" with O'Donnell, who loudly stated that "he esteemed not" the earl's forces yet was quietly gone the next day. In another strike south, into Limerick, O'Donnell passed through Clanricard "without any blow offered him either forward or backward," despite the earl's claims that he was on alert and ready to intercept. "Surely there is some mystery in it," reported an agent suspecting collusion.

But in fact, O'Donnell and O'Neill were impatient as well, wanting a commitment from Clanricard to join them in throwing off the English. His wariness received a nudge in 1597 when O'Donnell punished him by despoiling the entire barony of Athenry, burning Rathgorgin and probably Moyode as well. The castle and walls of Athenry were scaled—some say the Irish stuck their swords into masonry joints and used the protruding blades as steps—and the town once again was reduced to ruin, empty of villagers, merchants, and garrison. Its devastation stood complete, and never would a promise or hope for the place amount to anything. Earl Ulick reminded the queen of how much he was losing in her cause.

Elizabeth replied that Ulick would be suitably rewarded, the reports of which would give others "comfortable examples to imitate you." He probably did not have in mind the military position of commander in chief for all of Connaught, which the queen appointed him on January 9, 1599, especially as this honor pointedly excluded command over the resources and English troops of Athlone and Galway City. There was more burden here than seeming profit, though Ulick prepared himself to seize whatever opportunities might come his way.

The stiffening factor, and a far more successful result for English policy than that of Tyrone, was Ulick's son, Richard, baron of Dunkellin. Like Tyrone, Richard had been sent to England as a young boy, matriculating at Christ Church in Oxford in 1584 at the age of twelve. There he learned English and civilized habits, wore proper clothing, and affected the air of a gentleman. At sixteen he informed Elizabeth's secretary of state that his father wished his college debts to be paid and himself removed to court.

We cannot but wonder what Richard thought of his father. In Ulick's eulogy the monks used words like "sedate, mild, august, affable, gentle, and impartial," including but a single phrase to describe his warlike persona—"fierce to his neighbors." More likely is that Richard, newly returned to Ireland, found the earl a tough, gnarled, and uncouth warrior plunged to the neck in byzantine negotiations, treasonable intrigue, and perilous escapades out in the bogs. The young Tyrone, to the regret of all England, took to this ancient atmosphere immediately. The young Richard did not.

Richard, baron of Dunkellin, had become what the court had wished for all along, a major landlord who was "English." He regarded Ireland with distaste, the local Celts as wayward, his true home to be Britain, and his loyalty owed completely to the Crown. Whenever the opportunity arose, he sailed to England and civilization; when duty called, he put on his armor and returned. "If I might be so happy as to be able to settle any reasonable quietness in this place and to leave my father in any security," he wrote in 1599 from Connaught, "Ireland should not long lodge me. All the fortune this land can afford me cannot make me disloyal to Her Majesty, nor a stranger to my worthy friends in England."

We will also never know the degree of affection, if any, between father and son. Ulick's matrimonial affairs, while wayward, were a decided improvement over those of the first earls. He may have fathered an illegitimate child, and records indicate that for some slight period the earl might have slipped into bigamy, but for the majority of his career he seems to have retained a single wife, who in fact survived to the noteworthy age of eighty plus.

The Irish, of course, are known as affectionate, often sentimental parents. (Thomas Uniacke burst into tears the day his elder daughter married.) But chieftains customarily practiced fosterage, whereby sons were placed at a very early age in the care of other families, usually as an expression of treaty or alliance. Ulick followed the essence of that tradition by sending Richard to Oxford. Perhaps he never expected to have any feelings for his son nor care whatever for any return of warm attachment. The only quality he demanded of his son may well have been loyalty, and that Richard certainly provided.

Richard seems the typical Elizabethan professional: cultured, brave, reputedly handsome, with a dash of Irish temper and bravado, a skilled horseman and undoubted devotee of the hunt. He was the first Clanricard to comprehend a life beyond the borders of Connaught, the first to understand that his potential inheritance, enormous by any standard, could subsidize a very grand life in faraway England. It was a patrimony worth fighting and dying for. Where his father may have considered treason many times ("He has given his word to Tyrone!" a spy reported), his son never wavered. Ulick probably sensed that with Richard around, his only course was service to the Crown, however devious the route.

RICHARD'S INITIATION

The utter failure of Robert Devereux, earl of Essex, to bring Tyrone to heel in the spring and summer of 1599 largely accounts for that young man's spectacular disgrace and later execution at the Tower of London. Connaught, like every other wild corner of Ireland, crumbled into further disorder.

These were not auspicious times for the baron of Dunkellin either. He saw his first action in full-scale battle at the disaster of Curlew Mountains on August 5, 1599, a fight precipitated by Sir Conyers

Clifford, ordered by Essex to advance out of Connaught to relieve a strategic castle besieged by O'Donnell in Sligo. Richard, in command of the "battle," or primary battalion, was positioned in the middle of a small army of about 2,000 men as it negotiated a wooded and boggy pass through the Curlew Mountains. The advance guard, suddenly attacked and routed by O'Donnell clansmen lying in wait, tumbled back in complete confusion and threw Richard's command out of order. Panic ensued, and the army disintegrated in a frantic race down the mountain they had just climbed with their ensigns flying and trumpets blaring. English reports of the catastrophe highlight the rage of various unit commanders, cursing their "vile and base men," along with the unfortuitous deaths at key moments of major officers. One of these, an Irishman, enraged at the cowardice he saw all about him, in essence committed suicide, "braking from them in a fury, alone made head to the whole troops of pursuers, in the middle of whom, after he was stroked through the body with a pike, died fighting." Clifford also lay mortally wounded on the field. A rebel commander recognized him among the casualties and had him beheaded, whereby his corpse "passed not in one direction from the battle": His head was sent to O'Donnell as a present, his body to a neighboring monastery. MacDermot, a rebel, delivered the English a letter informing them of the disposition of their brave commander's remains, "barbarous for the latin, but cyvill for the sense."

From the general tenor of eyewitness accounts, Richard was probably among those slapping and shouting at his men to hold their ground. As the army fell apart with rebels closing in to slash and harry the fleeing men, it was reported that those from Connaught fared better in the retreat, being Irish and knowing the terrain. Most of the casualties were English. The baron of Dunkellin, it is said, "had a narrow escape."

The battle ensured the utter collapse of royal authority in Connaught, though Ulick, with the keen eye of a scavenger, took advantage of the chaos by ruthlessly harrying his personal enemies, with Richard usually in the vanguard of horsemen spurring on the chase. Father and son together were equally severe with members of their own feuding family. On orders from Ulick—"Dispossess a base sister of mine"—Richard threw the woman out of her castle in Mayo. As the void deepened, Ulick, sensing in the wilds that intoxicating aroma of freedom, manipulated his new war powers to stockpile arms and munitions and snubbed his English masters, impotent in a countryside swarming with armed bands. An English company billeting at Dunkellin found themselves rousted by the earl's men after dark, stripped of their weaponry and even one or two killed. "These beginnings will have a worser end if it be not looked to in time," a report on the incident concluded. In fact, officials deplored Elizabeth's grant of emergency commissions to the Clanricards. "It is to be feared," wrote one of her counselors, "that by time Connaught might grow wild and Irish, and so to be chargeful to the Crown to make English again." Worse still, what if the father and his son should "list? What footing hath her Majesty in Connaught then?"

As Ulick grew expansive, arrogant, and boastful, however, he may have despaired of his son, no matter how brave a young warrior he might have been. Richard was sulking, resentful that provincial command did not entitle his family to the captainship of English garrisons at Athlone or Galway. "I cannot but acquaint your lordship with the inconveniency of this course," he wrote to Charles Blount, a professional soldier sent as Essex's replacement. "The Province is all out. There is no service of importance here to be undertaken, but for the most part must have their means and directions from those places [Athlone and Galway]. This will quite weaken and disable my reputation with my own friends, whom God knows I have long labored in this mischievous and troublesome time to hold firm and steadfast to Her Majesty. I am limited and restrained from the means of doing good." In a fit of pique, and stressing the dishonor of this slight and lack of trust, Richard resigned his official posts, much to the amazement, no doubt, of his father.

Blount, better known as Lord Mountjoy, respected Richard and in fact may have known the young soldier from court. "I do believe him," he reported, "that in his own particular he is afraid to stay amongst his own countrymen without more power to give them the law. And I think for himself, you shall never hear that he will quit his allegiance to the Queen." He accepted the resignation reluctantly, because "of that province I am afeared more than any part of Ireland."

Richard's frustration and sense of wounded honor would be vented with passion some two years later on the day before Christmas, 1601, outside the walls of a town called Kinsale in County Cork.

Kinsale, 1601

For all of Elizabeth's reign, both Gaelic rebels and English policymakers had shared a single opinion as to what might tip the scales of fortune in either of their directions—foreign intervention, the very talk of which "threw the Irish into great jollity." After years of dangerous sea voyages back and forth, furtive negotiations between envoys and spies, and finally pleas to honor and preservation of the faith, a significant force of veteran Spanish soldiers, numbering almost 4,000 men, landed in Munster during September 1601 and sent word to O'Neill to join them.

Mountjoy reacted with relief—the worst had finally happened!—and wrote with vigor that "I cannot dissemble how confident I am to best these Spanish Dons as well as ever I did our Irish 'Macs and Oes' and to make a perfect conclusion of the war in Ireland." He saw, as did O'Neill, that a climactic battle would now be fought, and he hastened his forces south to lay siege to Kinsale. O'Neill was undoubtedly grateful for the long-awaited assistance from Spain. He was grateful too to have Mountjoy drawn off from Ulster, where an English strategy of slash and burn, containment, year-round warfare, and nettling garrisons thrown up at key points in the north had all seriously threatened his strength. Yet he may have been fearful as well. Irish success in battle had been predicated on surprise, terrain, and mobility. As he marched south, he may have wondered which of these ingredients would be sacrificed by fighting on ground he knew nothing of, with allies as formal and dogmatic as the Spaniards.

There would be no question to which camp Richard, now fourth earl of Clanricard, would report. The death of his father in May of that year and his burial in the family vault of ruined Athenry Abbey had only solidified the Clanricard's allegiance to English interests. With a levy of Connaughtmen, including his Dolphin retainers, in tow, the new earl stood in close attendance to Mountjoy's person, and on December 24 his rage and vehement exhortation evidently initiated the decisive action of battle.

O'Neill and O'Donnell, hoping to catch Mountjoy off-guard, attempted a night action that would have brought them right upon their enemies at first light, squeezing the English between Spaniards rushing out from Kinsale and their own Irish forces. Through misadventure and O'Donnell's having lost his way, the three main bodies of Irish soldiers, organized as never before into formal, disciplined battalions—and expected by O'Neill, rather naively, perhaps, to behave as such—arrived at dawn in a disorganized state to confront an enemy far from surprised. O'Neill drew the men back to better position, an action that continental soldiers would have carried off routinely. But his irregular horsemen, lacking cohesion, hampered the maneuver, and as Mountjoy's cavalry units reconnoitered in force, the Irish horse retired right through the middle of O'Neill's battle, sowing confusion and giving the impression to other units that a disorderly retreat was under way. The rebel army stood at a fragile psychological moment, caught between the two emotions of uncertainty and fear. Dispatches from English observers indicate that at this instant Richard Clanricard created a scene at Mountjoy's command post.

Whether Richard had some special insight into the Irish psyche or perhaps sensed that the strictures of formal tactics were a drain on the temperamental Celtic personality we shall never know. Maybe it was pure instinct or contempt for his countrymen in general, aping the movements of professional armies but botching the imitation. For whatever reason, Richard began howling that now, at that particular moment, Mountjoy must attack.

We may, from the tone of reports, sense that Mountjoy initially was not prepared to do so, but after listening to more harangues he gave the order to advance. Every cavalryman under his immediate command charged O'Neill's column, which, "thinned and discomforted," came apart.

The battlefield clearly advantaged English horsemen, offering no bog or woodland to which the Irish kern, in tight trouble, were prone to flee. In a set battle formation ill suited to their special qualities as guerrilla warriors, in a lie of the land perfectly suited to conventional maneuver, the Irish were clearly in a terrible position. The left and right wings of the rebel army were then attended in the same fashion with similar results. Red Hugh O'Donnell, incensed to see O'Neill's men scattering to the four winds, is pictured a hysterical warlord reduced to utter impotence as even his followers evaporated around him. "Manifest was the displeasure of God," groaned the annalist.

Richard, earl of Clanricard, equally possessed, was the scourge of rebels that day. Mountjoy, dictating dispatches to the queen, signaled him out for special praise. "The Earl," he said, "had many fair escapes, being shot through his garments, and no man did bloody his sword more than his Lordship, and would not suffer any man to take any Irish prisoners, but bid them kill the rebels." It was reported he personally stabbed and hacked twenty kern. In a mere three hours, the rout was complete, almost 1,200 enemy lying dead in the field, another 900 captured, most of whom were strung up from nearby trees. Amid this carnage Lord Mountjoy personally knighted the earl, which landed for him the moniker "Richard of Kinsale."

Red Hugh O'Donnell died in Spain, allegedly of poison, one year after Kinsale. The whereabouts of his grave have never been pinpointed, though his deathbed will, with elegant and stylized signature, was recently uncovered. Raymond, baron of Leitrim, heir to the dispossessed Clanricard issue of John (the third earl's murdered half brother), also fled to Spain. The Great O'Neill spent fourteen lonely, boring years in Rome until his death in 1616. He lies buried in the Spanish church of San Pietro beneath the Janiculum. Richard of Kinsale survived the great battle thirty-four years, reaping honor and wealth beyond measure. In the end, however, he may well have questioned just what it was he had fought for.

PRAY FOR THE SOUL OF THOMAS UNIACKE

The quarter century in which I have observed this small patch of countryside has probably seen the greatest concentration of social change ever witnessed in Irish history. When I first met Thomas Uniacke, the tenor and pace of life here was little different from those of his father in the 1930s. The Uniacke farm had no electricity, no indoor plumbing, no telephone. He delivered his milk to the pickup lorry by bicycle. I often saw him plowing the big field with a horse, reins around his neck. His children, isolated from the wiles and temptations of a modern world, stood in awe of the various automobiles that I drove into their yard. When I sat in the Uniacke kitchen, the hours passed like minutes with tall tales, wry humor, the pure gush of beautiful language that coursed through idle chitchat. It was a poor world in many material ways but a rich one nevertheless in harmony, generosity, and, as obnoxious as this may sound, innocence.

The 1970s witnessed a complete upheaval, primarily through Ireland's membership in the European Common Market. For a brief period, the influx of money and capital investment engorged the economy, and cash flowed like water. Old backcountry pubs where in former times you'd see gnarled farmers paying for Guinness with pennies and tuppence suddenly saw these same customers hauling out wads of five- and ten-pound notes. The apparition of farmers behind the wheels of brand-new, honking Mercedes as they herded their cattle became suddenly commonplace. Modern tractors by the hundreds appeared around the countryside, with the donkey population declining exponentially. "Take a picture of that," a wag told me from the doorway of an Athenry pub as an old-timer passed by in ass and cart. "That's the last you'll ever see of those, thanks be to God!"

The Uniacke household held a mirror to these times. The normally tight-fisted and conservative Thomas was finally talked into electricity and plumbing, to the delight of his wife, Margaret. A traditional homemaker and mother, Margaret had, for as long as I'd known her, suffered from a degenerative hip condition, walking with a decided limp. She had once taken a four-day charter trip to Lourdes for a cure, but the 1980s brought more substantial relief in the form of high-tech surgery and a new plastic hip joint. Ten years later she attended the opening performance of Brian Feil's *Dancing at Lughnasa* in New York City, seeing the play well before I ever did and giving me a very canny appraisal (She disliked the portrayal of Irish women. "I never wore boots like that, never knew anyone who did, and as for wearing men's socks . . . !").

The two Uniacke girls, growing up in a changing world, matured into sophisticated young ladies with bank jobs and executive positions in Galway City. As my 1972 Citroën began to sag and lose its spark, with gaping rust holes and broken mirrors proclaiming its decline, these two colleens would pass me on the road in dazzling new Hondas. When the younger daughter married, she and her husband built a sparkling new home right next to that of her parents. This building was no farmhouse, featuring just about every American-style convenience that anyone could imagine. As embodied in this creation, Ireland had finally entered the twentieth century.

Old Thomas was slow to convert, but in the end he made some accommodations to the new order. Although he was just as delighted to see me on my visits and just as quick to sit me down by the stove for a cup of tea and cake, the rituals of hospitality nonetheless had altered, for with electricity came television. Instead of having long, witty talks, we watched TV, mostly American programs such as *Dallas* or police shows. During commercial breaks we might chat and joke, but the story line always held his attention, and he watched his dramas from start to end. The death of old Ireland, begun centuries before by the Normans, will be completed in the next twenty years or so by the television set. Thomas was recalcitrant or clever enough not to go too far, however, refusing to join in the general free-for-all that engulfed so many country people. He remained in his heart a 1930s conservative: No milking machines, tractors, automobiles, or new bungalows for him, and when the economic reckoning hit Ireland like a hammer in the early 1980s, he survived without a hitch. "The problem with Ireland," he once told me, "is Arthur Guinness. It makes people Catholic and careless." This reminded me that I had never shared a drink with Thomas Uniacke, nor ever seen him in a pub.

Thomas Uniacke with daughter Frances, c. 1955

On a 1987 visit to Moyode, I dropped by the Uniacke farm as usual. I knew something awful had happened when I saw the old yard overgrown with weeds; the flower garden untended and withered away; the farm dark, forlorn, uninviting. I found Mrs. Uniacke next door, living with her daughter. Thomas had dropped dead in the big field in February of the previous year. To me his loss was prophetic; he was the last of a breed that Lady Gregory and other antiquarians had searched for all those years ago in the lanes and decrepit hearths of Galway, the reliquaries of old tradition. Nothing Thomas Uniacke ever said to me could or would resonate from a printed page. It evaporated into the Irish air the minute he opened his mouth. Listening to him was more like music, a symphony from the accumulated eons of a remote Celtic countryside. His like are gone now forever.

Mortal Threat to the Land, 1633

Richard, fourth earl of Clanricard, prospered on both sides of the Irish Sea as his titles, awards, offices, and dignities attest: governor of Connaught, constable of Athlone Castle, keeper of the King's House, lord president of Connaught, governor of Galway, baron of Somerhill, Viscount Tunbridge, earl of St. Albans, baron of Imanney, Viscount Galway, member of both the English and Irish Parliaments. His continued and unmolested practice of Catholicism, moreover, speaks of power as well as mere status. He was, or so it was thought, immune to challenge either in Ireland or, more important, in Britain, where Earl Richard now resolved to live.

Initially, the great snobs of court disregarded him as a roughneck Irish lord. The French ambassador thought him ignorant, backward, and insufficiently astute in taking advantage of the queen's gratitude to him for holding Connaught. But most regarded the earl as "a goodly, personable gentleman," and he mingled well with the retinues of both the queen and her Stuart successor, James I. In 1604 he married, advantageously, the hitherto unfortunate Frances Walsingham, daughter of Elizabeth's secretary of state, both of whose previous husbands had met untimely ends: Philip Sidney, the poet Spenser's Astrophel, killed in a dirty and needless melee in Holland fighting Spaniards in 1586; and Robert Devereux, earl of Essex, beheaded for treason fifteen years later. Lytton Strachey called her "a shrouded figure, utterly unknown to us," though gossip of the times reported that her marriage to Sidney had been a happy one, but with Essex, a notorious philanderer, less so.

The entire societal web of Clanricard's in-laws and new relations stretched to the limit whatever personal feelings he may have had for Ireland. Official duties forced upon him posts and assignments in

Connaught, but he longed to leave them behind and did so at first opportunity. "Good my lord, hasten my leave," he wrote to Viscount Cranbourne in England, "for there is a great difference between the sound of a harp and the tune of a cow, and here there is no music." His reports to London were plaintive: "All quiet, very poor, a great deal of waste, and many idle knaves."

Frances, wife of Richard, fourth earl of Clanricard, with daughter, Elizabeth (from her marriage to Sir Philip Sydney)

As for poverty, of course, Clanricard was speaking for others, not himself. As the principal landlord of Connaught, he could count on revenue that far exceeded even that of the Crown in western Ireland, though much of this income was of in kind. This was remedied in the early years of James I's reign, when Richard complained that since his bills in England were never paid with cows, butter, eggs, or pigs, he should be allowed, as others were not, to special treatment in the export of "3000 barrels of corn and one thousand oxen yearly" to England for quick sale. The king agreed. Richard, at garrison duty in Athlone, lived the day-to-day existence of an English gentleman "in very honorable fashion." The well-documented misconduct of his immediate forebears, the first three earls of Clanricard, in their matrimonial affairs prompted Frances Walsingham's friends and family to make certain that rumors reaching England of her mistreatment by the fourth were false, which various spies confirmed. "Saw my lady of Essex very well contented," one wrote, "and every way as well served as ever he saw her in England." In 1605 Richard and his family left Ireland, for all intents and purposes never to return.

This seems strange when one wanders about the grounds of Portumna Castle, on the shores of Lough Derg, some 17 miles southeast of Loughrea. Most historians agree that Richard never saw Portumna, built at the then exorbitant cost of £10,000, though of course we should probably see in its construction at least the idea that he would one day be back, if only to check his accounts and ledgers. That he never did more accurately illustrates that his affairs in England, like the country itself, were of a grander scale and consequently more complex. Just six years before starting Portumna, for example, Richard had completed Somerhill, a vast Jacobean mansion in Kent that supposedly swallowed a far greater proportion of treasure than Portumna ever did.

Despite the honors and estate that his marriage brought him, however, Richard was always aware that the bedrock to his fortune lay in Connaught, and his power and influence there were pervasive no matter where he chose to live. He received favors and special treatment, being granted leave from sitting in the Irish Parliament (as was his duty) or levying fines on Roman Catholics (which was the law) or attending Protestant services (certainly impolitic). Commanders of the garrison at Galway regularly reported to him about conditions there and rumors out in the countryside ("Disorder reigns in many things"), along with pleas for the earl not to forget them ("If you do not come, send us a word of encouragement"). His land agents and relatives controlled, in effect, the entire agricultural economy. Even the Privy Council in London kept him abreast of all reports they received from Ireland, in case the earl, at a time of future unrest, had to be shipped back "to keep the natives in order" (though on no account was he to be allowed to favor Catholics, "lest they be too much puffed up").

By 1610 some were questioning whether Clanricard was of any use to the province that had again become "very tottering and unassured," but they were brushed aside. Well in the tradition of all the de Burgos, Richard remained a palatine lord. Nothing shook him until rumors surfaced that the land was threatened, and with it his entire source of authority.

In 1626 Clanricard received a letter from Connaught. "There is talk of a plantation here," his confidant warned, "which I regret. It causes more fear than the Spaniards," and gossip had it that the earl was encouraging people to surrender their titles once again to the Crown, hopeful of getting them back secure, no matter the cost. Aghast,

Richard replied, "I should rather put my hand in the fire." He may have finally realized what the implications of Kinsale now truly were.

The history of Ireland during the seventeenth century, especially its last fifty years, seems superficially one of rebellion, war, religion, an Ireland finally pacified. In fact it is the story of property. In 1600, Catholic nobles and chieftains owned 95 percent of the island. By 1625, in large measure because of the confiscation of O'Neill and O'-Donnell patrimonies—over 750,000 acres—and their subsequent redistribution to Protestant settlers that figure had decreased to about 60 percent.

After Cromwell the percentage was more than halved to 22 percent, and by the year 1700 a mere 14 percent. In essence, the land was taken out of the hands of one constituency, that of Roman Catholics, and put almost completely into the hands of another, the Protestant faction. What Henry VIII and Elizabeth only dreamed about the Puritan zealots of Great Britain achieved. Those who felt most grotesquely betrayed were descendants of the Norman adventurers, ground into poverty by institutions and men of authority they had traditionally considered their friends. These aggrieved men were, of course, the Old English.

Richard de Burgh was among the greatest of these, being Catholic, lineaged, and loyal to the Crown, as witnessed by his heroism at Kinsale. In the year 1625 he and his class owned one-third of Ireland, the richest agricultural portions without doubt, mostly around the Pale and in Leinster. The Gaelic Irish also possessed a rough third, certainly the poorest lands, primarily in far reaches to the west. The last third was held by a new class of landlord, popularly known as the New English.

These New English took many forms and personalities. Most were farmers; many were Scots. Some were former soldiers from Elizabeth's armies, now largely settled in the six counties of Ulster. Others were entrepreneurs, like the spectacular Richard Boyle, earl of Cork, who bought land cheaply from previous grantees, men too flawed or whimsical to find success, then pushed their potential toward enormous profit (where Walter Raleigh failed, Boyle eventually earned £20,000 in yearly rents alone). Some were fervent Puritans who saw it as their duty to extirpate papism by appropriating benighted bogs and farm fields; others were speculators who used religion to disguise their greed. All were propelled by a certain energy, whether specious or divine, that seemed voracious in its desire to strip old Ireland of everything left her, an appetite that horrified those whose families had been there for centuries and who were themselves no strangers to cupidity.

The efforts to "line Connaught thoroughly with English and Protestants" coalesced around the remarkable person of Thomas Wentworth, earl of Strafford, a lord deputy unlike any other in Ireland's history, who ruled tenaciously and often tyrannically from Dublin Castle for seven years beginning in 1633. Theories of plantation were by no means novel with Wentworth, however. Ever since Elizabeth's day, Ireland had been tested with colonies here and there, most of them failures. These experiments culminated in the grand design for Ulster in 1610, which eventually saw the entire character of that province utterly transformed. Wentworth viewed Ulster as only the beginning, Ireland being "unsound and rotten at the heart," and when the difficulties of his lord and master, Charles I, deepened, he envisioned the confiscation of Connaught not only as sound Protestant policy but a financial tool whereby the king could survive and prosper.

The reign of Charles, of course, marked the great struggle of Parliament versus the divine right of absolute monarchial rule. Charles, a mediocrity, self-dramatized the situation in grandly heroic, solitary terms, burying himself in prayer and approaching his myriad of crises as miniature Golgothas. When victorious, he attributed all to God and nothing to his ministers; when defeated, he accepted the rebuke as divine, trials his Lord had made him a king to shoulder. In fact, the source of his problems was fairly crass: He needed money.

By 1635 Charles had ruled without Parliament for over five years, and the service he most appreciated from his advisers was the wherewithal to continue in this same unobstructed fashion. Wentworth, from an ancient family in Yorkshire, had originally opposed in Parliament Charles's authoritarian tendencies, but growing Puritan extremism eventually threw him into the king's cause, which he pursued with characteristic vigor. His highly successful duty as governor of the north of England convinced Charles that Wentworth was perfectly suited to the continually unproductive kingdom of Ireland. It was to be Wentworth's greatest challenge, and no one could ever fault the intelligence and expertise that he brought to this most thankless post, which eventually consigned him, as it had so many others, to the execution block in London.

The situation he faced upon landing on Irish shores was certainly chaotic. He simplified matters, however, by rejecting altogether from his considerations one of the three "estates," the defeated Gaels. That left the New and Old English, and his facility as a parliamentary tactician served him magnificently as he called, ran, and dismissed various Irish forums. He was by turn conciliatory, condescending, firm, duplicitous, forthright, furious, and above all ruthless. His guiding principal, which he took no trouble to hide, was that in all affairs of government the king would consider "himself first, his people afterwards." This was not comforting news to either Irish camp.

Wentworth's mission was to raise money for the king, and to accomplish such a goal the country had to be settled, quiet, Protestant, and amenable to the strong hand of its economic master, the infallible lord deputy. He immediately saw that the current imbroglio concerning "graces" was poor policy and socially disruptive. To ease the king's financial woes in the past, Old English landlords and merchants had pledged and, more to the point, paid to the Crown thousands of pounds over three years in return for promises (or "graces") that guaranteed, among other things, religious toleration, commercial concessions, and a moratorium on plantations.

Even in peacetime, however, the budget remained out of balance, and with new rumors of war with Spain everywhere rife, the added expense of mobilizing a new army to keep Ireland under control promised even higher deficits. Men like Boyle, the rambunctious earl of Cork and the greatest of the New English entrepreneurs, bristled at the suggestion that they finance such a force. Why should Protestants pay for soldiers whose necessity was dictated by the possible, indeed foreseeable, treachery of the country's Roman Catholic population? His suggestion was simple: Make the Catholics increase their payments, which were little better than bribes for the maintenance of their status in a society that was now in the position, and the mood, to threaten them.

The Old English, especially those from the Pale, united in their feeling of betrayal. For centuries, they had spilled blood to develop Ireland, for all those generations maintaining at the very least a semblance of loyalty to the Crown and often a great deal more. The test of an Irish lord, as several historians have pointed out, was how close to his own level of self-interest he might place the king's business. If the two were even remotely matched, the test of loyalty was considered met. Men like the Clanricards, Ormonds, and Gormanstons were regarded as the king's men through whatever crises might arise. Their anger at the extortion of money by the king's government was considerable.

Wentworth did not in the long run appease these magnates by his initial agreement that such payments were not a businesslike way to rule Ireland. He preferred better customs law and other forms of tax collection, but what he abhorred most were the graces, which tended to benefit and entrench Catholicism. He saw to it that the feckless king, who had not previously fulfilled his end of such bargains, never did. He took the further step of proceeding with plantations, which naturally struck at the very existence of the Old English.

Wentworth was certainly no romantic. Whatever Clanricard's previous service to the Crown, which Wentworth dismissed with derision, the earl was an anachronism. Clanricard, in the lord deputy's view, was no longer required as a mainstay for the king's peace. O'Neill and O'Donnell had long since disappeared from the Irish scene; the threat of Catholic gallowglasses surging south from Ulster into Connaught seemed empty. What Clanricard now represented, twenty years after Kinsale, was lack of revenue. "It would be both to King and Subject a mighty safety and ease," he wrote to Charles, "to have the Earl at once handsomely removed forth of the way." The king, distant and unconcerned with details, agreed.

Wentworth proceeded to Connaught in the summer of 1635, his intention to invalidate all its property titles in favor of reestablishing, by law, the king's vested ownership of the entire province. The charade proceeded through Roscommon, Mayo, and Sligo before handpicked grand juries who tamely assented to Wentworth's presentation of "some nice points of moth eaten record" dating back to Richard de Burgo; the Brown Earl; and Lionel, duke of Clarence, all of which funneled down to the person of King Edward IV and, by extension, to Charles as the true owner of Connaught. "By reason of continual wars and rebellions, the Crown made little benefit of these lands," argued the lord deputy, "the profits wholly taken by the inhabitants, most whereof were rebels. For remedy, it should be lawful for the King to enter and seize all manors, honours, castles, tenements, rents, services, moors, meadows, pastures, waters, and mills in the Lordship of Connaught." What of the Old English position that sixty years' possession of property should amount to legal title? What about the agreements, indentures, and "compositions" the landowners had entered into with the Tudors? "The inhabitants were intruders," Wentworth replied, "and had no such estates as could either be surrendered or confirmed." Wentworth's terms for settlement were offered discreetly. Each county would automatically lose a quarter of its land for new

Portumna Castle

plantations; the remainder, at higher fees and rent, would be settled, with proper title, among the current landowners.

The earl of Clanricard, naturally enough, realized from his lawyers and agents just what was afoot and commenced a furious search in London for old documents and letters, squirreled away in the Exchequer, that would support his various titles. These he sent to Ireland along with detailed instructions that were carefully followed.

Wentworth, never known for discretion, chose Clanricard's own seat, Portumna Castle, as the venue for his County Galway proceedings, an insult much resented by Ulick, the earl's son, who complained that the lord deputy "cast himself in his riding boots upon very rich beds."

The day of inquisition saw Portumna's great hall lined with Wentworth's soldiers, whose muskets, in the observation of a juror, must certainly have been loaded, since their matches were all lit.

The jury, duly assembled by the sheriff, heard evidence, the lord deputy presenting his case for the fourth time in two months. Lawyers for the earl then proceeded at some length to establish Clanricard's position, much to the contempt of Wentworth, who was heard to mutter in Latin, "What great nonsense from so great an effort." Three days later, however, he was much discomforted by this jury, which "most obstinately and perversely refused to find for his Majesty."

Clanricard's men, naturally enough, knew beforehand what the judgment would be. They had, in far from subtle fashion, showed their contempt and disregard for Wentworth by packing the jury with the earl's friends and relations, who blatantly overawed the one or two unsteady jurors who, out of fear for their land or the lord deputy's person, seemed inclined toward finding for the king. Public response to the verdict (cheers from the crowd) and boasts from Clanricard's nephew further incensed the lord deputy. But he was not "a great and wicked man" for nothing. If the proceedings he had orchestrated were of dubious legality, as he well knew them to be, then such could equally be said for his response.

Nothing, he informed the king in a furious letter to London, would deter him from a "business of so great weight and consequence." The unfortunate sheriff who had chosen the jury was fined £1,000 and arrested, his "pertinacious carriage" thrown into prison, where, to the lord deputy's embarrassment, the unfortunate man died. Each of the jurors was fined £500 and threatened with total ruin—"We conceive to seize for his Majesty their lands." Various lawyers and agents of the earl were disbarred, harassed, and threatened with charges of conspiracy. Wentworth reneged on his earlier terms of settlement, now pledging to expropriate half of Connaught for new plantations, exclaiming "there is scarce a Protestant freeholder to be found to serve his Majesty on this or any other occasion in this county, being in a manner altogether compounded of Papists, Priests, and Jesuits," a situation he would remedy. He then directly attacked the earl.

The powers of Clanricard, he told the king, "are greater than in reason of state ought to be allowed any subject, especially in so remote a corner of the kingdom, and amongst a people so ill affected. The power of Government should be no longer continued with him, much less with his son, but rather be dissolved, and the county reduced back as it formerly was" under Elizabeth. Clanricard's commands in Galway should be "quietly removed," the forts of Galway and Athenry repaired, the lord deputy's troops sent in as replacements, and neither the earl nor his son allowed back in Ireland for the foreseeable future.

Then the lord deputy should proceed with confiscation. These were not the results Clanricard intended from his victory in court.

Richard was by now seventy-two years of age and serving his third monarch, a man to whom battles in faraway times and places meant nothing. The fourth earl, in failing health, took the bullying tone and unrelenting hostility of the lord deputy to heart, especially as it became apparent that Wentworth had the king's ear. On November 12, 1635, he died at Somerhill, to the grief and rage of his son, Ulick, who became the fifth earl. The earl of Danby, a friend of the family, wrote bitterly to Wentworth two weeks later:

> I came very lately from my lord of St. Alban's funeral, who died . . . full of honour and days according to David. And yet his people report that the apprehension of your Lordship's discourtesies and misrespect hastened his end, whereof my Lord his son seems very sensible. And is also possessed with many other causes of complaint under your government, wherein I presume he means in person to crave redress from your Lordship's own hand, so soon as the season and some English occasions will permit his journey into Ireland. In the meantime, give me leave I humbly beseech you to remember the extraordinary merits of that nobleman deceased, far above any of his nation in our times.

Wentworth was amazed and annoyed at this sentimentality: "I am absolutely innocent of the death of Lord Clanricard and St. Albans. They might as well have imputed unto me for a crime his being three score and ten years old." But Wentworth had made yet another powerful enemy, one who would rejoice at the vote on his fate taken by Parliament six years later.

CONCERN FOR THE LANDSCAPE

The condition of Moyode's great field often concerned me as work on the castle progressed—not the ruts and mud hollows created by Paddy's van and other vehicles, which the relentless touch of Ireland's rampant fertility would erase in a matter of weeks, but the ubiquitous thistle.

The thistle plant, if left unmolested, can choke a field no matter how many livestock might graze upon it. Neither cows nor sheep will touch its long, thorny branches, and I had noted with dismay that since Thomas Uniacke's death the field had never had its customary mowing. By mid-August 1993, after the thistle had grown up and bloomed for its brief season, a dead and dying scraggly mass disfigured all 30 acres of Maigh Fhód. From afar the pasture looked brown and barren, in mordant contrast to the many hues of green surrounding it.

This presented the usual Irish dilemma: what to do about something gone amiss "across the wall." In the modern agricultural era of the 1980s and 1990s, this has mostly involved farmers who began fertilizing their fields using slurry, or liquid manure, which is delivered as a spray from behind tractors. If your neighbor is partial to slurry, close your doors, lock your windows, and stay inside for a day or two. "The odor of that will knock you off your feet," one of the Hartys told me, "and if they store it near an underground aquifer, you better check your tap water every few days."

Even worse are those few farmers who spread their lands with offal, picked up cheaply from commercial slaughterhouses or neighborhood abattoirs. There are prohibitions against the use of raw animal innards as manure, but no one ever remembers an arrest or prosecution for doing so.

In the 1800s there was a law against the thistle. "If you didn't cut it down each July," I was told by a farmer, "you could be fined six pence, quite a sum, I suppose, in those days. Because once the seeds sprout and get carried off by the wind, it crops up everywhere." The field was becoming a neighborhood scandal. Seamus Taylor, down by the gatehouse, scythed about an acre around his house by hand. "Mrs. Uniacke will do it one of these years," he said. Then Godfrey Skrine, my Dublin solicitor, came down to cub hunt with the Galway Blazers. He said the field looked burnt from afar. "You have your reputation to uphold," he said. "Pay someone to do it."

"It's not my field," I reminded him. Besides, I had other bills to take care of.

In the course of various negotiations with Mrs. Uniacke over sharing water and rights of way, I often brought up the matter of thistles. "Oh, I'll take care of that," she promised, and true to her word the field was eventually mowed in proper season, and now is again a jewel in Ireland's crown. The experience reminded me once more of the prominence land plays in everyone's consciousness here.

"My father never had a car or a tractor, or too much else to shine up or polish," one of Thomas's daughters once said to me, "but he had his cattle and he had his farmlands, and he was awfully proud of them."

One evening an old-timer who lives in a thatched cottage on the demesne walked the newly mowed field with me. "A grand sight, it is indeed, and when you think just a couple of generations ago, when I was a boy, no one had anything. To think of owning a field this size was beyond all reckoning. Only lords and ladies could ever dream of it, and they lost out in the end, didn't they, and had to turn it all over to us. Well, now, you're looking at a lost soul at the moment, because I never had an acre myself. But I never stopped in the admiring of it, I can tell ye that."

As we approached the old man's cottage, a mangy old sheepdog ran out and bit me on the leg, breaking skin through my dungarees. "God damn that worthless beast. I'll give him the boot for ye." Over candle-light we poured some precious whiskey over the fang marks, then had a swallow apiece to seal his apology.

Last year when I visited his cottage, I was again greeted fiercely by the dog. "He killed eight sheep last winter, and that cost me dear. I hadn't the heart to put him down, so I paid the neighbors, though it's you I blame. He decided when he got a taste of you in the summer-time that he needed more mutton!"

CIVIL WAR, 1641

In the career of Ulick de Burgh, fifth earl of Clanricard, a century's worth of English policy reached fruition. Though born in Ireland, Ulick grew to be the prototypical English gentlemen in every respect save religion. A youth spent on his father's great estate in Kent, his mother's noble English heritage, knighthood in company with the prince of Wales at Windsor, and marriage to the daughter of an English earl, all helped to mold a man of fastidious habit and honorable intent. He was about as far removed from his buccaneering forebears, riding about the untamed Irish countryside stealing cattle and firing castles, as could be imagined. The court and presence of the king were no novelty to him; he ranged smoothly through the channels of power and society as a polished courtier.

These refinements stood him well as he negotiated the wreckage of his father's financial affairs. The fourth earl had been a lavish spender, and Ulick found himself encumbered with debt that he could not relieve, in large measure because of Lord Deputy Wentworth's continuing vendetta, which left bankers unwilling to forward the new earl ready money. "Rumours of my estate being questioned hath given occasion of wonder to many," he wrote Wentworth politely in March from London, no doubt gritting his teeth at the same time, "and to speak freely of the danger I am in, a continuance of that belief will much impair my credit here with those to whom I am deeply engaged, which proves much to my prejudice."

Wentworth replied in solicitous terms, satisfied he had the earl in his grip. The Galway jury had, with much wringing of hands, completely come apart, reversing themselves to find unanimously for the king's title. Clanricard himself had obsequiously presented Charles with their humble apologies and utter surrender. The king airily answered that "he could not tell how fit it might be for him to take that of a courtesy which was his due" but in the end allowed the jurors "to confess themselves mistaken" in their initial verdict. Wentworth in effect told Ulick he would not help him, that the king, through his minister, would procure "all that is of right belonging them. Your own wisdom will set you in the rightest path for yourself." The earl could approach the king from the position of either "Justice or Favor," and Wentworth was confident that Ulick would receive satisfaction from neither.

But "you do not lack for friends," the king's secretary informed the Irish lord as word of his continuing difficulties spread, and indeed Wentworth was to learn firsthand how fickle divinely inspired monarchs could be.

Charles, like all kings and queens before him, could at times barely function within the confines of his own household and court, so bitten with intrigue, gossip, and narrow self-interest that policies could vary as the day progressed. Wentworth, at a disadvantage in far-off Dublin, could not compete with Ulick, standing at the king's elbow, importuning him time and again with the iniquities of Wentworth's behavior, a man Charles rather ironically did not personally care for.

Archbishop Laud, Wentworth's ally in court, sent distressing letters to Ireland warning the lord deputy that "St. Albans has moved the King." Wentworth wrote stiffening letters in reply, cautioning the king that plantation was paramount to control of Ireland and its subsidiary mission, the eradication of papism, a position Charles's wife, a Catholic who disliked Wentworth, ridiculed.

After two long years of endless supplication, Ulick and Wentworth appeared before the king, whose boredom was much remarked, to argue their respective cases for the course of an entire afternoon. To Wentworth's fury, Charles ruled in June 1639 that Clanricard's estates were to be exempt from confiscation. An Irish lord had bested an English lord deputy by being, for the first time, at the hand of his king on the politically correct side of the Irish Sea. In 1641 Ulick sailed for Ireland to take control of his estates there. Portumna Castle was to be his seat. The news of Wentworth's execution later that year personally cheered him, but he realized how poorly this boded for the king, in whose cause he too would suffer.

HIS WITHERED HAND

Thomas Wentworth was no soldier, but he met his death with dignity and great composure, a conspicuous prize in the growing dispute between Parliament and the king. Charles, whose bungled attempts to save his chief minister make for painful reading even today, was embarked on his own tortuous path to ruin, led there by yet another rebellion in Ireland.

Historians no doubt abuse the word "chaos" when they attempt to describe many of the tumultuous eras of the Irish past, but for the decade of the 1640s no other word applies as well, if for no other reason than that all of Great Britain's components were individually explosive and, more fatally, inextricably entwined. Ramifications in one corner of the kingdom affected conditions in the others, no matter the hundreds of muddy miles that may have separated them. Irreconcilable points of view, especially those of religion, produced in the public arena a state of nearly complete anarchy. Never have the affairs of men, even those of today's world, seemed so excruciatingly muddled.

The rebellion of 1641, though planned to some degree, became a matter of spontaneous combustion as rumor and hysteria raced through the countryside. It originated in Ulster, as the indigenous Irish rose to torch and scatter the plantations, and it spread everywhere in the traditionally Gaelic kingdoms. Ominous reports reaching Dublin Castle, loaded as they were with tales of revenge and massacre, took greater note of a possibly radical development. The Old English of the Pale, nearly all of them Catholic, appeared to be wavering. No automatic pronouncements of loyalty to Crown and country were flooding into the capital, only fugitives.

The position of King Charles was originally promising. To crush rebellion, he informed Parliament, a new army was required, but of such numbers and strength that Parliament surely understood against whom it could eventually be used. But then came word from Ireland that the Old English were petitioning the king to confirm the graces once and for all before they committed to suppressing the revolt. The very idea of the king's negotiating with papists threw London into turmoil and put Charles in an impossible light. The careless disregard, indeed the ignorance, of his behavior toward the Irish barons during Wentworth's tenure now hampered the king's ability to maneuver. Those who should have been his staunchest support in Ireland now veered to rebellion, and the New English ran for cover.

Alone of the great Catholic landowners, Ulick of Clanricard stood for the king. As disorder inflamed Connaught, his castles of Portumna, Loughrea, and Oranmore stood flooded with hapless Protestants, driven from their estates and looking for a protector. Convoys of New English families struggled through hostile lordships toward Galway, relying on dubious safe conducts or assurances from local Catholic magnates, who endangered themselves by doing so, given the temper of the times.

At Shrule in County Mayo, just 19 miles from Galway City, an Old English landowner left such a group of stragglers at the boundary line of his territory, an ancient bridge and castle, wishing them good luck

Ulick de Burgh, fifth earl of Clanricard

for the remainder of their journey. As he turned and marched his men away, Gaelic marauders suddenly appeared from the Galway side of the bridge and proceeded to rob and strip the refugees. In surging commotion to and fro, over screams of fright and protestation, a blade was unsheathed and bodies began to fall. Over 100 unarmed people were slaughtered, but many escaped to find shelter in Catholic towers nearby. In one of these, a Protestant vicar was found hiding. Friars and priests wanted to kill him then and there as a heretic, but he was slipped away under cover of night by a wild Bourke to Clanricard's care.

Clanricard never wavered in sheltering those of the apostate faith, a stance that endeared him to no one in Connaught. His principled dedication to Charles, in fact, wholly inexplicable given the torment by Wentworth, guaranteed his status as the loneliest man in the province.

To catalogue the problems he confronted as the primary foe of insurgency would be an exhausting task, as thankless to recite as it was for the earl to face. Let us just summarize the state of Galway City at one stage of these events, the single year of 1642. At first the town was split: gentry in favor of the king, rabble and friars for rebellion. Clanricard, ever the diplomat, secured a tenuous truce between these factions, and the city declared initially for Charles. Ostensibly, so too did the fort and garrison, always the bastion of English sentiment in Connaught. But at the time the fort was under the command of an unstable and violent young officer named Willoughby, over whom Clanricard could exercise little control, and various scuffles broke out between the soldiers and tradesmen. Taking advantage of hot tempers, friars incited their congregations to open the city's gates to area clansmen, in effect declaring for insurrection, and the fort was duly attacked. Clanricard in turn gathered his levies and surrounded the entire theater, both besiegers and besieged, finally compelling the townsmen to declare again for Charles.

Ulick returned to Portumna just in time to hear reports that Willoughby had since gone berserk, lobbing shells into the city, hanging people indiscriminately from the fortress ramparts, and looting the countryside. Clanricard, furious, nonetheless had no time to move against him, as a flotilla of seventeen ships suddenly appeared in Galway Bay, sent by Parliament and looking for spoil. Clanricard again mediated a withdrawal, but not before English sailors, in a show of Protestant solidarity, defaced some churches and dug up a graveyard, scattering bones and coffins in every direction. They were followed by a colonel representing rebels of another sort—the Catholic Confederates, headquartered in Kilkenney—who inflamed the neighborhood into attacking the fort, again now held for Parliament and not the king. After a brief siege, the Confederates prevailed.

Galway City by year's end stood ambiguously for the king and freedom. "I have had no rest since the rebellion broke out," Ulick wrote despairingly, "but at least my endeavors shall be sealed in my best blood." The situation barely improved with the outbreak of genuine war in England between Charles and parliamentary forces. Who was now in rebellion against what? Men like Ormond and Clanricard, with all available forces and supplies, were to join the Catholic Confederates against largely Protestant armies made up of English parliamentarians and Scots from Ulster. Yet whereas Dublin Castle had refused to trust Ulick the papist, now the Confederates shunned him because "he still had more conversation with heretics than with Catholics." As a mediator once again, he engaged in endless, futile, and exhausting negotiations with the Kilkenney Confederates, attempting to find some common basis for an alliance between them and the king. For Clanricard, that basis should have been "duty and moderation," meaning of course the continued relationship between Ireland and the Crown, with toleration for papists. The rebels, under goading from a newly arrived papal nuncio, Archbishop Giovanni Battista Rinuccini, had a more radical idea in mind: an autonomous Catholic Ireland. Again, Clanricard found himself in grievously awkward positions, aggravated by his close association with Butler, earl of Ormond, the highly capable lord deputy (whom he admired), whose disgust for the Confederates was heartily returned. No one, in the end, had a kind word for Ulick. "He trusts no one but himself," wrote a Confederate. "God will never bless his withered hand."

Unlike the personal devastations and battlefield woes that many of his ancestors had suffered in Ireland during the preceding four centuries, and recorded laconically by scribes and annalists, Clanricard's ruination can be traced in his own words. His letter books and dispatches, laboriously copied by secretaries, chaplains, and relatives, give an intimate picture of this collapsing world as Charles fell from power and the Confederates found themselves crushed by Cromwell's New Model Army. These were all grave events, varied in their particulars but with a single effect for Connaught. "My estate in this Kingdom," he wrote,

> has continued in bad condition, spoiled and pillaged both by English and Irish, what one left always destroyed by the other; nothing that I could properly call my own but small territory between my castles of Portumna and Loughrea, for which the charge of defense did much exceed the revenue. In brief, my lord, this has been my condition: a vast debt and a constant growing charge upon me, no estate, no pay nor entertainment, nor no forces, nor powder trusted to me, no arms worth the mentioning, forsaken or forgotten by my friends in England, suspected and discountenanced formally by the State here, hated and scorned by the natives for my opposition to their ways, and nothing regarded for it by the others. And, lastly, the disturbance of my own thoughts being disabled from performing any considerable service to his majesty in this general time of trial. Yet I must acknowledge some inward consolations by the assurance I have received from his majesty of his favor and good opinion and the testimonies of a clear conscience for to justify the reality of my intentions.

Three years after the king's execution, Clanricard stepped away from the world of politics and intrigue, disappearing into that gray expatriate oblivion that has swallowed up so many disappointed Irish statesmen and soldiers over the generations. He had spent his last few weeks in command of Irish forces in the west in a kind of delirium, issuing calls for fighting to the end, last stands, and promises that Galway City would be held for years against the regicides. The mayor and council of Galway thought differently, especially when favorable terms were granted nearby Limerick. If similar proposals were offered them, they informed the parliamentary general Sir Charles Coote, they would surrender immediately, and in April 1652 they did. Clanricard washed his hands of that affair, retiring to one of his castles. In time he too came to an arrangement with his enemies. "The Earl may transport himself," reads the official order, "with eight servants, their horses, traveling arms and necessaries" to England, there to remain six months, after which he was to remove himself to whatever European country would have him. Because of the protection he afforded Protestants during the earliest years of rebellion, he was never forced to fly to France, but his great estates in Kent were seized and given to John Bradshaw, the president of court who had sentenced Charles to death. Portumna, with its farms and villages, passed to Henry Cromwell, the Great Protector's fourth son. Ulick, with no income, found himself harassed by debtors. A more generous Parliament voted him a small pension some months later, but he died in 1657, impoverished, unlamented, and without a son to succeed him.

To Hell

The Cromwellian settlement of that midcentury continued the redistribution of property that would, by 1700, utterly disenfranchise the Irish Catholic. At Moyode the process of transferal seethed with bitterness and frustration. Parliament, as a means of financing its wars with Charles and, after his death, the residue of his scattered papist following, bluntly promised to strip its enemies of all they owned to repay creditors and soldiery alike. Those in England who had "adventured" monies to the government or served in its armies had 2,500,000 Irish acres to despoil among them. Elaborate mechanisms of investigatory inquisitions and baronial surveys were set up to judge all the property owners of Ireland, their political behaviors and boundary lines receiving equal attention.

One Philip FitzGerald, though not a traitor of the same caliber as the earl of Clanricard or the baron of Athenry, nonetheless was a papist now confronted by that famous command, "To hell or Connaught." He was ordered to surrender his ancient estate in Munster and remove family and dependents to a property specified by English agents, which itself would be confiscated from its current occupants. In FitzGerald's case, this happened to be Moyode Castle, a gutted ruin inhabited by the cattle, sheep, pigs, and family of Edmund and Myler Burke. The Dolphins of Moyode by this late date had been dispersed, some transported to Barbados, others to the Continent as foot soldiers in Spanish or French armies, a small handful to roam the forests and bogs as landless beggars, day laborers, or bandits. The Burke brothers unhappily became tenants of the equally unfortunate FitzGerald, whose farm in Munster was then disposed as payment of an English debt. Forty-four thousand Catholic landowners shared this fate, and over 30,000 Irish soldiers, peasants and nobility alike, emigrated overseas with no possessions at all.

Eight years later FitzGerald's spirits rose when Charles II returned to claim his throne. Cromwell's body was dug up from its grave at Westminster Abbey, dragged through the streets to Tyburn, there to be ritualistically hanged and dismembered. His head graced a pike in front of Westminster Hall. News of this startling development cheered some Irish Catholics, who, not unnaturally, expected the restoration of their property, little realizing the fragile position of the new king. FitzGerald rushed to establish his innocence of treason. He was one of only 500 Catholic landowners to succeed, as he recovered the bulk of his estate. The Burke brothers of Moyode tried the same route but failed, tainted by their association with Connaught's historical enthusiasm for rebellion. They became tenants of James, duke of York, to whom the new king issued large grants of land all over Ireland, including Moyode.

Ulick's widow, Anne, received her reward, the return of Portumna and several hundred acres, but her possession of the house was blocked by the new earl, the sixth, a cousin of Ulick's and no friend. This gentleman was an unsentimental individual who had languished in the Tower for participating in various Cavalier plots before escaping to join the future Charles II during his exile in France. He was not pleased to share his patrimony with Ann, whom he sabotaged whenever possible. Their feud, punctuated by appeals from both to king and court, dragged on until his death in 1666.

Somerhill, from the painting by J. M. W. Turner, 1811

On Ulick's maternal side, the estates of Somerhill were also restored, their Cromwellian owner, "that bloodhound" Bradshaw, having similarly been disinterred from his grave and publicly torn apart at Tyburn. The great mansion and grounds of Somerhill proved a welcome diversion for Charles II and his retinue, where trysts and parties and seductions were routinely pursued, and eventually that estate regained, if only for a few years, its former profitability. Clanricard's daughter, described by a French courtier as "the Princess of Babylon," was noted for both her ugliness ("She had the shape of a woman big with child, without being so") and great wealth ("loaded with fortune"). Three husbands eventually impoverished her, and Somerhill fell into decay. Today it is a boy's school.

THE BATTLE OF AUGHRIM, 1691

Now that progress was finally being made on the tower, I allowed myself to veer off toward more domestic tasks, such as finding a chair or two and maybe a table. I struck pay dirt, or so it seemed, in a derelict tower that stands over to the northeast of Athenry. Although it had been lived in until just a few years ago, I stopped by one day when I noticed crows flying in and out of broken windows, a sure sign of abandonment. Inside was a pile of residential refuse—smashed up furniture, rotted mattresses, manure-encrusted crockery, and one piece that caught my eye immediately, an old peasant dresser. Most every farmer's cottage from the 1930s featured one of these, a type of china cupboard tacked together out of scrap wood and generally painted in bright, primary colors. They featured two or three crude drawers down below, topped with a display case with open shelving, the doors of which were paned with glass, usually cracked. No one would mistake any of these for fine furniture.

This particular specimen seemed in good shape, as did one or two spindly chairs that I thought could be repaired. The dresser would fit perfectly in Moyode's small kitchen and could hold my odd bits of silverware and plate, most of it purloined from various airlines. But the farmer's wife who owned this junk refused to sell, more from surprise at the offer than anything else. When pressed, the only explanation she could muster was that she needed something to hand down to her children. I reminded myself upon leaving that I should never approach anyone in Ireland to sell me anything. I just do not have the touch.

As usual in matters Irish, I consulted my immediate neighbors for advice, most particularly Marie and Alphonsus Harty, whom I saw daily either at their water pump in the morning during washup or over tea in the evening. Marie especially is free with her generally good counsel and was aghast that I could be interested in such déclassé debris as a dresser. "There you are now, pouring your money and sweat in the castle, and what are ye doing but for filling it up with old worm-eaten sticks that no one would pick up off the road if they happened to pass them by?" Marie talks so rapidly that I often haven't the slightest idea what she's saying, but the tenor of her voice is usually unmistakable. I reminded her that she had no right speaking to the lord of the castle in so disrespectful a fashion, but differences in our social standing rarely deter her. "If it was the king of England, I'd tell him the same." Marie thinks I should buy new furniture for the place and not waste time running from one derelict wreck to another, picking over stuff that most people would throw away. Alphonsus was more understanding. "If it's a dresser you want, talk to a gypsy."

I can remember as a child of seven seeing caravans of gypsies camped out in the Irish countryside. I also recall watching farmers nearby here roust a colony of gypsies from their roadside encampment in 1968, not a pretty sight at all. The "itinerant" problem has changed in its particulars but remains nevertheless a thorny issue. Government policy has been to domesticate these people, almost by force, penning them up in housing estates, normalizing them through the dole, educating their children. On the outskirts of Athenry, a cluster of low-income apartments was built with generally calamitous results. The place became a blight on the landscape, an instant slum with urban-style social problems that angered the townspeople and area farmers, who contemptuously called it "Riding Hill." Several of the units were thoroughly gutted by their occupants. When a gypsy heeds the yearning to hit the road, he may well decide to take the bathroom and kitchen along with him, fixtures and all. "No one can pin us down," one of them told me.

Nowadays tinkers camp at roadside rest areas on the main roads. Nobody likes them there, of course, and periodically violence breaks out when local people turn up and push them down the highway. After a few months they generally return to squat again in the same favored places. The horse-drawn caravan, though, is a thing of the past, as most gypsies live in trailers and vans. The naked, filthy babies are the same, however, and a gypsy's reputation will never change. "They be lads so bold they'd steal the cream right out of your tea," says Alphonsus, "and when they be done with that, come back for the sugar." To a man like Phonsie, who drinks tea at seven distinct times of the day, this is serious business. He said if ever I bought something from a gypsy, not to have it delivered to the tower or, for that mater, to his place. "They like nothing better than to spy on what you have." On the main Dublin road I stopped at a gypsy camp one evening to look for Johnny, a famous hustler. "A dresser is it? Thanks be to God, I'll find it for ye. I know every corner of the country. I know every barn, shed, and garage there is. You're in great hands with me." Without a second's delay he piled into my Citroën, and we were off.

"A dresser. Now that's a queer thing to be wanting, but let every man's taste suit himself, I always say. Now see that farm there? That old man, God rest his soul, had a fine dresser, but he wouldn't part with it. We'd go out back, and no matter what I'd bid ye, he'd give no fire. After they buried him, though, I got it from his wife. Patience, I says to myself, patience will always win the day."

A few miles past Loughrea, we entered the little village of Aughrim, noteworthy for nothing other than what happened here in 1691, when for a single day thousands of men converged to grapple in its fields, then to stagger away to somewhere equally nondescript to fight some more. Johnny directed me to a small house where, in the rear garage, some local man had accumulated around forty dressers that I picked through. Without a doubt these were utterly worthless pieces of driftwood, crudely banged together by hapless bachelors or worse by the looks of them. All were ridden with worms. By the dim glare of my flashlight, I picked the least decrepit of the lot and signaled Johnny to begin.

I let the gypsy do the talking and stood apart. The two men, natural conspirators, were either discussing ways of carving up my wallet between them in a grotesque rip-off for this piece of junk, or else my man was using every wile, deceit, and trick in his sly repertoire to get me the best deal he could. There are times in this slippery land where I really don't care. The night was ink black. I crossed the road toward the bloody hollow.

In all my years here in the neighborhood, I had never walked the fields of Aughrim, the great battle that finalized Ireland's fate for almost three centuries. I've driven by it enough times to know there's nothing here to remind anyone of what happened on that July afternoon of 1691; just another landscape of bog and pasture, thistle and hedge, an unremarkable anonymity that could pass for any collection of farmsteads in the country. Seeing (or not seeing) it in the pitch dark seemed an apt reminder of the great void of futility and heartbreak that has so often engulfed this island. Many observers are so overwhelmed by the litany of Irish disasters that they term her history tragicomic. But 6,000 men died here, and surely there is no comedy in that dreadful fact.

The battle of the Boyne, twelve months previous to Aughrim, is the more famous struggle that most people recognize as decisive in this final phase of the Glorious Revolution that ousted the Stuarts from England in favor of the Dutchman William of Orange. Charles II had successfully maneuvered his way through twenty-five years of post-Cromwellian compromise, but his younger brother James, though a man of many strengths, enjoyed precious little subtlety of character to succeed in his own right after he was crowned in 1685.

James II is undoubtedly the most maligned English king of the modern age—George III at least was mad—and much of his behavior strikes us today as unbelievably misguided, unattractive, distracted, foredoomed, stubborn, almost farcical. That James was a brave man and religiously principled (though he shared with his brother a voracious sexual appetite) does not excuse him in the eyes of critics for spoiling just about every enterprise of importance that he touched. In Ireland's case his bad reputation is even blacker, and deservedly so. After all of Catholic Ireland had been ground to stubble in the Stuart cause, Raftery, the blind poet of Connaught, called him "James the Pile of Shit, the curse of God upon him."

Ireland represented James's last throw for his crown, though he did not realize this at the time. Later expeditions organized by his patron, the exalted Louis XIV of France, were discussed, planned, organized, and even launched but because of ineptitude, awful weather, and the English navy never progressed beyond the harbors of France. If James had known all this beforehand, perhaps he might have tried harder at the Boyne, where the faulty disposition of forces and his own lack of resolution led to a dispiriting defeat. Whereas William III had joined his troops in battle and gained the honor of a wound, James spent the afternoon aloof from the fray with his best troops, French infantry from Louis, kept in reserve. James was among the first to leave the field, entering Dublin in flight well before his army, there to have a famous (though no doubt apocryphal) exchange with Lady Tyrconnell, sister of Sarah Churchill. "Your countrymen, Madame, are skilled in the art of running away," said the king. "And you, Sire, gave them great example, winning the race."

The Boyne convinced James that Ireland held no hope, and he decamped for France, to the amazement of Louis's court, who had expected him to triumph or die. William, equally swayed in his opinion of this battle as conclusive, called for the Irish to surrender unconditionally and was shocked at their refusal. After desultory operations, he too found reason to leave. But in fact the Jacobite forces, albeit routed, had not suffered crippling losses in either men or material, and though they abandoned Meath and Leinster to William, they established themselves strongly at Athlone and the Shannon line, intending to maintain their enclave in Connaught, there to await reinforcements from France, expected at either Limerick or Galway.

Instead of armies, however, they received generals, and one of these, Charles Chalmont, marquis de St. Ruth, failed utterly at the again famous bridge at Athlone, where on June 30, 1691, the polyglot forces of William—Dutchmen, Danes, French Huguenots, English and Ulster Protestants, all under the command of Lieutenant General Godart van Ginkel—stormed across the Shannon in a surprise attack. The breech into Connaught had been achieved.

St. Ruth, anxious for redemption, chose a slight ridge running southward from Aughrim village as a strong, advantageous line to break Ginkel's advance. He had decided to risk everything on a climactic battle here, "to bury his body or win," as a modern Irish poet wrote, though his Gaelic allies were less than enthusiastic. Still, in the late afternoon of July 12 they dutifully aligned themselves to receive the Protestant attack.

Warfare had by now evolved into a more organized, set-piece affair, where fixed regiments and tactics, disciplined musketry volleys, artillery, and fields of fire had entered the consciousness of commanding generals and theoreticians. St. Ruth stretched his infantry in two long, neat, and formal lines across the ridge, guarded in front by extensive bogs and skirmishers. He arranged cavalry at both flanks and three batteries of artillery spaced evenly along his front. He intended a defensive fight, looking for that one fragile moment when he might break the enemy with a sudden attack of his mounted reserves. That moment arrived. St. Ruth was heard to yell, "We have them, *mes enfants!* The day is ours. They are beaten," as he prepared to lead the fateful charge himself. A cannonball then ripped his head off.

I am reminded here of an incident from U.S. history, involving the unfortunate Major Marcus Reno in General George Custer's command at the Little Bighorn disaster. Under grievous fire, he consulted Bloody Knife, one of his scouts, as to strategy. As they spoke, a bullet tore into Bloody Knife's skull and splattered Reno's face and tunic with bloody pulp. It is said that Reno's commands were thereafter confused and contradictory.

St. Ruth's headless trunk, a ghastly apparition to those about to charge, evidently drained the will to fight out of all the Life Guard cavalry. A cloak was thrown over his body and the bundle heaved on a horse. The guards then fled the battlefield with their dead general.

This was enough too for the cavalry on the Irish left under Brigadier Henry Luttrell, who was labeled from that time on the arch traitor of Aughrim and whose path of retreat remains known today as

Luttrell's Pass. Without engaging the enemy in any significant way, Luttrell deserted his post, leaving the entire Irish flank exposed, which the Williamites attacked immediately. Three hours after fighting had commenced, the Jacobite army in Ireland collapsed forever.

In the middle of this catastrophe stood John Burke, who eleven years later would become the ninth earl of Clanricard. He and his brother, the eighth earl, had thrown everything they had into the cause of James, both having raised a complete regiment of foot from their estates and both having been formally outlawed by the Williamites. The earl's levy had absorbed the entire power of William III's frontal attack at the Boyne, and here at Aughrim John's regiment now stood largely destroyed. With only a few men left, he refused to flee the field. Unsupported by any cavalry, finally encircled by the enemy, he yielded his standard and was taken prisoner.

As night finally settled, the pursuit and slaughter of fleeing foot soldiers ended. There are tales that Williamites then scoured the battlefield searching for booty, sabering all they found still alive.

Ginkel descended on the earl's town of Loughrea the next afternoon, finding it utterly ravaged by the Irish themselves as they had retreated. Moving onto the great plain of Moyode, he discovered quantities of grain and fodder (quickly appropriated) and then, at Athenry, a pathetic assemblage of wretched cabins huddled within the old stone wall, quiet as a graveyard, with not an inhabitant in sight. At Galway he received the city's surrender from an exhausted Clanricard, who threw himself on Ginkel's good graces. Although most of the Catholic garrison marched out to join their confederates at Limerick and from there to banishment in France as the celebrated "Wild Geese," the earl stayed behind to see if an accommodation could be made with the victors. This earned him a Jacobite's vituperative remark that Clanricard had "inherited neither the courage nor the loyalty of his ancestor, the great Earl of St. Albans."

When the eighth earl died childless in 1702, John succeeded to the title but not the estate, which had been attainted. The new earl, who after surrendering at Aughrim had been imprisoned at Dublin Castle, then transported to England, filed for his restoration, both of property and good name. In fact, he begged for mercy. The father of ten children and with virtually no income to speak of, he did all he could to revive his family's fortunes, even attempting to bribe Arnold van Keppel, earl of Albemarle and an intimate of William III's notorious homosexual cabal, the *chateau de derrière*. When authorities heard rumors of John's promise to Albemarle of £7,500, his petition was denied. The earl then renounced Catholicism and submitted his two eldest sons to education at Eton under the supervision of Protestant tutors, thus joining a lengthy list of apostates who would do anything to gain or retain their landed wealth.

In 1702 he saw his reward, "acquitted of all treasons and attainders, restored in blood and estate." This by no means guaranteed emotional stability within the earl's family, however, now riven by religious discord. His sister, widow of the great Sarsfield, had married James II's illegitimate son the duke of Berwick, and three of his sons fought on the Continent under Catholic colors (two of these dying in combat, one at the murderous Battle of Fontenoy in 1745, where Irish infantry won the day for Louis XV).

One result of Aughrim was that James II lost all his lands and revenues in Britain and Ireland. What had been known as the Duke of York's Estate, including Moyode and 6,000 acres, passed to William of Orange. It then became known as the Private Estate, and William used the income much as James had, to pension off ex-mistresses. According to an old Irish friend of mine, William continued the payments to his father-in-law's ladies, as well as to his own. "Really rather decent of him," he commented. In due course, however, the English Parliament seized back from William all the property confiscated from Irish Jacobites, including the Private Estate, and in 1703 sold it at auction in order to recoup the cost of defeating James. Sir William Scawen, a London merchant who had outfitted the future duke of Marlborough's regiment, received thousands of Irish acres in return, 4,700 in Galway and, again, including Moyode. His agents roamed the countryside establishing leases and collecting rents.

As for Henry Luttrell, he was murdered in 1717, and despite rewards his killer was never found. Local people cursed his passing coffin. A hundred years later his grave was dug up and the skeleton hacked with picks.

That evening I drove back to Moyode with the dresser roped to my Citroën. The price had been pretty bad, but I gave Johnny a £20 note for his trouble. He spat on the bill before putting it into his pocket. I was, I must admit, fearful as to Marie's response to this purchase. Sure enough, she was amazed I would buy such a thing. "And the worms!" she announced. "You either treat that with a worm killer or it will be dust in six months' time." Next day she went to town and returned with disinfectant. Marie's mood was not generous, despite my compliment on her efficiency in showing up so soon with just the needed item. "We are very efficient around here, your highness, you just fail to see it. Now since you bought that incredible monstrosity, you can paint this on yourself and good luck to you." In opening the jar and catching my first whiff, I must admit that I instantly recalled just about every public toilet that I had ever been in through my years of travel in the British Isles. That particular odor is unmistakable, and as I dabbed it on the moldy wood the entire castle reeked. Marie's revenge.

Select Chronology

1691–1703	Williamite confiscation of Catholic properties.
1700–1800	The Protestant Ascendancy.
1713	Jonathan Swift appointed Dean of St. Patrick's Cathedral in Dublin.
1767	Moyode purchased by the Persse family.
1798	The Great Rebellion.
1800	The Act of Union: Ireland absorbed into Great Britain.
1821–1822	Famine in Galway.
1845–1849	The Great Famine.
1880s and on	Land League agitation. Moyode House deserted.
1914	World War I begins.
1916	Irish Uprising.
1922	Civil War and "The Troubles."

Perse and Mellows

1700–1922

Dean Dudley, he was called a madman to quit Dublin and go to the wilds of Connaught among wolves and other wild beasts.

Gleanings from the Local Paper

Most historical sights in this country, particularly those that are obscure to begin with, have pretty much been left alone by the national government and even regional councils over the years. Until the explosion in land prices in the late 1970s, when an acre of prime agricultural land might fetch nearly £5,000, farmers rarely bothered with them, whether they were raths or "faerie forts" or inconvenient standing stones—they merely plowed around them. Remnants from the past that had shown the Irish cause or personality in any sort of unfavorable light, however, often suffered, especially as Common Market grants and government initiatives from Dublin flowed down the pipeline, discouraging the notion of idle land. Something like 52 percent of the remaining Norman mottes or earthworks in four southern counties had simply disappeared by 1980, mottes having been deemed symbolic of foreign domination and thus barely valued. And in Dublin the subliminal distaste for an architectural style essentially Protestant (i.e., Georgian, which most of Dublin's finest buildings are), allied with the reckless desire to modernize at any cost, unleashed in the

Irish a destructive impulse that is never far from the surface. For years, the demolition of Georgian Dublin was the preservationist scandal of Western Europe.

Pillars and obelisks, especially those thrown up by the English, also suffered. In 1966 the IRA used explosives to remove Admiral Nelson from his column on O'Connell Street in the capital, and luckily he was not replaced with a Virgin Mary enhanced by fluorescent halo, a suggestion seriously discussed at the time. Likewise the Boyne battlefield looks much the same as it did to William of Orange and James II two centuries ago, the triumphal pillar there also dynamited by the IRA. No one would know anything untoward had ever taken place there, which is the whole point.

I was inordinately curious, therefore, to learn that half a million pounds had recently been spent to develop a new "interpretive center" at the Aughrim battlefield, arguably more of a fiasco for the Catholic cause than the Boyne. Reading a copy of our local newspaper in Marie's kitchen one evening, I spotted a photograph of the incomparable Mary Robinson, Ireland's extremely handsome president, snipping the ribbon and signing the guest book at this new manifestation of emotional unity. "The President expressed the wish that the center would help Irish people to reach out in friendship in a pluralist way, especially to our friends in the North of Ireland, whom she hoped would come to visit Aughrim in great numbers."

If Northern Irish soccer fans are any indication of the types of people who might wish to take an excursion bus for Aughrim to celebrate what was certainly an overwhelming Protestant triumph, I have a feeling the good shopkeepers of tiny Aughrim might wish for some other kind of commemoration. But the desire for profit, any sort of profit, out here in the west of Ireland drives people to all kinds of convoluted rationalizations. The notion of looking at Aughrim as a place "to create links of friendship" boggles the mind.

The newspaper, of course, is not to be blamed. Anywhere, no matter how incongruous, that Mary Robinson visits, the media will be there too, cameras rolling—"President launches world wet fly championship" is standard fare on her calendar. And although her office is largely ceremonial, Robinson has come to wield tremendous psychological power in a land where the repression of women has long been standard procedure.

"Listen to this now, Jim," reads Marie. "Here's a lad from Tuam, a right blockhead if ye ask me. His ideal is 'one of those Eastern women who sit when you tell them and wait there until you order them up.'"

"Well, that's better than some of your holy saints," I reply. "I remember seeing somewhere that St. Kevin in his cave would whip away with nettles the young women who came to bother him and then push them into the lake below, where they turned into fish, thanks to a curse from him."

"I'd like to see him try that with Mary Robinson!"

The newspaper keeps me well up-to-date on other local happenings. I read with interest of a survey that indicated "Galway best for breastfeeding mums." Fifty-four out of fifty-five local cafes and restaurants in that city had no objection to patrons' feeding their children "the natural way" on their premises. Mother's milk, after all, "is always available in the right quantity and at the right temperature." This largess, however, did not extend to nude beaches, the requirement for which may be forced upon Galway by the European Parliament. "Not a bob," said one city counselor over a proposed expenditure for directions and signs.

Several adjacent items chronicled the devil drink at work again—"Had 20 pints of cider, Judge told." One patron evicted from a licensed premises took his revenge by throwing a bicycle through the pub's window. His sentence was "adjourned" when a solicitor for the defendant claimed "his client had been going through a bad time, and has since given up drink." Even a local lad from here in Moyode made the papers—"Stay away from discos, Judge advises"—after a brawl one evening. "You are walking the shortest route to Mountjoy Prison!"

More distressing are recent crime figures for County Galway: all categories up. In Galway City 2,069 indictable offenses, mostly auto theft and burglary (only forty-eight drug-related arrests, however). The most heartless of these crimes on the police blotter involved an Italian couple on holiday who had an accident on their new, expensive BMW motorcycle. As they were taken to hospital for treatment of cuts and bruises, the motorcycle was pinched. "It was rather a big bike," said a police spokesman. "It would have taken a number of men to move it." The Italians' shock at being rear-ended by a car was now "compounded" by this "cold-hearted" deed.

"Four die in weekend Connemara car crash"—nothing amusing here. The carnage on Galway's roads is horrific. The last time I noted figures, 350 people had been killed in the county over the previous five years. Some of the wildest driving I have ever seen in my life has been along Irish roads, particularly the newer highways connecting Dublin with the hinterland. My theory here is that the ancient Romans had the Celts down perfectly two millennia ago. They are "high spirited and quick to battle, but otherwise straightforward and not of evil character." Now that swords and shields have been put away, along with cudgels and axes, that pent-up energy for the rush pell-mell into battle has found its release behind the wheel. I have seen normally mild-mannered and restrained Irish people lose all control of their faculties the moment their foot touches the gas pedal. It's a kind of furious release from the cares of any given moment, an exhilarating charge into the unknown. Finding three cars each passing each other and running fully abreast on the Dublin road at 65 mph or more is a common, heart-stopping sight to those coming in the opposite direction. Head-on collisions are the usual fare.

"Decline in the West" is a frequent cry in local papers here, generally described as all talk in Galway, no response from Dublin. Real facts, dutifully reported, all underlie the sad though traditional Irish story of emigration and then abandonment of bleaker portions of the countryside. Today's paper laments the decline of yet another traditional Galway subsistence crop, seaweed. Whether collected for its low-end application as fertilizer or the more futuristic usage as a component in certain cosmetics (its high point as a source for iodine was described in the nineteenth century by Thackeray), the laborious harvest provides almost 500 jobs in a hard-pressed economy. But the question really is, who wants to work like that anymore? Evidently the French do, having processed half a million tons of the stuff in 1993, compared to only 36,000 tons here in the west of Ireland. "We want computer jobs, not grunt work," one man is quoted as saying.

In the nick of time, the Arabs are coming with a projected forty new jobs. First it was icebergs they planned to tow from the Arctic to provide drinking water in the desert, but Lough Corrib, next to Galway City, is a good deal closer. The current proposal is to pump 10 million gallons a day from the lake into Greek supertankers, underutilized cows that are starving for cargo during the current oil glut. Sport fishermen and environmentalists are understandably horrified, and even economists are dubious of the figures they've seen, one noting that the deal is much too sweet: For the cost of a single pint of Guinness, the sheiks will be buying 100,000 pints of Corrib water. Not much of a surprise to one observer: "The Arabs have been screwing us for years."

Meanwhile, Julia Welby recently celebrated her hundredth birthday. The bishop of Galway said mass for her at the St. Francis Home, with friends, family, and staff in attendance.

The Protestant Ascendancy, 1700

Frank and Mick Broderick, bachelor brothers, now live alone in the former dairy of Moyode House. Whereas in 1968 over fifteen people resided back in the various outbuildings of the old mansion, today only Frank and Mick are still here, and Mick at times rarely so. He has the habit of disappearing for days to pursue his livelihood (or so it is thought) of buying and selling Connemara ponies. Frank, in his seventies now, is always home, however, and always ready for a chat.

Each year I come back we generally go on a tour of the ruins, starting with the noble archway, with Persse crest, that leads to the former work buildings of the old farm, where the stables, smithy, barn, milk sheds, and gardens all stand in semiruinous condition. The garden, with tracings of the old boxwood hedge still visible (and still full of scent), is especially impressive, a 3-acre enclosure now bare and given over to sheep. At the dog kennels, I hear the usual story, familiar to every great estate, of the night when the keeper, dead drunk, made two fatal mistakes: He forgot to feed the pack, and he passed out walking home through the pen. Next day only his shoes and three toes were left. Frank generally apologizes when a junked car lies abandoned in the yard, for in general the area is kept clean of refuse and garbage.

What is left here in this great complex of skeletal fragments only hints at the former grandeur of Moyode House, and the rubble, all stone and masonry debris, gives no aura of human personality. The only familial remain I have been able to unearth after rummaging about through these ruins for the past twenty years are faint tracings of ornate initials scrawled by various Persse youngsters on the attic plaster of a coach house, now roofless and smothered in ivy. In some strange fashion this warmed my heart. One does not read or hear

Triumphal archway, Moyode House

much in Ireland today that speaks well of the Protestant Ascendancy. Their virtual disappearance from the Irish scene caused few tears and little regret, though for every despotic and grasping landlord of whom we have records, there were others who ran their estates with compassion and tolerance, known to this day only by their local reputation as orally preserved in the neighborhood. Frank has nothing bad to say about the Persses.

There is no question, however, that the Persses were by and large diehard Protestants intractably opposed to the popish religion. From the first who came to Ireland, one Reverend Robert in about 1610, to the last of the Moyode line, one Burton Walter, who died in 1935, there was seldom any question as to where the family's emotional and, to be blunt, commercial interests lay. Robert arrived in Ireland with grants of livings from Queen Elizabeth I that originally belonged to

Persse Initials

the Church of Rome, and Burton Walter specifically voided his bequests to anyone mentioned in his last will and testament who may have been foolish enough to convert to Catholicism, a condition he equated with death (he may have had his housekeeper or day laborer in mind).

The Reverend Robert Persse was an Englishman, reputedly from Northumberland, but little else is known of him regarding family, education, training for the clergy, or political astuteness. He came to this beleaguered island at a time when the Reformation had gone too far in England to be reversed. Queen Elizabeth over her long reign had withstood the many challenges to her position, and Puritan zealotry was sufficiently rooted to survive the many difficulties that lay ahead in the 1600s. Ireland, of course, presented a different picture. Catholicism and local political control became so intermeshed that religious allegiances assumed a racial, and thus intensely emotional, character—the old gentry and smaller landowners, largely Catholic, trying to fend away aggressive interlopers, the New English Protestants. In the wake of continual warfare and dislocations, scavengers descended on Ireland, and Robert Persse was one of these.

The earliest Protestant ministers of the sixteenth century had been universally scorned and hated. Some were Catholic turncoats eager to survive, others entrepreneurs indifferent to spiritual concerns, seeking profit. Their abysmal training, lackluster sermons, disinterest in learning the people's language, and often dissolute lives ensured that few of the native Irish ever converted. Even in England these clergy were considered *excrementum mundi*, or the scum of the earth.

The Reverend Robert added a third living in 1605 from King James I and comfortably ensconced himself and family within the Pale, near Maynooth in Kildare. Two of these appointments were inherited seven years later by his son Edward, who styled himself a "minister of God's Word." This unfortunate man's not inconsiderable accumulation of goods was utterly scattered during the rebellion of 1641, when on the night of December 7 a gang of ruffians burst into his vicarage "displaced, despoyled, robbed, and deprived" him of property worth nearly £2,000. As a means of salvage, the Reverend Persse entrusted to some Catholic neighbors his herds of cattle ("English breede") and many of his possessions—"three great Brewing Pans, one great chest full of Lynnen, three great Brasse Pots, one feather bed, saddle and bridle, and other household stuffe, 2 Car loades worth, all to keepe safe." This trust proved naive at best; all these men slipped into treason and the reverend lost everything. Perhaps in compensation his nephew, the Reverend Dudley Persse, the third generation of his family in Ireland, prospered mightily.

Dudley entered Trinity College in 1641 at age sixteen, but the same upheavals that had ruined Uncle Edward interrupted his education so haphazardly that he did not receive a degree until 1661. He seems to have commingled in his personality the best and worst of the Protestant cleric of his time, a modern Persse descendant calling his portrait the picture of a thorough "scoundrel." That he was more than adequate as a preacher is attested by his appointment to St. Michan's in Dublin while still a student at Trinity. St. Michan's, the first church

Dean Dudley Persse

built on the north bank of the Liffey, was at that period most fashionable and well endowed, and Dudley probably owed his advancement to connections made there, such as the duke of Ormond, who called him "an eminent cleric."

But avarice was another of his traits. Beginning in 1662 he amassed a string of advantageous livings, many in Connaught, culminating in his designation as archdeacon of Tuam and then dean of Kilmacduagh, an ancient Celtic monastery. This did not deter him from seeking betterments, as he wrote to a powerful friend in 1682:

> His grace the Duke of Ormond hath spoke his kind resolutions to many persons promoting me. Lately in England he spake very kindly of me to the Duke of Drogheda and other friends of mine. I am of the opinion that ere long there will be an opportunity, for the Archbishop of Cashel is almost at death's door. He cannot live many days. I was in those parts about ten days since and he was very weak. Upon his death I know

> there will be removals and then it will be, I presume, a fit time for his Grace to appear, and if you please to be a remembrancer to his Grace in my behalf I shall own it with all thankfulness and, upon the success manifest my gratitude. Pardon this trouble I beseech you and be assured, etc.

Dudley had an equally fine eye for property. Successive grants from both Stuart kings and authorities in Dublin generated over 1,100 acres in Galway, the nucleus of which would be the estate of Roxborough, immortalized as the birthplace of Yeats's mentor, Augusta Persse, better known as Lady Gregory, cofounder of the Abbey Theatre and a distinguished playwright herself. Roxborough at its height numbered some 6,000 acres. A Catholic writer of the last century could not believe Dudley's luck. "Fortunate, if not distinguished," he dryly noted.

Dudley lived to seventy-five years of age, fathering two sons and seven daughters. Five of the latter he married off to other deans, thus perpetuating the Protestant habit of intermarriage. The later Protestant Ascendancy, and the Persses in particular, made this a dangerous habit, frequently sanctioning first- and second-cousin alliances, "interbreeding of almost Habsburgian dimensions," according to one of them. Plenty of eccentricity, he added, but only a little idiocy.

As the Persse family of Roxborough developed their estates, they kept a keen eye on the locals. Dean Dudley had warned Dublin that Catholic monks and itinerant priests were reinhabiting the old ruined monasteries. At nearby Kilconnell, trashed by Cromwellians fifty years before, "I am credibly informed that friars reside and live there, walk in their habits and solemnly, at all usual hours, chant their offices. They grow in numbers and are daily debauching souls." Such clandestine manifestations of unrest disturbed the Persses, as indeed they did all the new Protestant gentry of the country, speedily enriching themselves, and intensified both their clannish sense of isolation and a deeply rooted insecurity. "I hope this will be kept in all secrecy," the dean requested Dublin at the end of his report, "lest I receive some prejudice or incur some danger by reason of this relation."

Over the years the Persses of Roxborough bought neighboring properties for younger sons, thus establishing separate and often competitive branches of the family. When Dean Dudley's great-grandson Burton came of age in 1767, a large chunk of Scawen's holdings, including Moyode, was purchased for him. He built a modest country

Kilconnell Abbey

seat, called Persse Lodge, and proceeded to improve his estate, which eventually grew to 3,000 acres, with several thousand more scattered elsewhere through the province.

Little can really be ascertained as to the intimate character of Burton Persse. By the time people came to jot down their impressions of him in the 1820s, he had already passed into caricature, known locally as "Old Burton," the sporting gent who even in his eighties mounted up for the hunt on wintry days. That he was a successful farmer is beyond doubt, if only because for sixty years he lavished a fortune on the only thing that ever really mattered to him, the chase.

Old Burton was actually better known by a more distinguished accolade, "the Irish Meynell," in tribute to his stature as the premier huntsman in all of Ireland, if not the equal to Hugh Meynell himself, one of the early giants of the English sporting scene. Let others worry about religion and Wolfe Tone and United Irishmen. Old Burton spent his time studying bloodlines of horse and hound, setting out his servants in orange plush while he, the master, rode about in scarlet

A contemporary miniature of "the Irish Meynell"

coat with a mother-of-pearl stickpin. These were the Regency days of high living and great extravagance. To be Protestant and rich meant living like a feudal king. The earls of Clanricard, for instance, no longer had any illusions as to religious preference. By the mid-1700s they had become doctrinaire adherents to the established Church of Ireland and great absentee landlords. The eleventh earl, dubbed by London's gutter press "the Hibernian Hero," led the gay and licentious life of an English nobleman, a habitué of the theater and society of Bath, a collector of actresses and women of leisure. Indiscretions in love continued to haunt their line: Reports of an illegitimate son of the fourteenth earl and his mysterious, all too incriminating "latchkey" were enough to bring down a government led by Palmerston.

To be Catholic and a landowner, however, was something else. Worry, insecurity, and the prospect of a dissolute relative's using religion to steal the farm all tended to nurture the deeply conservative and suspicious attitudes about land that farmers like Thomas Uniacke held throughout the twentieth century. Men counted their farms by the square yard. "Nearly all the inhabitants of the district are Catholics," a visitor to Galway wrote in 1797:

> Only the rich submitted to the Anglican form, in order that they might possess their goods in peace. Thirty years ago, the proprietor of a very fine estate called Oranmore, fearing that some cousin might turn Protestant in order to filch it away from him, sought the bishop and offered to renounce the superstitions of the Church of Rome. "What motive my son," said the pastor, "urged you to enter the fold of the faithful, and to abandon the Babylonian Woman?"
>
> "Oranmore."

Pillar and Post

It had been my intention those many years ago when I first purchased Moyode to rebuild the small bawn, or wall, that once circled the tower, the outline of which can still be traced from the battlements 50 feet above. The expense of such a project, however, would run to the thousands, and long ago I reluctantly gave up the notion. Some sort of barrier was required to keep livestock out, however. Thomas Uniacke once told me that in his uncle's time a bullock managed to climb right up to the top of Moyode, negotiating not only the circular stairway to the third floor but the far narrower rampart steps as well. When he reached the walkway, he stood and bellowed his confusion until all the neighborhood knew what had happened and came running. As the small crowd waited, Uniacke's uncle sent word for the butcher to bring his tools, and when the unfortunate beast finally stumbled and fell, the carcass was rendered on the spot and freely distributed.

I decided, after consultations with Phonsie, that a good and sturdy Galway stone wall would do nicely, and he knew just the lad to do it. This left me with another item to forage, a set of proper gates. The original iron gates of Moyode House had long since disappeared, and to judge by the size of the granite pillars that had supported them, purchased by monks of the nearby Esker monastery and reinstalled there, they would have been far too grandiose for my needs. Modesty of scale was what I required, and once again as I drove about I kept an eye out for anything that might suit.

Success came where I least expected it, right around the corner. A side entrance to the Moyode demesne had a set of perfect gates on two finely shaped and graceful pillars only 7 or so feet high. The gates themselves, remarkably, were salvageable, and the question, as usual, was who owned them and would they sell. A few discreet inquiries revealed that in fact one of Phonsie's cousins had them and that this gentleman, one Robert Harty, planned to replace the gates with larger, more modern posts that would facilitate the maneuvers of lorry and trailer more efficiently. To sum up, they could be had.

Robbie is the odd man of Moyode. A stout fellow of great physical strength, he lives the bachelor life in a trailer down the road. Ordinarily I would conclude this to be a prescription for aesthetic disaster, but in fact Robbie's place is most fastidiously maintained, and he is respected in the neighborhood as a man of impeccable taste when it comes to judging a horse or cow and as having very high standards in general. It was clear when I first broached the matter of the gates that he would not sell them to just anybody—no, no, no. Others had called on him to inquire, but those gates were not meant for modern bungalows or blacktop driveways. Their projected use would have to meet Robbie's criteria of appropriateness. When I explained their perfect scale for the castle, his eyes lit up. "And they would stay on the estate, which is proper, correct, lovely, perfect, in every way to be desired, and exactly what I think should happen in the first place." Talk of price was disposed of in ten seconds. They were mine or, in Robbie's words, Moyode's.

The next week I hired Michael Nolan to help me dig them up. This would be a morning's work, I told him. We removed the gates, not the simple task I thought, since in the course of two centuries they had tended to sag and settle. We put them aside for Phonsie to take into the blacksmith in his trailer. Then we started digging. At first I went at it with gusto, to the amusement of Michael. "Wouldn't it be a shame now, Jim, to go home without the feel of a shovel in your hand?" he said, and as I tired he continued expertly. The French make soufflés like no other people, the Germans brew their beer the best in the world, no one knows pasta better than the Italians, and the Irish wield a shovel with the skill of brain surgeons. Michael deftly circled the pillar, neatly folding back the earth and making precise little piles of dirt around him. When he was down below his knees he shook his head, however. "I don't know, Jim. We could be here for a couple of days, and then what are we going to do? I'd say there's more of this below the surface than above." We called over to Robbie for his opinion.

"Oh dear God, lads. You'll never get her out that way." Turning to me, "And tell me, Jim, how are you going to lift it?"

"Well," I began lamely, "I thought three or four of us maybe, hauling it into Phonsie's trailer."

"And how much weight do ye think is there?"

"I don't know."

"Well, I'd say over a ton each, to be sure." Michael and I took the rest of the day off.

Meanwhile, I interviewed the day laborer Phonsie thought could do my wall. Or more precisely, he interviewed me. The subject of labor is a sore one with farmers today. In the 1920s and 1930s, the wild men of Connemara would come to Athenry during springtime for hiring fairs. They were called *spalpeens,* Gaelic for "a scythe for a penny." Knowing little English, wearing homespun, often with nothing to their names save spade or shovel, they would gather on an appointed Sunday after mass in the village square, there to be looked over by farmers who would offer slave wages, £30 a season plus their dinners to the strongest. Today the going rate is £20 a day. Marie gets all hot and steaming when outsiders or do-gooders pay day help up to £30 a day, which tends to inflate the local scale. Tim, the candidate for wall builder, plans to charge me £250 for my job. He'll do it over the winter while I'm away, he'd like the money up front, and he wants to know what I think about God and sin.

"Well to be honest, Tim, at the moment I'm more intent on the wall."

"Ah, to hell with the wall. If I don't do it, it's because I'm dead, on the other side of the sod, there to meet my maker and be damned."

"You're pessimistic, Timmy."

"I'm concerned. Not worried, mind you, but concerned."

"That distinction kind of eludes me, Tim."

"It needn't, master, it needn't. I see the better way, but I fail to follow it. Now look at me. I'm dirty, correct? But this is dirt I never worry about. It's outside—soap and water, it's gone. It's the dirt inside that matters."

"True, Tim, very true. Now about the wall . . . "

"Ah, to hell with the wall altogether."

I later asked Phonsie if Tim was really the right man for the job. "Oh, spot on, Jim, he is." I took his word for it.

Later, when the trench was dug connecting the new water line to Moyode, I borrowed the backhoe, and we went back down to Robbie's gates. After thirty minutes of digging, we finally freed up one of the posts, put a chain about the top, and hoisted it out. I was amazed at what I saw, and Robbie had been right. The carved and finished portion was only half the piece. The bottom was a rough cutout, its lower end an engorged, bloated mushroom cap of solid rock. Michael laughed when he saw it trundled up to the castle. "Now in fairness," he said, "the power is the boy. You can't beat the power. We were going to pick that up all by our little selves?"

The next year, needless to say, Timmy had not finished the wall. Phonsie was to have doled out the money I gave him in bits and pieces as the job progressed, but Tim was apparently in the process of starving to death, so Phonsie had given him everything. "This is Ireland," Phonsie explained. "He'll get to it." When I arrived at the start of the second year, I paid Tim a visit one evening. His house, north of Athenry, had once been the proud centerpiece of his father's prosperous farm. Through drink and indolence, Tim had frittered all that away. In the dark, stumbling about the overgrown path to his cottage, I could see Tim sitting by the hearth smoking a cigarette, his only light a small turf fire.

Actually, not by the hearth but in it. Dragging up an old feed tin, he offered me a seat at the other end of the fireplace and resumed his, hunching directly over the smoking fire. The house was a dreadful mess, open plastic buckets catching rainwater from the leaking roof, tins of rotted tuna and salmon lying on the floor, moldy bread from weeks ago in the otherwise empty larder. "You need a wife, Tim, to take care of this place."

"No, I need a servant. Actually, what's the difference? Ah, I don't give a damn. If I was in the States, I'd be on the bowery and that's it. This was a grand house once, but I made bad provision. It's a race between me and the roof. If I win it, your wall will get done. If not, well, you needn't worry. I'll get my just reward."

"How about we go out for a hot meal, Timmy, down in Athenry?"

"Man cannot live on bread alone, master, only on the body and blood." On that weird note, I left. That winter Tim finished the wall.

RELIGIOUS MATTERS

When the weather is fine, I generally hike or bicycle to mass at Esker on a Sunday. Nowadays my bike is generally the only one there. "Old people used to walk 4 or 5 miles each way to mass in times gone by," Frank told me, "and the younger ones on their bicycles, hundreds of them. But everyone has a car now."

Esker, guarded by Burton Persse's granite gate pillars from Moyode, is a nondescript assemblage of church and monastic buildings equidistant between my place and Athenry. It sits hidden in a copse of trees surrounded by some of the poorest land in the parish, boggy and wet. The Dominicans came here in Elizabethan times when various lord lieutenants evicted them from their abbey in Athenry, and it became, quite typically for Ireland, a kind of underground station for itinerant monks on the run. All the country people, naturally enough, knew of its existence and generally gathered here for mass or sent their children for education at the "hedge" schools that friars and masters haphazardly held in nearby fields or cabins. Local Protestants were also aware of Esker, but mostly left the place alone. In extreme times during the penal days, the monks would scatter, though when authorities loosened their grip or decided out of necessity to look the other way, the Dominicans returned.

Bribery was always useful, of course. Account books still in the Dominicans' care show the friars paying off sergeants, most particularly for their "Christmas box," with money and sometimes "claret, to treat the sherrifs." An indignant official in Galway upbraided the constabulary for their venality. "Disperse those restless popish ecclesiastics," he wrote. "Let me not meet them in every corner of the street where I walk as I have done. No sham searches, as to my knowledge you have done. Your birds have flown, but they have left you cake and wine to entertain yourselves."

Today there are no Dominicans at Esker. As with most religious orders in these modern times, retrenchment is the rule. "When I was a boy," Phonsie told me, "on Sunday afternoons the novices from Esker would take a grand walk from the monastery over here to Moyode.

They'd come in by the old gate, up the avenue past the castle, over there to the old bridge and then up to Kilconierin Church for a prayer, circle around then to the Athenry road, and back to Esker in time for compline. There could be 200 of them at a time, and you'd see them coming on through the demesne like a flock of black crows, clattering away in their talk. It was a great sight, really. If they have four novices over there now I'd be amazed, vocations being so thin on the ground."

By "they" Phonsie means the Redemptorists, who took over Esker in 1901. They were once known as especially dogmatic and aggressive preachers. "They used to talk about Satan and Hell altogether too much," an older woman told me. "We'd come out of church all afeared, to be honest with you, but those days are all done. The only thing you hear now is, 'Your Divine Lord is not a judge. He says come to me. He is love,' and all of that. Being a person of penance, I prefer the old way."

This morning's sermon was typical for the 1990s. The priest called for all the men to join in a weekend retreat, and his pitch made me think I was heading off to the Costa Brava for vacation. "We want you to withdraw from noise, the noise of work and play, the noise of children and scurrilous politicians, the noise of disco and television. We are here to listen, to give you peace. And remember, this is no fasting experience; you won't go hungry. We have a modern kitchen and a great cook. There's no bog tea at Esker."

After mass some of the men were dubious. "They just want to get us in there, then turn up the screws," said one. "He talked the wind."

My friend Seamus, master mechanic, had me over to dinner that afternoon. Times are changing, it appears, for the true saints as well. "My sister, now, she's a recluse with the Sisters of Clare, or what they call 'enclosed.' Once a year we get to see her, or to be truthful, talk with her. They had a 2-by-2-inch hole in the door, and that's what we talked through back then. Just enough space to lock fingers. But now they've relaxed some of the rules. The opening is about 6-by-6 inches these days, and you can really see a bit of her face. I miss the girl, I do, but she's happy, and I guess that's what counts."

"People seldom want change, especially in their forms of worship," a youngish priest was later to tell me in Athenry, "but the life of the spirit demands it. The old people now, it's difficult for many of them in the Church today, but for our ministry to thrive here in a modern

Ireland, we have to adapt to some degree to the concerns and difficulties of our young people. I think we'll never bend on the big issues like abortion, but things like meatless Fridays and the Latin mass and all, it's history. And a married clergy is a distinct possibility."

"You make it sound very cozy, Father: 'Let's all become Episcopalians.'"

"You're just angry about the old mass, but frankly I've no use for people always looking behind."

"Is Christ behind us or before us, Father? That's an interesting question."

"Look, the Vatican II mass is theologically correct, and it's historical. If anything recreates the spirit of the Last Supper, that does. I'll wager you hate the kiss of peace."

"I certainly do."

"I knew it! Incense and Gregorian chants, that's all you want! There's precious little in any of that to help out some poor Irish girl in London or New York, pregnant and friendless, with nowhere to go."

"As we say in the States, Father, 'Take away the pain and you take away the gain.' Confession is the next thing to chop out, I'd guess."

"In twenty years you'll see a general or public confession built into the mass, along with a general absolution, yes, I'll agree with you there."

"I'm just amazed, Father, to be having this conversation in Ireland."

"And in a pub of all places," the priest answered, ordering another whiskey, which I paid for.

Some days later I visited the old bag factory, now an automobile repair shop, a few hundred yards beyond the North Gate of town. "We found these statues here when we moved in," the young proprietor told me, pointing out a St. Joseph, a St. Patrick, and a Jesus of the Sacred Heart. "They were in the old church, and when the bishop tore it down to build the modern one, they removed these from the grounds and they ended up here. Ah, they must have been in use for generations, these things. My father and I had a painter come by and he redid the Savior in a beautiful way." We both admired the refurbished statue, which, I must admit, was indeed immaculately done, the new colors of Christ's garments a subtle blend of mauves and purples, quite in contrast to the gaudy splash these images generally receive in Irish churches. "We had one of the parish priests come over, and my father said, 'Look, isn't this lovely? We can bring it down to the new church

The Sacred Heart, McNamara's Garage

anytime you say, and we're ready to restore the other two as well.' The priest went on for a few minutes saying how nice they were and all, and he'd get back to us. That was two years ago."

"It's the Sacred Heart," I replied. "They don't want those old-fashioned notions anymore, bleeding and raw and messy. It's too embarrassing. He'll never call you back."

THE DARLING ROOT, 1821

An acquaintance of mine who lives near Loughrea has gone into the auctioneering business, and word has it that he has landed a buyer for the main gates of Roxborough House, just about the only thing left of that formerly magisterial estate, which are to be dismantled and shipped away to God knows where. Other friends of mine, mostly American, consider the sale indecent and disgraceful, the spoliation of the countryside and so forth. Having become an expert on gates but forgotten what the Roxborough behemoths looked like, I drove over one afternoon to see. Although certainly impressive in their Irish context, they hardly seem sufficiently powerful to grace much more than the rear entrance of some minor English country seat. Their attraction to me was more ironical in nature. They beckon us to enter and contemplate the cruelties of fate, the hollow ruins and tumbled masonry of evaporated pretension.

More interesting in its way was a small arched bridge over the stream that flows through the Roxborough demesne and the little carved inscription that explains its purpose: "Erected in Memory of Ireland's Emancipation from Foreign Jurisdiction, 1783," followed by the name "William Persse, Esquire Colonel of the Roxborough Volunteers" and, incidentally, Old Burton's brother. It reminds us, or should, that generalities about class and social attitudes must never be swallowed whole.

The eighteenth century in Irish history is known by some as penal times, that span of several generations when a dispirited Catholic population, deprived of its leaders, land, and the legal practice of religion, slid into a state of virtual serfdom. Although it is certainly true that anti-Catholic laws and prohibitions slackened as the 1700s progressed, this in fact simply reflected the Protestant perception that their victory was complete.

The American Revolution, however, whose impact and influence on Ireland we may find hard to imagine today, shook the Ascendancy world as much as any other of its time, though in a confused and in some ways contradictory fashion. To some Irish minds, like that of William Persse, it served as a reminder that he was Irish, not English, and that his affairs, along with those of his county and nation, might be better served if the power of government reigned from Dublin, not London. In this sentiment most Irish Protestants agreed. But William Persse took the lessons of America one further step: All men were created equal, and perhaps some small measure of political privilege could now at last be entrusted to responsible Irish Catholics, many of whom were neighbors and tenants of his and decent men altogether. In this sentiment he came to grief.

Most of the Protestant elite saw a free Ireland in narrowly sectarian terms. They could become excited at talk of British tyranny, both in

America and Ireland, but still declare their allegiance to the Crown. They could endorse rebellion in the colonies yet still enlist in British forces to suppress it (William's brother-in-law was shot at Bunker Hill). And they could advocate the notion of Rousseau's "noble savage" born to freedom but sincerely deny that status to Irish papists.

William Persse, with his notions of admitting Catholics to the bar or the legislature or even, most dangerous of all, the army, was truly suffering from a "strange madness." The New English had now inherited that Old Irish disease, cultural schizophrenia.

The brief period of Ireland's legislative independence, achieved by men like Persse, who formed their regiments of armed volunteers and pressed for home rule and a genuine parliament of their own, foundered on the rebellion of 1798 (which terrified all Protestants) and the subsequent ability of London to exploit religious prejudices. The Act of Union in 1800, which saw the absorption of Ireland and its governmental functions into the Westminster orbit, in fact ruined Dublin, destroyed Irish industry, and guaranteed that for another fifty years great estates like Roxborough and Moyode would continue their almost feudal role as the nation's economic and cultural mainstay. Connaught in the eighteenth century remained totally undeveloped, backward, and isolated. The now-fabled Connemara district, for example, was a virtual wilderness to outsiders, with no roads and no means of overland communication. The almost hysterical enthusiasm of the volunteers wholly dissolved. Men like Persse, so imbued with the idealism of George Washington, Benjamin Franklin, and the Marquis de Lafayette, were thrown into despair, especially as Ireland's mercantile activity simply shriveled and minor county cities like Galway followed Dublin into decline. Ireland more than ever was seen as a land with no future.

William Persse, at least, was an eldest son, the squire of Roxborough. He had his great estate to keep him busy and the pleasures of the hunt to console him. For younger sons who had no income, however, prospects could be dim indeed. Old Burton had been lucky; his father had provided for him. As the Persse family multiplied in the dead economic climate of old Ireland, many of their brood were cast aside. The reigning principle, of course, was primogeniture, or at least that of the favored son. A generous father could help launch a younger son to a career if he chose, but there was seldom any inclination to divide the land. William Persse's younger son, Henry Stratford Persse, was a case in point.

On William's death, Roxborough was handed down intact to the eldest son. Henry, though his father loved him, had no future allocated to him on the estate, and through family connections (the Persses were fourteen times high sheriffs of Galway City) Henry secured a position at the customshouse. There he struggled to make ends meet, helped in little measure by his fathering twenty-two children (of whom twelve survived infancy), all of whom were thus minor gentry of a minor son with no inherited wealth to sustain them. The notion of a Protestant aristocracy living off the sweat of Irish helots simply does not hold up if we examine the life of Henry Persse and his family.

Henry's letters from the 1820s show a man disgusted with the state of Ireland: its ruination by Britain, its social fabric torn by sectarian bigotry, its landlords idle and often dissipated. For him, the future lay over the seas in America, where to his own personal grief he sent off three sons, his "dear boys," as indentured apprentices to various farmers in New York State. These lads did not go to oversee fieldworkers, ride to the hunt, or develop a "head and stomach to twelve tumblers of Punch or four bottles of wine." They went and shoveled manure, much to the pride of their father, who rejoiced at their flight from "the vagabond climate of Ireland, full of overtaxed, famishing, cut-throat people," to a land where "industry receives its just reward."

Certainly the brood who stayed behind gave him little solace. There was William, "who does nothing, gives himself too much to the bottle ever to reform. A place in government? He has been upon the list for the last nine years. I see no hope whatever of his getting any situation." Henry Jr.'s prospects were not much brighter: "He goes on quietly at the Post Office and is worn. He went to Loughrea, to the hazard table, and received a fine painted face so bad he could not show for ten days. I certainly will turn him out of the house. I will not put myself to support him in vice and drunkenness." As for Robert,

> This boy is full of wildness. He wants to be a Constable under the new act, a man employed to hunt down the peasantry and see that they are in their hovels after sunset, and not out before sunrise, and force them to pay rent, tithes, and taxes, a fine trade for what is called a Gentleman. He is only fit to be a driver over slaves. He would not for £500 a year spoil the shape of his nails by any unfashionable enterprise.

Parsons? "I know not what Parsons is about. I advanced £100 long ago to bind him to an attorney, but I declare this moment I know not whether he is bound or not, so silent is he." Poor Sally! "I am sorry to tell you that she has made a very hasty match." And his three younger sons? "It is not to idle the boys that I take them to hunt. It is to make them hardy men, fit for Yankee land, for determined they are to go" (they never settled there). Only Mattie, his eldest daughter, made a good financial match, marrying Old Burton's son and becoming mistress of Persse Lodge, soon to be renamed Moyode.

Burton de Burgh Persse, Mattie's new husband, was given Moyode before Old Burton died. Old Burton went into retirement, as it were, wandering from one address to another and finally ending up in a cottage on the Roxborough estate. Henry asked why Old Burton was behaving this way in his ancient years. "I am like the hare," he replied. "I was started at Roxborough. I ran my ring, the world hunted me. And now I am coming home to die near my old farm." ("Not bad from an old Sportsman," remarked Henry.)

His son Burton de Burgh Persse totally transformed Persse Lodge. He was an entrepreneurial man with farms and rented properties throughout the province, largely given to sheep. He invested heavily in wool and became the full owner of Persse's Irish Whiskey, an enterprise begun by his financially strapped father-in-law some years before. Moyode House, as he renamed his estate, a baronial contraption of pseudo-Gothic design, was built wholly on Burton's sketches. No architect or consultant advised him. The multiple turrets and Tennysonian battlements all covered in ivy came straight from Burton's fantasies, the details of which we know nothing. The Camelot he created was naturally the most visible manifestation of his success and wealth, though its extravagance greatly burdened the family at a time when rents and generally hard times were proving worrisome to all.

The four years of Great Famine from 1845 to 1849 provided some of the most horrific episodes in Irish history, but few people recall the precursors of that disaster twenty some years before in Connaught. Henry Persse, from his desk at the customshouse, saw the disaster unfolding, with "people dying like rotting sheep," and his observations, had they been noted at the time, might have prevented some of the greater misery that enveloped the entire island at midcentury.

To Henry the explanations were manifold. As famine started in the 1820s, he bemoaned the helpless condition of the Gaelic peasantry, a class for whom he had great and commendable concern. "The Irishman and the Pig are here upon the same level," he commented bitterly, "the same food, the same bed of straw, the same hovel." British

Moyode House

policy had contributed to this social misery, having drained the economy through selfishness and punishing taxation, leaving all to beggary. Crops "as cheap at any period for the last thirty years" resulted in "the riddle or paradox of people starving in the midst of plenty," precisely the condition of 1846–1849. More basic to the problem, however, was the reliance of common people on a single crop, the potato. "I am the only Irishman who has ever exclaimed against potatoes," Henry wrote prophetically. "I would wish to see this root abolished from general use."

The killing famines of 1821 and 1822 were directly related to the failure of this solitary crop, the sustenance of all the poor. The potato was easy to grow and economically suited to the exceedingly small farm plots that the average farmer could barely afford to rent. Its pervasive cultivation coincided with an explosion in family growth throughout Ireland, commented on as early as the 1780s. "I asked a peasant who had a dozen pretty children, healthy and flush as roses, 'How is it your countrymen have so many children?'" a Frenchman wrote during a walking tour of Connaught. "It's the potato, Sir," he replied.

But to Henry Persse, this dependence was fraught with danger. True, grains take more land to cultivate, but does the potato keep? As Henry put it,

> If an unpropitious season follows one that has been superabundant, the whole people starve. Can potatoes, like wheat, oats, barley, rice, or indian corn be held over for even fifteen months to make up the deficiency in a short crop? If they could, where could stores be got to lay up by that unwieldy article. Not so with corn and grain. They can be preserved for many years and lie in a small compass too. So the famine of one year may be guarded by a hoard in the previous one.

The result of one crop failure in 1821, therefore, was "distress of this county beyond description, when there is not a single vile potato to be had around us. It is impossible to give a just picture of such misery as now walks abroad, the moving specters are like walking deaths. A woman just now expired from want at my window."

Henry and his family took in strays from the street and ran a soup kitchen to help feed over 1,000 families.

> I am up every day at four or five o'clock. I buy wheat at the market, get it ground, pay a baker for making it into bread, buy small bullocks at the fairs, and with some oatmeal, pepper, and onions I make excellent soup. The parties applying have tickets, signed by the priest. As they come in I give them their portion and when all are served I open the doors and all go away. A quart of soup and half a pound of meat is the allowance. This barely keeps them alive. Such a scene is not to be looked at in any other spot on the globe except here, at soup shop, when the door which I call the flood gate of misery is opened, and although I have now regulated it so the last in are the first helped, yet such is the anxiety that the moment the door is opened, if I had not three or four great, strong men at the door to keep the pressure back, I should have scores of men, women, and children trodden to death. Some have their legs and arms broken.

Unlike many of his country brethren, he did not take the occasion to harangue the starving people on the evils of papist Rome. Henry was also active in generating public work schemes to employ the poor. The markets were full of food, but no one had money to buy any.

At Moyode Burton de Burgh Persse also assisted the tenantry. The medieval ruin of Moyode Castle was tidied up as an ornament for the formal lawn. Missing lintels were carved and inserted (some with miniature angels sculpted for decoration), window mullions replaced, broken stairways repaired. Over a doorway I found two masons had chiseled out their names in 1822: M. Brady and J. Doyle. Burton was proud to the day of his death that no tenant of his in 1821–1822 or in the horrific 1840s, when about 30 percent of Connaught's peasant population died, had ever been evicted or forced to the workhouse. And he had the common touch, able to converse with his people in their native Irish tongue, a condescension that most of his contemporaries would have regarded as well beneath their station. He died in 1859, and the usual flood of panegyrics as to his worthy and estimable character are all, for once, perfectly believable.

His son Burton Robert Persse succeeded to Moyode. Initially some dispute had caused a rift between the two, as Burton Sr.'s first will had instructed trustees to sell the estate and divide its proceeds among his six other children. He had, in effect, disinherited Burton Robert. But a codicil added fourteen months later reversed these instructions: An illegitimate son, previously provided for, was cut off; Moyode House was retained and given to Burton Robert; the distillery granted another son; and the meager leftovers then split among his remaining children. Someone, probably Mattie, had worked her way with the elder Persse.

Burton Robert now stepped forward to a world beginning its decline. The famine had proved a commercial as well as moral disaster for many of the great Irish landlords. As much as the peasantry depended on potatoes, so did landlords require their rents, especially as many had over the years financed their excessive indulgence on buildings and hunts through mortgaging at reckless proportions. In many cases, in good years, rents barely covered interest debt, providing nothing to live on after expenses. To miss even a single year's revenue from their impoverished tenantry spelled severe disability; four years' worth meant ruin, and many estates were sold out by creditors in the 1850s. Successive years of poor harvests, depressed agricultural prices, and terrible weather hard pressed many others.

Even worse, the news from London was disquieting. The Great Famine had done more than kill off over a million Irish peasants and

The Persse Family of Galway
Simplified Genealogy

Dean Dudley Persse
d. 1694

Henry of Roxborough
d. 1733

Robert of Roxborough
d. 1781
7 children

(of whom 2)

William of Roxborough
d. 1802
5 children

(of whom 1)

Henry Stratford
Customs Official
Persse Whiskey
d. 1833
12 children

(of whom 1)

Dau. Matilda
m. Burton Persse
of Moyode (his 2nd w.)
d. 1862

Burton of Moyode
"The Irish Meynell"
d. 1829

Burton de Burgh of Moyode
m. Matilda Persse
d. 1859
15 children

Burton Robert of Moyode
Master of the Hunt
Galway Blazers
d. 1885

Burton Walter
d. 1935

bankrupt some few score Protestant squires. It had destroyed the reputation of the Irish landlord. Ordinary Englishmen, as fed up with the Irish problem as any of their Elizabethan forebears, still could not, in equanimity, stomach the horrible tales of eviction and deportation that flooded from Ireland during and after the famine years. Absentee landlords, who had drained out of Ireland over £6 million in rents alone for the year 1842, were especially singled out for shame, and powerful agitation for reform began that eventually, over the course of Burton Robert's lifetime, effectively destroyed the Persses and their way of life at Moyode. Even the normally quiescent Irish peasant was moved to act, and this awakening hastened the end.

Initially these momentous changes caused little stir on the estate, as Burton Robert took up with a passion seldom seen the sport of his grandfather Old Burton, the chase for fox.

The Underclass, 1830

As the Persse family road to hounds and entertained their fellow gentry with lavish house parties and horse races (for "the Moyode Cup"), interspersed with jaunts into Galway, where various of their number maintained townhouses, the Catholic peasantry buried themselves in toil, debt, and heroic memories. Their own aristocracy, both military and religious, were dispersed all over the world, though primarily on the Continent of Europe. The saints and scholars of ancient lore no longer studied at Kells, Clonmacnoise, or the Aran Islands, but rather in the Flemish lowlands surrounding Louvain, the sunbaked universities of Spain, along the Tiber in Rome. Their soldiers fought and died in countless wars for pay and glory, but as Sarsfield said memorably at his death on a faraway battlefield in the Spanish Netherlands, "Would this wound had been for Ireland!"

The long years of the 1700s, the penal years, in many ways dried up the nation's soul. No one will deny that the old ballads still churned out their steady reams of romance and despair over Ireland's sad fate and its many tragic heroes, and no one will deny how profoundly the Irish wallowed in these deep-running streams of melancholy. But in many ways this struggle to survive drained the Gaelic character of its profound, spirited, wayward, and often playful intellectual curiosity, that drive and tenacity of will that at one time had spiritually influenced many of the more substantial and populous societies of Western Europe.

Deprived of natural leaders through war and exile, Irish religion and society devolved to the lower stratum of peasant custom. Where before the Irish could look to their chieftain for leadership in battle, now they often gathered round a local outlaw or bandit or "whiteboy" to maim a few cattle or leave the master's gates open at night to cause some confusion. Where before they could hear their bishop preach or a hermit deeply versed in St. Antony or Cassian or Evagrius, now they had fugitive monks and barely literate parish priests to minister them through life's miseries. Where before they could sit at the feet of *filid* and bards, men trained in the timeless traditions of poetry and national saga and subsidized by royal patrons such as O'Connor Don or the O'Heyne or the O'Kelly, now they listened for a knock at the door of a windy, wet night to behold the spectacle of a beaten-up, homeless itinerant, the blind poet Raftery.

Raftery was little better than a tramp, a whiskey-loving, lecherous, dirty, and evil-tempered man who roamed the lanes and byways of the old baronies in central Galway. The vast classical heritage of an Irish education back in the days of great monastic schools, with their resident scholars and busy scriptora, reached a bedraggled conclusion in the meandering doggerel of Raftery's poems. A polemicist and poet for hire, Raftery maintained himself composing panegyrics and salutations, eulogies and political broadsheets. He was a rhymester and satirist whose malicious tongue, harking back to the ancient tales of pagan bards who could raise a blister on anyone they singled out for ridicule, was much feared by the country folk of Galway. He was the kind of man an Elizabethan soldier would have hanged and a Burton Persse thrown out the backdoor should he have found him skulking about in the kitchen. An old couple living in dire poverty on a backwater lane of Dunkellin, however, would have sat him down at table, fed him, and put drink at his hand, all in the hopes that Raftery would spin a few lines of praise comparing their hovel with Hector's palace at Troy, one of a staple of classical references that he rambled through daily with each and every meal that came his way for free.

Culturally, of course, a man like Raftery played a vital if unintended role in maintaining a Gaelic identity. Just as the fugitive priest kept the rudiments of Catholicism alive among the people, so too did Raftery nourish, in however ragged a fashion, the old tug of learning and erudition that had so marked Irish life in centuries past. Instead of wandering from one royal *tuath* to another, he roamed from cottage to cottage. Rather than address kings and warriors, he orated before farmers and publicans. Instead of gold or cows for reward, a glass of whiskey and perhaps the caress of a country girl did nicely. However much his life lacked in moral stricture, nonetheless the marrow of tradition was nurtured: respect for the scholar, joy of recitation, the marvel at memory, the appreciation of delivery, the soul warmed by allusion, historical pride, fervor, love and anger, the bittersweet sorrow of heroic defeat.

Raftery and men like him reinforced the imagery and symbolism of their Catholic past. While the Persse family built a school on the Moyode estate (called the Nest) to proselytize their tenants' children, a Raftery could mock such pretension and call to order any slippage toward "the foreigners." Pride and arrogance have been noted as a customary Celtic posture by writers from as long ago as before Christ. Even through the darkest years of penal servitude, Raftery maintained for his audience the notion of their superiority. Like the underground friars at Esker, Raftery sustained his people.

When he died in 1835, the poet was buried in an unmarked grave at the ruined churchyard of Killeeneen, 3 miles down the road from Moyode. Lady Gregory, riding about in horse and carriage collecting folklore from her Irish-speaking tenantry, heard his name mentioned often and scraps of his poetry recited by hearth and fire. She had a tombstone carved and placed on his grave at Killeeneen. Douglas Hyde and William Butler Yeats, burrowing about the countryside, listened keenly too. Hyde collected manuscripts and published many of Raftery's poems, seldom intended though they were for the printed page. Yeats, along with other poets, wrote variations on Raftery's verse. These rarely succeeded.

A friend of mine at Loughrea lent me a book of Raftery's work. "It's hard to read these in English," he told me. "The translation seems stiff and bulky. They were meant to be recited in the rolling cadence of hyperbolic Irish." Still, one famous poem on the delights of Mary Hynes, the Rose of Ballylee who so held the imagination of Yeats, struck me as particularly fine, and I copied its first two stanzas:

Going to mass of me, God was gracious
The day came rainy and the wind did blow,

Raftery's grave

And near Kiltartan I met a maiden
Whose love enslaved me and left me low.
I spoke to her gently, the courteous maiden,
And gently and gaily she answered so:
"Come Raftery, with me, and let me take you
To Ballylee, where I have to go."

When I got the offer, I did not put off its acceptance
I laughed, and my heart bounded.
We had only to go across the field,
And we only brought the day to the back of the house.
There was laid for us a table on which was a glass and quart,
And the ringletted colleen beside me sitting,
'Twas what she said, "Raftery be drinking, and a hundred welcomes,
The cellar is strong in Ballylee."

About 2 miles away, more of Raftery's poetry has been carved in stone, at the foot of a Celtic cross set up on Seefin Hill, a low eminence that gives a surprisingly expansive view of all the surrounding county. Castles and towers by the dozen lie about here, but Seefin is known for something else, a place of execution.

Raftery's lines, in Gaelic and thus indecipherable to me, commemorate one Anthony Daly, who was hanged here in 1820, accused of attempting to murder a landlord, the squire of nearby St. Clerans. Two memorable quotations came out of Daly's ordeal. At his trial in Galway, he denied the charge with bravado: "If I had shot at Burke, he would not have lived to tell the tale." Many thought him innocent, but local landlords refused to sign a petition for reprieve. Daly sat on his coffin during the long ride from Galway back to the meadows of his birth.

At the gallows he was offered commutation if he revealed the names of local outlaws. His mother, standing in the crowd, yelled to him, "Anthony, you were born a Daly, now let the world see you die like one." When the hangman hauled the body down after Daly died, onlookers saw him kick the boy's head into a pulp.

A RIDE TO RUIN, 1881

Now that reports have circulated through the neighborhood that "Jim's come home," I receive from time to time impromptu visits from friends, mostly children so bored from watching television that an excursion to Moyode seems like fun. They turn up at the gate or heavy oak door at odd times, totally awed that anyone could possibly live here, and seem more interested in my spartan accommodations and bare kitchen larder than in climbing to the top for the view, something they had done all their lives when the tower was a ruin. Today I receive another young visitor, who arrives in different fashion.

Working on the wall, grunting and sweating and pretty oblivious to my surroundings, I am suddenly aware that a great thunderbolt is

Execution Hill, Seefin

about to catch me from behind; or is it a freight train, like magic coming out of nowhere to rumble through Moyode? Turning around, I see Edel, a neighbor's daughter, hurtling across the great field on what appears to me the largest horse I have ever seen, hooves drumming through the turf, ground quivering, an absolute kaleidoscope of fury and commotion heading directly for me. I am overwhelmed at this display of magnificent physicality and wonder why horseback riding has always left me cold.

To the kids around here who can afford it, the hunt is their great passion. For many adults, it's more serious than that, the great open road to insolvency. Nowadays the renowned Galway Blazers rely on rich Americans and other well-to-do foreigners to bankroll the hunt, people like John Huston, who lived for many years at St. Clerans, regularly entertaining his Hollywood friends with an afternoon's sport. The club is no longer religiously exclusive either. Some seasons back the Catholic mechanic who works on my old Citroën was a member of the hunt committee.

Irish hunts have always been noted for their boisterous ways, and the wild gentry of Connaught more than any other sustained that image. In 1840 a hard-drinking group of Galway hunters held a banquet at Dooley's Hotel in Birr, during which they set the place on fire and burned it to the ground, hence the sobriquet "Blazers." Today, however, the scene is relatively tame. Godfrey Skrine, my solicitor in Dublin, scorns his own pack, the Killing Kildares. "If anyone here ever killed anything, they'd faint dead away," he told me. In his opinion decline set in when hunting became a hobby, not a way of life.

In the old days of the Irish Meynell, country squires generally kept private packs of hounds and restricted themselves to their own estates. The desire to hunt more frequently, as many as four days a week during winter months, required additional territory if foxes were not to be exterminated, and subscription hunts were formed. In 1839 John Dennis, first master of the Blazers, was given £450 per annum to maintain his field. In just ten years the Blazers were hunting over 1,400 square miles of central Galway. The county, of course, was at the time perfectly suited for the chase, as it was largely made up of vast estates of open fields, unrestricted by wire or fencing, with fine stone walls 4 to 6 feet high for jumps, little tillage or plowland to slow the going, and certainly no farmers insolent enough to complain about trampled chickens.

The greatest hunt master of all was the celebrated Burton Robert Persse of Moyode, who became master in 1852 and held that post for an unprecedented thirty-three years. Everything in his life revolved around the chase. A superb hound breeder—his leather-bound kennel register went back a century to his grandfather's pack—Burton ran the field with tremendous skill and discipline, observers constantly amazed at the rapport between master and pack, the sense of unspoken communication that existed between them. No less skilled as a rider, Burton was noted for his "fine seat" and his indomitable courage. During one chase, having jumped a wall lined with stakes, he was gored in the groin but continued in the saddle. "Disregarding the wound," wrote a correspondent, "he went on, killed his fox in the open after a fast forty-five minute spin, but on attempting to alight he found himself a cripple, and fell."

The hunt assembled at different venues daily, the pack of fifty to seventy dogs arriving in Burton's hound van pulled by three horses. Burton himself had twenty hunters in stable to support his rotation, as a good hard day in the field could exhaust a mount over time. Runs of

Burton Persse, master of the hunt, Galway Blazers

10, 15, even 20 miles were not unheard of. A Blazer at the end of one day's hunt found himself clear across the county in pitch dark. He road into Galway City and had a cattle car hitched up to the Dublin mail train, which conveniently dropped him off at his estate by midnight.

Everything was possible in Ireland then. Burton always entertained on a grand scale. Royalty from England visited Moyode, were mounted at the master's expense, and had the privilege of watching him, horn in hand, at the head of his hunt, afterward to repair "to a groaning table," as an overwhelmed reporter from the *Galway Express* related in 1877. Moyode, he wrote, was "magnificently furnished and decorated, reminding one of the ancestral halls of some Italian prince, with the heavy marble mantles, the splendid carved mahogany and rosewood furniture, the exceedingly large windows with deep gilt moldings before you; and behind, the huge covered tables, all odorous with spice and wine, the tapestried halls, and the magnificent pictures, all tending to remind one of Oriental grandeur."

Frank's father used to tell me that as a boy it was his job to keep all sixty fireplaces in that great mansion well supplied with wood and turf and to ensure that not one ever went out. I remember at the time thinking this was an exaggeration, but I'm not quite sure anymore.

Agrarian troubles, however, stained Burton's last years. Land League agitators organized the peasantry, whose memory of the famine was still fresh, and boycotts, demonstrations, and animal maimings grew steadily. In London Parnell came to power at Westminster, and Gladstone's bills for land reform began making way. In 1881 local farmers blocked the hunt. Burton Persse, out of respect,

Persse graveyard, Moyode demesne

was allowed to pass through the mob, but all the other Blazers were prevented from taking the field. To Burton Persse this insult was intolerable. He was no absentee! He never ordered goods or materials from London! He had never evicted a tenant! In a pique he sold off his hounds, sixty-five of them for £375, and auctioned his entire stable at Rugby in England, where he himself decamped as soon as Moyode could be shuttered and closed. He hunted that entire season as the guest of various titled families in the English countryside, riding to hounds five days a week. His most fabled chase took place in the company of the duke of Beaufort. A field of over 300 riders tracked their fox at full speed to the banks of the swollen Avon, but only one dared plunge ahead into the racing, frigid stream to cross to the other side, alone to close in for the kill, and that was Burton Persse.

Burton died in 1885 at the relatively young age of fifty-seven, appropriately enough from injuries sustained in a fall from his mount and a chill he caught thereafter. He was buried in the small family graveyard that lies on a knoll overlooking the main avenue to the mansion. Over my twenty-odd years at Moyode, the condition of this cemetery has varied considerably, at first completely overgrown and buried beneath yards of nettles and growth, later totally bare and dusty when local farmers herded calves or pigs in here. I recall a small heifer scratching himself on Burton's headstone. I told one of the locals that I found Irish disrespect for graveyards quite unattractive. "They let our people die in ditches and rot unburied by the side of the lane. I'd bulldoze the place if it was my land," was his reply. Today, maybe thanks to me, the Persses lie again unmolested, vegetation and fallen trees making the place once more impenetrable.

In ready cash, after his debts, Burton Robert left behind a modest £12,335, 15 shillings, 1 pence. His younger brother, de Burgh, who had emigrated from Ireland years before with his small legacy to seek fortune in Australia, returned in 1889 to rent Moyode for three years. It was a moment of some triumph for him, as he arrived with money in his pockets. A pioneer rancher in the outback of Queensland, he eventually built his holdings to include a 20,000-acre cattle spread 50 miles from Brisbane. Intermarriage with other cadet branches of County Galway gentry (especially the Joyce family, who converted to do so) produced a miniature and religiously correct Ascendancy out in the arid wilds of Australia, but with many of the same problems. In place of Irish Catholics, the Persses had aborigines to deal with. De Burgh rescued the Blazers, assuming most of the financial burdens his brother had shouldered, but in the end, after spending the astronomical sum of £40,000 on the hunt, he took ship again with wife and daughters back to Australia. He surely saw the troubles that lay ahead.

The fifteenth (and last) earl of Clanricard proved less prescient. Known as "Clanrackrent," the earl was the perfect target for vilification. Owner of 56,000 acres in County Galway that generated an income of £24,000 per year (30 percent of his annual income), Hubert George de Burgh–Canning had hardly set foot in Ireland over the course of his long and peculiar life. Keeping to rented rooms in London, complaining whenever his club dues went up a few shillings or more, the earl struck a ridiculously eccentric figure in fashionable society, often dressing little better than a street sweeper and smelling worse. When his tenants refused to pay their rents, he ordered agents to evict them all. The Blazers could, and did, go on as usual (Andy Dolphin, threadbare survivor of that clan, died on horseback when his rotted gear came apart over a jump); Ascendancy balls could proceed as scheduled, the Galway gentry dressing up in tableaux as "A Greek

Slave," "An Australian Cricketer," "The Colleen Bawn," "Moonlight," and best of all "The Evicted Peasant," but publicity of the sort coming out of the Clanricard's farms proved devastating.

Clanrackrent ("Old Wares") by Spy, 1900

The end for Moyode and men like Clanricard came steadily over the Irish Sea with each successive land reform package passed from Westminster, culminating in the Wyndham Act of 1903 that enabled tenants to buy their farms from landlords at what in the long run proved to be ruinous prices for the Ascendancy. Coats of mail from Norman times, still serviceable after centuries in the attic, were suddenly resurrected: Worn under leather jerkins, the mail was useful protection against buckshot, as the Wyndham Act was not compulsory under law and some landowners refused to sell. "My uncle Walter was shot," Major Walter Joyce, my old Catholic neighbor, once told me. "He was very impolitic, told the peasants he would never sell out, and that was that, so they ambushed him one day on his way to market. He was one of many."

At the turn of the century, all that remained of Moyode was the immediate park and demesne grounds; after independence, nothing. The Persse family had dispersed all over the world—Australia, New Zealand, South Africa, the United States, and of course England—their fates similar to those of émigré civil servants from all over Britain's colonies, a syndrome one of them labeled "nowhere to call home." In World Wars I and II, they fought and died from Ypres to El Alamein.

Easter Week, 1916

Events of the Easter Rising in 1916 are probably better known to greater numbers of non-Irish observers than most other highlights of Ireland's story, with the possible exception of St. Patrick's more grandiose exploits, which people recall once a year on March 17.

Disheartened by its horrific losses on the battlefields of France, Great Britain had trusted moderate nationalist leaders like John Dillon and James Redmond to keep the Irish house in order. Promises that Ireland would be satisfied after the war by some form of home rule seemed so eminently reasonable to most in England—and to most of the Irish as well—that news of rebellion in Dublin was universally greeted by anger, cries of betrayal, and a thoroughgoing disgust with all things Irish. The appalling truth that thousands of British war dead were in fact Ireland's war dead as well was quickly forgotten in the heat of passion, and the few armed insurgents who had heeded the call to revolt were brushed aside by British soldiers who spared little firepower as they leveled portions of downtown Dublin.

Hardened by the war with Germany, entirely given over to thoughts of revenge and punishment, Britain then committed its greatest political blunder of modern times by putting fourteen insurgent leaders up against a wall in Dublin and executing them. Though severely wounded, James Connolly, the labor leader, was hauled out in a chair and shot. One mother, called twice to Kilmainham Jail to say farewell, lost two sons to firing squads. Joseph Plunkett married his sweetheart a few hours before his death. Roger Casement, the last to die, was convicted and hanged under an ordinance written in French by the Normans in 1351. Ireland, said a British general, did not deserve the velvet glove.

All of these individual moments of death and pathos created an aura magnetically attractive to the Irish temperament. Traditionally, what Ireland never achieved on the battlefield it has more than gained by spellbinding oratory from the prisoner's dock, piteous last letters full of overwhelming sentiments of love for Ireland, followed by unflinching heroism at the moment of execution. Britain has always provided Irish revolutionaries a second, posthumous chance, and the Irish, to their credit, have generally taken advantage of it. Instead of shipping these hapless warriors to some modern equivalent of Botany Bay, English authorities created yet another panoply of martyrs by slaughtering them. The victims, inevitably, were then canonized by a people

Execution yard, Kilmainham Jail, Dublin

prone to romantic melancholy, and in just a few short years Ireland was lost forever to Great Britain.

That the Rising had been a botched affair few will argue. The combination of surreal idealism, incompetence, bad luck, missed communications, and impossible odds makes for a tale of almost farcical proportions. As things turned out, only Dublin erupted in serious fighting. The west, far from being "awake," as one writer put it, instead was a dither of hesitation and irresolution. A rebel force of some 700 men, armed with a few rifles and about 300 shotguns (many of these loaded with roasted wheat because of a shortage of buckshot), gathered at Moyode House on Wednesday, April 26, two days after the capital rose. They were under the command of a twenty-three-year-old hothead from Dublin named Liam Mellows.

Mellows, like so many of the Rising's leaders, was a fine individual of great moral stature, despite his extreme youth. Enthusiastic, committed, doctrinaire, and brave, he suffered if anything from the twin

Celtic streaks of excitability and lack of restraint. An organizer in Galway for months prior to the Rising, he pedaled all over the county on missions that frequently produced not a single recruit or cell. He was all motion, rushing from farm to farm, crossroads to crossroads, bar to bar, issuing and receiving dispatches from headquarters that were obsolete before the ink dried. Like everyone else in Ireland that week in April, he knew little of how events were unfolding in Dublin. When news of fighting in the east was received, he unhesitatingly issued the summons and prepared for battle, choosing Moyode House as the center of rebellion in Connaught.

Moyode had by that time been long deserted. Gone were the days of eighty servants and beautiful hunters. Only the solitary peasant caretaker greeted Mellows, who was resplendent in green uniform, and his ragtag assemblage of farmers and small-town rabble-rousers. Lookouts were posted on the top of Moyode Castle, a kitchen set up, marching drills undertaken on the front lawn, and cars loaded and unloaded as practice for the moment, soon to come, when British convoys were to be ambushed and looted. Local girls dressed up as nurses and practiced tying up wounds with torn sheets to the cries of stolen cattle as they were butchered and tossed into pots. Amid the hubbub, a cannonade could be heard from Galway Bay; British cruisers were shelling the city (with duds). Everyone wondered if Galway was in flames yet again. At night, with fires blazing in its many hearths, the Army of the West stretched out on Moyode's floors. Rumors flew. One volunteer sang a patriotic song to steady everyone's nerves, but the next morning 200 men left camp.

Mellows's only link to the outside world was a local priest, who cycled madly about the countryside seeking the latest word. British troops were known to be prowling about. Mellows was determined to fight at Moyode no matter what, but others, sensing disaster, disputed him. Arguments and factions sundered the command. On Friday, the 28th, Mellows drifted south in great despair with all who were left, 150 men. The talk now, strangely, was to follow the example of Patrick Sarsfield 200 years earlier and retreat to Limerick. What awaited them there, other than a lesson in old history, was not altogether clear to any of them. Nine miles down the road they were met by Father Fahy with grim news. The Rising had been smashed. Mellows's tenuous hold on the men evaporated, the priest advising all to return home. Mellows and three remaining diehards fled to the bogs of Slieve Aughty, hiding out in a bothy for four months as the army

Foundation stones, Cait O'Shaughnessy's barn, Slieve Aughty

and "peelers" scoured the countryside for rebels. Someone at Moyode House identified twelve men of Athenry—the Twelve Apostles, as they became known—to the police, who arrested and deported them. In time Mellows, dressed in various disguises, including a nun's habit, escaped the country for England and eventually to America.

On a lovely fall day, I drove up to Slieve Aughty to look for Cait O'Shaughnessy's barn, one of Mellows's hideouts after the debacle of Easter week. Tom Ruane has spent much of his sporting life in these hills with shotgun and dogs, but again the pastoral perfection of our walk up here is ruined by his keen and telling eye on what is missing. "The only species of bird you don't have to worry about is the pheasant. You can raise them as easily as chickens, and snipe are still quite plentiful. But take partridges, now. The west of Ireland used to be famous for them, but they've practically disappeared. Chemicals poison them, clearing land robs their habitat, changing farm habits for silage wrecks their nests, and natural predators like gray crows prey on them. The corn crake, you'd hear them all of a summer's night craking along. Well, they're gone from the scene as though overnight. The little pine martin is a thing of the past. Even the poor old house sparrow is in decline. Falcons, both the kestrel and peregrine, are virtually extinct. Farmers used to spray a chemical on the corn crops, pigeons would eat the corn, and the falcons would prey on the pigeons. The funny thing is, this spray didn't affect pigeons at all, but in falcons it rendered them sterile. If there are twenty pairs left in Ireland, I'd be amazed.

"But last of all, my favorite bird, the native Irish red grouse. You'd go stalking on Slieve Aughty and raise dozens of good packs, eight or twelve birds to a pack, and you'd have fine sport and all. Now you'd be lucky to find a pack at all, more likely a few old barren pairs. The last grouse I shot I remember it well. He was one of a brace that got up, and I had what we call a two-barrel on it, a right and a left. The right barrel, lighter shot for the near bird, the left is heavier for further range. As they went up, I hesitated on the right—too far away. For a moment, I wasn't going to fire the left at all, doubtful range, but at the last moment I decided to give it a try and I got him. It wasn't right, though. There are just too few left. Conifer plantations up here on Slieve Aughty and predators, they're to blame here. In the old days of estates and gamekeepers, you know, predators were kept under control, but not now. You even hear sometimes of sick sheep being put down by a great crow. They sit on the poor animal and peck his eyes out, peck him to death."

Tom took his red grouse to a taxidermist in Dublin and had him mounted. He's not shot a grouse since, nor ever will again.

BLUE BANGERS

A great deal of my time over the past year or so has been spent pottering about the neighborhood looking for salvage and getting ideas from old ruins. Cut and dressed stonework is especially difficult to find these days. The old cattle stalls to the rear of Moyode House, for example, were beautifully crafted back in the early 1800s. The manure

The last Irish grouse Tom Ruane ever shot

line consisted of smoothly carved runs of block from 3 to 6 feet in length. The window and gate lintels were delicately fluted, and several drain spout receptacles lay as they have for almost two centuries, chiseled and polished from a single large stone—the cows, it would appear, had better housing than the peasants. But Phonsie's cousin, who owns this deserted section of Moyode's detritus, would not part with any of it, planning, I was told, to restore it. I did manage to buy a couple of lintels from an old nineteenth-century workhouse being torn down, but the effort was hardly worth it. In the end, Paddy and I went to a local headstone dealer, and he agreed to bang out three sets of medieval window embrasures at a truly God-awful price. "They'll look a thousand years old after three winters," he told me cheerfully.

I was also looking for old roofing slates. In the Middle Ages the first roofs were evidently straw, hardly sensible when a burning arrow could turn the whole upper third of a tower into conflagration. There are stories of people covering their thatch with wet hides as a defense, but eventually they determined that a more resistant material was required, and slate proved the answer. The additional weight, of course, called for a more sturdy timber framework to support it, and the National Monument people in Athenry, whom I consult now and again, know of several variations, many of which would be worthy of Windsor Castle in England and require a bond issue to finance. On their advice I took a run up to Knockmoy Abbey, an obscure ruin some 11 miles north, to look at something they call a scissors design. As always, I kept a sharp eye out for falling-down buildings.

The slate I needed are generically called "blue bangers." In the building parlance of modern Ireland, blue bangers are small, thin, lightweight, uniform, and almost prefab tiles that anyone building a traditional cottage would prefer over the more common plastic styles. These are not the blue bangers I was looking for.

In the old days blue bangers were big, thick, heavy, irregular, and easy to come by. Weighing from 10 to 15 pounds each and ranging in size from 1 by 3 feet to 3 by 4 feet, they could be seen on churches, gatehouses, shops, farms, hospitals, jails, and nearly all municipal buildings. Since the 1950s or so, they have gradually been replaced and today are unobtainable except from wrecks. They have no commercial value—unless you happen to need some. On the way to Knockmoy, I spied one or two collapsed houses. Rummaging through the debris, I salvaged four or five big slates. The old Citroën groaned as I loaded them in. Since I estimated needing around 200 of these, this was clearly not a very expeditious mode of collection, but near the abbey I spotted a derelict tumbledown with lots of blue bangers. I turned into the drive full of confidence. There was no question that whoever owned these would sell out in a second at a dirt cheap price. What other choice had he?

The proprietor of this crumbling relic gave me a decidedly sullen greeting. This surprised me; he clearly had no idea of his coming good fortune. We chatted a bit, and then I popped the question. How much for the slates?

"Who told ye I'd sell them?"

"No one," I replied. "I just happened to notice the building driving by."

"That's a lie. Was it the man at the head of the lane?"

"No one told me. I was just looking around and stopped."

"Well, they're not for sale. I'm restoring the place."

"You're what?"

"I'm restoring it."

I was incredulous. "You and who else?"

"Me and myself alone. I'm working on it."

"Are you kidding me? This thing is about to collapse!" The door was then slammed in my face.

I walked about the yard in disbelief, snorting and puffing and muttering. Irish bravado is at times amusing and at times innocuous, but there are also times when enough is enough. This place was being restored? Was I such a fool that I would swallow that? If promises ever met the deed, surely there wouldn't be a ruin in this entire country.

The next week, closer to home, I was driving over to Loughrea and passed a large poultry operation. In the factory yard, surrounded by lorries, stood an old, deserted farmhouse, nearby a thoroughly modern bungalow—the Irish transition from old to new, but in this case I approved, since the former was loaded with blue bangers. I pulled over.

The plant was large and cheerless. Truckloads left here before dawn to deliver poultry to Dublin, Limerick, Galway, and a thousand points in between. Liam Lawless, the owner of all this, greeted me, and I plunged right in. Did he want to sell the slates? His reply, "I might"; he'd think about it; come back tomorrow. This was both good and bad. He could be enticed into parting with these worthless bangers, and that was all to my benefit, but delay allowed him to brood on the matter, which meant their value might inexplicably rise. I went away depressed.

The next day he gave a price. I was rocked, but I also knew the Irish are horse traders, and countered. "No, no, no," he said. "The price is the price."

I could not believe this. All I had read about the Irish character and all I thought I knew about them was evaporating before my eyes. An Irishman who would not dissimulate, hedge, barter, and bargain? Not possible. So I went up a bit, but still below his first proposition.

Suddenly he got the wind up. "Leave 'em off to me for all the wrong ye've done me," he said, taking up some papers on his desk. Was the subject closed? I wondered, and panic set in. What if I lost the slates?

"Mr. Lawless, you know the bangers aren't worth anything."

"They are to you."

"But you have no need for them. You say you're going to demolish the old house, correct?"

"Yes, that's so."

"What are you going to do with the slates?"

"I'm going to watch them fall down and break into a thousand pieces as the bulldozer flattens the old hearth."

"Exactly. You're going to throw them out."

"Yes."

"So, will you lower the price?"

"No."

"Why not?"

"You're a contention to me, Mr. Jim Roy!"

"Can we negotiate a little over this?"

"You're beginning to vex me, Mr. Jim Roy!"

I pause. "Will you come down a lousy £10 to make me feel better?"

"Of course I will. They're yours."

"You know something, Liam," I said as I handed over the cash, "you've just plucked me as clean as one of your birds."

"Yes, I have, Yank, so I have."

The next week, with two local lads, I scaffolded the old house and began a long day disassembling the roof. As noon passed it started to rain. The slates got heavier. Some were so brittle they cracked in half; others slipped out of my hands and clattered to the ground. At dark, however, we had finished. Over 250 blue banger behemoths, neatly loaded on an old lorry, were now ready, as I was to learn, for their journey back home.

"You know where those came from, don't you?" Liam told me as we prepared to leave. "They're from Moyode House, from the Persses'. After it burned, my father went over with a horse and cart, brought them to put on his own wee house. And now you're hauling them back. Ireland's a queer place now, isn't it?"

BLACK AND TANS

British retribution after the Rising entirely alienated the Catholic population of Ireland. Moderate politicians were swept from office in the general election of December 1918, which saw Sinn Fein capture

70 percent of all Irish seats. None of these appeared in Westminster to take their "degenerate places" but instead sat in Dublin. An entirely shadow Irish government took shape, assuming the duties of normal officials. Again England reacted in wrath, and a genuine shooting war broke out. The Irish, disappointed their case would not be championed at Versailles by the United States, took to terrorism and guerrilla-style attacks. British forces, composed of disgruntled and ill-disciplined renegades known as the Black and Tans, responded with similarly irregular tactics. One result was Tom Egan's bullet-ridden body.

Nora Egan, eighty-six years old, stood in the kitchen of her old family home at a lonely crossroads just a few miles north of Athenry. Today was the seventy-second anniversary of her father's death. Across the lane and sloping up through several courses of enclosed fields was the once great demesne of Castle Lambert, an estate of nearly 5,000 acres, and down the road from it by a few hundred yards, another Protestant manor, Moor Park, and from there a short ride to Belleville and then Castle Ellen.

In the early hours of a chilly March morning in 1920, Frank Shawe-Taylor of Moor Park was on his way to the cattle mart in a horse-drawn coach. Passing Tom Egan's pub, his driver found the lane obstructed by a donkey cart. Both he and his master were then shot, Frank Shawe-Taylor to death.

"We had the public house back then," said Nora Egan. "Shawe-Taylor's children often played with us at the old ash tree in front—the governess used to bring them down. But when Shawe-Taylor was shot, his wife thought it was the French Revolution or something, and she fled that afternoon to Galway. The Tans took her in by convoy, and when they came back they were in a dark mood entirely. We be playing outside, but my mother, when she heard their lorries down the road, called us in right away and a good thing too. They were drunk and they poured rifle shot into our house. A friend of Dad's warned him to go on the run, but he wouldn't. He hadn't done anything wrong.

"A week or so later, Sonny came into the pub to tell us there was a rumor the Tans were about that night, on a rampage, and later on they showed up at our door. Mary, Jane, and I were upstairs in our room over the bar. Dad was in the kitchen reading a newspaper. Mother answered the knock, and it was soldiers. They said, 'Who's in the house?' Mama said no one. They barged into the kitchen. 'Who is this

Where Tom Egan died

man?' they asked. 'My husband,' she replied, and they went for him to take him out the backdoor. But my mother, God rest her soul, ran to the latch and threw the bolt, because a Hanlon had been taken out to the back of his home just a week before and shot, supposedly because he was running away. And Mama said, 'You'll not make a John Hanlon of him.' So a sergeant, he had three stripes on his shoulder, grabbed my mother with one hand, holding her back, and shot my da in the temple, then again in his throat. Another Tan let off his rifle, and the hole was still in the wall for years.

"Mama collapsed then on the floor. The smoke of the shot smothered her. The Tans went outside, shooting their rifles in the dark. I was the first to come down—I was thirteen at the time—and my father was lying on the floor gasping. Mama came to herself, we lifted him up, Mama said an act of contrition in his ear, then he died.

"We laid him back on the floor in his own blood, which was pouring out the doorway. Mama got a mop and tried to clean it up. We couldn't go out. The Tans were going mad, shooting everything in the night.

We couldn't go for help, and no one could come in to us. Imagine, from half past ten at night until the next morning, Mama and us girls all alone in the house with poor Da stretched dead on the floor, and the Tans, twelve or thirteen of them, all drunk and sleeping on the straw in our barn. Mary Connolly, at half seven, was the first to come in to us next day. None of the lads dared come, and neither did the priest.

"Remember now what I'm telling ye, because I've seen some rough times. We had Da on the floor until Monday night because the man with the coffin was too scared to come. Finally Michael O'Brady brought a box up from Athenry on a cart. On Tuesday we had a mass at the house, on Wednesday at 4 p.m. he was buried. We had to go through Moor Park, Shawe-Taylor's place, to get to the graveyard, and we had to pass the Tans who lined up on the avenue. They were firing shots in all directions. When we got him in the ground it was dark, and coming home we were all frightened to death. It was a terrible, terrible time.

"How Mama got through it I'll never know. We children couldn't sleep for Mama's crying for Daddy, and every week or so there'd be a banging on the door at night, and Mammy going down in the dark to let the Tans in. They'd take whatever they wanted. Mama had us all sleep in the far room, not over the bar, so stray bullets couldn't come in from below. Really, no one could stop them.

"We'd say the rosary every night for Daddy. I lived on the understanding that he was in heaven, and so did Mama. Bill Fahey, one of the lads on the run and a fine person and all, once came by and said to my mother, 'I'm going to have revenge for Tom.' But my mother said, 'We'll let the dead rest now. I have to raise my family.' I really don't know why she didn't drop dead from it all, the poor woman."

Later that afternoon we visited Tom Egan's grave in an overgrown cemetery, once the site of an ancient abbey. "He was the father of ten," said his daughter, "shot dead by the Tans but an innocent man." In one of those ironies typical of the Irish landscape, Egan's grave is just a few feet from a mausoleum of the Lamberts, about as typical an Ascendancy family as one could find in Connaught. Local vandals long ago forced open the iron door to their vault, trashing the coffins and scattering about skulls and bones.

The next week Seamus Coughlin, an army reserve officer, took me along on shooting drills at a rifle range near Athenry used by the British army over a century ago. Local lads equipped with Lee-Enfield rifles from World War I fired off volleys into enormous earthen banks over

Family vault, Castle Lambert

20 feet high. I was amazed at the noise these antique firearms give off, and thought again of the terror, confusion, smoke, and flowing blood that engulfed the home of Thomas Egan those many years before.

THE TROUBLES, 1922

The acceptance of London's terms at a peace parley in the fall of 1921 recognized the strong sentiment in Ireland for a stop to the bloodshed, but the idealism that had fueled centuries of rebellion forbade

Liam Mellows (far right) and other officers prior to the civil war, 1922

many already in arms from accepting partition in the north. Civil war and the infamous Troubles ensued. Liam Mellows was one of seventy-seven veterans of the Rising who found themselves before firing squads made up of their former comrades. He was shot at Mountjoy Prison on December 8, 1922. "My dearest mother," he wrote before the dawn of his death,

> the time is short and much that I would like to say will go unsaid. But you will understand; in such moments heart speaks to heart. . . . Though unworthy of the greatest human honor that can be paid an Irishman or woman, I go to join Tone and Emmet, the Fenians, Tom Clarke, Connolly, Pearse, Kevin Barry and Childers. My last thoughts will be on God and Ireland and You. . . . I had hoped that some day I might rest in some quiet place, but if it be prison clay it is all the sweeter, for many of our best lie there.

These years of turmoil saw many great houses torched by the country people. Godfrey Skrine's father lost his seat, and Roxbor-

Great house, Killullagh

ough House was burned down as well. One of the Roxborough Persses now living in San Francisco told me her grandfather was eating breakfast one morning when a delegation of local farmers appeared at the door, caps in hand. Apologizing profusely they gave him one hour to salvage what possessions he could. Some helped him remove furniture, plates, his silver, and several portraits, including that of his family's progenitor, Dean Dudley. Roxborough was then set to flames. Next day a legion of peasantry descended on the smoking ruin. Dean Dudley, it seems, back in the seventeenth century had allegedly stolen the parish plate from one of his livings. Rumor had it the loot was walled up in Roxborough, and now the entire neighborhood sifted through debris in search of the hidden treasure. Moyode House also burned to the ground. Today everyone says it was an accident.

Ghastly events such as these were the last straw for the Ascendancy. Most of those who had not fled the country before did so now.

Those left turned inward, “opting out,” as one of my few Protestant neighbors was to write me, “from any political involvement. The result is the rabble now running the country.” The Dublin Horse Show is about the only remnant still left of their once considerable social presence.

Lament

The end of the world I knew.

The Train Station

If I happen to be in Athenry late in the afternoon, I will often go down to the railway station to watch the 5:30 Dublin train pass through. Some people, myself among them, are hooked on trains. Public transport is prohibitively expensive in Ireland, however, and with regret I know I'll never board this grimy, smoke-belching diesel on its rumbling voyage through the countryside into Dublin. Usually the passenger car is nearly empty.

The station itself, with its neat Victorian waiting rooms and wrought iron accoutrements, would seem English if there weren't so much dirt and trash around. Barriers at the crossings are still opened and closed manually, reminding me of Eastern Europe. Nothing here is particularly Irish. The railroad saved Athenry from complete decay when it came to town in 1851, but progress of this sort did not stem the trickle of people who fled the place in search of a better life elsewhere. At the time of the railroad's inaugural service, 1,487 people lived in Athenry. Thirteen years later over 200 souls boarded the emigrant ship *Rag a Dee* sailing from Galway to Boston. "They were the pity of all creation," an old man told a local antiquarian, "without a penny in their pockets." In 1875 smallpox ravaged the town and over a hundred died. There are still stories about the poor woman who buried her husband and three children in unmarked graves below the abbey's wall without anyone's help. Four years after that Great Britain, with its usual insensitivity to Irish economic affairs, dumped shiploads

Railway station, Athenry

of fertilizer on the local markets, ruining Athenry's trade in seaweed. By 1910 barely 700 people still lived in town.

One can walk about down here by the tracks and imagine William Butler Yeats getting off the train here with his family, then setting off by coach for his own restored Norman tower, Thoor Ballylee, just a few miles away; or see in the surging passengers the slight figures of Sean O'Casey or Bernard Shaw, just arrived from Dublin, being greeted by Lady Gregory at the start of a literary house party at Coole Park. But the picture that more often presents itself to me is one of departure, not arrival.

"I'll never forget the day in the early 1920s," Athenry's Aggie Qualter wrote, "when Sonny Hession left for America."

> The railway platform was packed. I was standing on the cross bridge looking on, and the crying and wailing of young and old left a scar on my memory. The train driver too gave his own farewell salute with a long shrieking whistle that lasted until Sonny and his waving handkerchief was well out of sight. In later years I endured the same heartbreak,

as the boys and girls I knew and loved followed the same trail. Emigration caused terrible mental anguish. It seared the souls of our people, and left an emptiness in their lives that could never be filled. America was then far away. It was the point of no return.

BLARNEY

One of the workers on Paddy's crew was a regular rogue, and as such perfect for the arcane art of striking deals with other rogues, an aptitude I clearly do not possess (witness my outrageously expensive blue bangers now rising beautifully to grace Moyode's roof).

I had kept my eye on Jimmy from the start. He was clever in his repartee, attentive, had a keen eye for what went on around him, was fulsome in praise of his own abilities, and enjoyed to the hilt that old Irish pastime of appearing busy on the job while at the same time taking it very easy. In essence, he was sly and Jesuitical. When a local teenage girl came to visit the site, he eyed her up and down while looking the other way, a feat only I noticed. I chided him for salaciousness, especially as he had married but three months before. He would have none of that. "Just because you're on a diet doesn't mean you can't look over the menu."

But what confirmed my every suspicion about Jimmy was an exploit he told us during lunch. An old woman faraway in County Tipperary had a car he wanted to buy, but the word was out she wouldn't sell. Jimmy's brother was a priest, and one day he borrowed his suit and collar, showing up on the victim's doorstep to convince her that he needed transport to cover the parish. "Ah, Father, I have just the thing for you out in the shed." He offered her £400; she gave it to him for £350. As he drove off, she asked for a blessing, which he thoughtfully gave her and did not refuse the £5 note she stuffed in his pocket for a mass.

"That's a disgrace," one of the other lads said.

"'Twas not," replied Jimmy, "I had the mass said right and proper, and it cost me the fiver." This was the man for me.

That weekend Jimmy and I drove out to the celebrated Cliffs of Moher, a series of dramatic sea ledges rising over 600 feet from the tempestuous Atlantic and probably the most photographed scenic attraction in all the country. The traditional viewing spot near an old tower is almost an institution, allowing visitors to see one cliff head after another geometrically lined up to its slightly more elongated neighbor in a cyclopean march into the sea. Busloads of tourists enter by way of a modern car park, walk to the dizzying edge, and gape in wonder. Then they depart for whatever is next on their itinerary, rushing past the narrow lanes that lead to the liscannor quarries.

Jimmy and I drove by the car park. I had to check my own reflexes to turn in, since a trip to Moher is automatic for every visitor to Ireland I receive. I had never realized what a warren of activity, past and present, lies all around it, at least not until today. Jimmy did, however. He had never been to the cliffs but to the quarries many times. He knew liscannor stone and guaranteed me a bargain.

Liscannor is moderately prized in Ireland. It is a gray-green stone with an understated though elegant gleam, best known for the large and seemingly bulbous streaks, rather like sea grass, that course through the mass in irregular meandering. It is used mostly in flooring, and I planned to lay it down on the top floor, over the arch. It varies in color ever so slightly in differing light. Many people ruin the stone by giving it a high sheen with polyurethane. "Lads who do that need marble, not liscannor," said Jimmy the connoisseur.

We turned down a dirt track toward the cliff edge and ocean, entering a world about as far removed from touristic glamour as possible. There will never be airline posters of this place. Rusted machinery, broken bits of metal and junked trucking, and enormous piles of scabrous, discolored rock lay all over several small pits. Most of the workings seemed deserted, but Jimmy took a right, down an even smaller lane, until we could drive no further.

Walking along we saw a lone man with pipe hammering away at a wall of stone. It doesn't get much more primitive than this. "Don't say anything," advised Jimmy, "but look severe."

The two men exchanged greetings, the quarryman chipping away. They chatted about this and that, skirting around and never coming to a point. Long silences ensued. I looked grim and uncomfortable. We strayed on like this for fifteen minutes until Jimmy finally took an opening. We might, he said, be interested in some stone. Impossible, replied the man, still hammering; couldn't even consider it. "I've nothing to sell," he said. I was tempted to ask about the thousand or so slabs that I saw carefully stacked all over this moonlike atmosphere but bit my tongue and looked out to sea. Unlike all the tourists, I was oblivious to the immense view. Jimmy started talking about cars, and his man joined in with vigor. Eventually he slid in a reference to liscannor—did he know of any about? "There's no liscannor to be had, and that's God's truth," was the answer. My groan was audible.

After another hour of this swordplay, we finally established that our man here was in the business of selling liscannor, had a fairly decent supply, would deliver the stuff in three days' time, and would accept a rather modest sum for his efforts. Jimmy was very pleased with himself and his oratory. "When he talked he had no liscannor, I'll wager you would have said OK and left," Jimmy crowed later in the car. "That's your first mistake. No Irishman will ever answer you direct. Dance first, make him feel important and clever, implore him to treat with you. I doubt any foreigner can really talk with a country man and get anything done." I began to appreciate the Elizabethan perspective.

The Old Days

One evening I took a walk through "the lonesome lands" of Moyode demesne, or "out in the country," as a local called it, by which he meant anything off the major roadways. Hacking through the fields, crossing an ancient stone bridge over a swollen stream that runs from Rathgorgin down to join the Dunkellin 2 miles below, and from there to the Atlantic, I hit a wandering lane barely wide enough for two cars to pass abreast. Several thatched cottages in various stages of ruin lay scattered about, some deserted for newer bungalows just a few feet away. Ahead was the old parish church built during penal times on the site of a Norman abbey and abandoned some twenty years ago in favor of a substantial concrete building put up on the main Athenry road. A local farmer uses it as a cattle pen, a rather curious and, to my mind, sacrilegious conversion at best, and indicative of a curious con-

Former parish church, Kilconierin

tradiction in the Irish personality. For a people so famed for their memories of things past and habitually nostalgic for the Ireland of old, they rarely give a second thought to plowing under ancient raths or walking away from testaments to their patristic faith. The shriek of beasts in pain being dehorned, injected, castrated, or God knows what else seems inappropriate indeed to the shell of this building, put up and sustained by their forebears in a noble attempt to keep Catholicism alive and functioning. "Penal times are times best forgotten," however, as an old man was to tell me. The Irish seem to think of those years as more of a degradation than the moral triumph they really were.

Some families do remain jealous of the past, of course. It has long been traditional for certain septs or clans to act as hereditary custodians of particularly treasured relics or manuscripts. A neighbor of mine

Penal crucifix

showed me a mass kit from the 1700s that had been scrupulously preserved (in recent times, under the family sofa) since the death of his ancestor, a penal priest who had spent his adult life saying mass outdoors behind hayricks. "I had an aunt in America who came over one time, said she was a closer relation and wanted the crucifix that was used on the mass rock. Even the local priest said I should give it to her. 'Pardon my Latin,' I said to him, 'but my family has guarded these things for over 200 years, and that old woman, she's not getting my fucking crucifix.' And she didn't."

Following old carriage trails through the demesne back toward Moyode, I came to the crossroads at Tallyho and Dermot Hynes's old farm. "I lived there forty-three years," Dermot told me of the thatched cottage and its snug little collection of outbuildings. "Me and the wife, we worked 36 acres by ourselves with no help at all. We made a grand living out of it, no money to speak of but a free and healthy life all the same. We sowed all our own food, the barley and spuds and carrots and cabbage. We had our pig and about twenty bullocks, a few sheep, the horse and cart. We never bought anything in

Dermot Hynes

the city but tobacco, tea, and sugar. It amazes me to see the young lads now who farm. They'd never think to have a garden or be self-sufficient when they can buy it all in a package at Athenry.

"They were tough times back then in the thirties, but good all the same. Many's the pitch-black evening we'd set off at midnight to drive the cattle to market when they had them set up on the street. We'd go early to walk them easy, but really it wasn't work at all—it was fun, an adventure. Today you couldn't get a young lad to do that. They know too much from TV, they're too well dressed, gone to too many places, driven too many miles down the road in cars when we didn't even have bicycles! The next corner in the road holds no mystery for them.

"Once in the city, we made our bargains in the street. Oh, what a crush that was, not like today's mart, where all the stock is put to auction and you never meet the lad who buys it. Back then we'd haggle and argue over a few pence for hours at a time. Do you know that before the war I sometimes only got £3 or £4 for a bullock? Or that in 1950 I made only £300 a year? It's amazing to think back on. It really is.

"You take religion then. The old people went straight to heaven they believed so hard. The priests were like our bosses: We did what they told us and never answered back. We had no TV and no entertainment other than ourselves. Here at Tallyho, on St. John's Night, we had a great fire and a grand dance out in the open air. What music there was! And we'd go visit our neighbors, something no one does anymore, and had wakes, another custom all finished with. Everyone has to get home by 7:30 to catch their favorite quiz show. Oh Lord, have I seen the changes. You know, I'm over eighty years of age, and I was never in Dublin. Seamus took me there last summer for the first time, and we went to the zoo. The Lord be praised almighty but wasn't that a grand sight!"

The Field of the Grassy Sod

Aer Lingus flight 132, an enormous jumbo jet originating in Chicago, proceeding to Boston, then flying on to Shannon and Dublin, had about forty passengers on a trip I recently took, symbolic to some degree of Ireland's fading allure in these times of economic depression. Aer Lingus itself is hemorrhaging millions of pounds a year, layoffs are threatened, and even Shannon Airport's future is grim, a potential calamity awaiting the west of Ireland, which has already suffered a significant decline in its tourist industry.

The new first-class compartment on this otherwise aging aircraft was to me a sign of desperation, as Aer Lingus has always been famous for utilitarian discomfort, configuring its planes to remind all of us just how our forebears came over to America in the first place. "This is steerage all the way," a frequent-flyer Irish businessman told me, stuffed in his minuscule seat. "You should see it in the summer. They cram people in here like cattle, not an inch to spare. The only other airline to service Ireland off-season from this hemisphere is, if you can believe it, Aeroflot from Havana. Sometimes I think it would be worth it just to fly to Miami, take a shrimp boat to Cuba, and try Aeroflot just to see the difference. At least you wouldn't get henpecked."

I fear he has a point there. Irish stewardesses do not take any guff. In keeping with traditional matriarchal stereotypes, they take absolute control of their sheep. The shrill command of an Aer Lingus stewardess is not to be ignored, especially when accompanied by eyeballs rolling to heaven in exasperation or incredulity. Though the plane is empty, we are all shoved together, shoulder to shoulder, in the first ten rows. No one is allowed to spread out until well after takeoff. I recall what my old friend Walter Joyce said to me when we were talking about the Normans one day: "The only people who could really handle them were the womenfolk here. Gaelic wives, especially if they came from royal blood, were very strong, masterful personalities. If they were punched or shoved about, I expect they got right up and punched back. In many ways it's still the same today. Sharp-tongued Irish women can draw blood from a stone."

Flight 132 arrived in Ireland at the uncongenial hour of 6 a.m. when the only people awake at Shannon were the customs staff. But the approach into Ireland had been worth it. During the takeoff from Chicago and then Boston, the blaze of metropolis below had been overwhelming, stretching for miles in all directions. In lonely Ireland the reverse was true. Coming in over the Atlantic, our plane went straight over the mouth of the great river Shannon, following it through to Limerick. Looking southward out my porthole, I found nothing but pitch darkness greeted the eye. Scattered small villages passed underneath, their single streets illuminated by one or two dozen yellow lights. A handful of dairy barns glowed in solitude, an occasional car could be seen navigating a twisty lane, but to all appearances the land was dead. Even Limerick City was deeply asleep.

That night, by the time I had arrived at Moyode, unlocked its ponderous door with a key that must weigh 2 pounds, and swept up after all the mice and bats that still manage to find their way into the keep, I was ready for bed, having been up for over thirty-three hours. A wintry wind off the Atlantic tore up the heavens, pushing immense cloud formations through an otherwise starry sky. I built up a coal fire in the stove in the third-floor bedroom and set up three kerosene lamps on a ledge over my sleeping bag, then went over the field to Marie's for a final cup of tea. We watched a quiz program on television, unfathomable to me in that it was impossible to lose, an incongruity that did not bother the Hartys at all, who sat on the edges of their chairs, tot-

Moyode Castle, 1992

ing up the money and prizes. Then came the news and a prototypical Irish weather forecast: "It will be warm and sunny tomorrow all over the country, with rain and possibly snow in many areas." I washed up, said good night, and ventured back out into the gale.

Moyode, as far as I was concerned, was finished now aside from odds and ends and a couple of appliances. I had called poor old Paddy to see if he could spare me a couple of days, but he was bankrupt and bitter, hounded by revenue agents for past taxes and fines, thinking of turning fugitive and flying back to England. "It's dead here for me and my friends," he said. "This country has always done that, driven us all to places we never wanted to go. If I leave here again, I'm never coming back." That's the way of it with Ireland, a country that has broken more hearts and spirits than any I know. Thank goodness I'm not Irish.

Sloshing through the green field of grassy sod, I felt my rubber boots sink into the muck and mire of this sodden land. Cattle bellowing all around me, unseen and unseeing, reminded me of my historical environment, surrounded as I am by Burkes, Brodericks, Hartys, and countless more of the lawless Celts, who will come in the dead of this tempestuous night to steal my fatted calves.

A short, sweet burst of odor passed me by, a commingling of dung and the smoke of a peat fire, perfume to a person like me who for some inexplicable reason finds himself happiest in the middle of a maelstrom such as this. Beyond, the lamps of Moyode Castle flickered from the upper floor, a sight that would amaze and startle the locals when they noticed it in the coming weeks. It would dawn on them, as it did for me standing in this pasture, that for the first time in over three centuries a lord of the castle was living in Moyode. Food would be eaten there, drink consumed, fires made, banked, and shaken down, waste would flow down the *guarderobe* in much the way its original builder intended, children would be scolded, a wife caressed. Like a fool, I suddenly felt a rush of contentment, luckily doused as the skies suddenly poured a torrent of showers over this lonely stretch of Connaught's plain. Hurrying to the castle, I recalled the Dolphins, long gone now and forgotten. They had it right as they rushed into battle yelling their war cry—*Firmum in vita nihi:* "Nothing in life is permanent."

Afterword: The Celtic Tiger

Something happened to Ireland when I wasn't looking, preoccupied, no doubt, with some construction detail or another: It changed. Before I knew it, in just three or four years, the economy erupted, and where it will end no one knows—except me.

Ireland is now the success story of Europe, its rate of growth dazzling, its unemployment falling, its long tradition of emigration to greener fields finally reversed. High-tech leads the way, and the countryside sprouts new houses like grass after a strong rain. No one examines history anymore; no one sees the crash that's coming.

Euphoria is everywhere and casually embraced (especially by the young), but skeptics die hard in the far reaches of Moyode. "The Celtic Tiger?" one of my neighbors asks. "We feel the brush of its tail once and again, but he doesn't live here. More often than not he's growled at us in passing." His son, sixteen years old, sits all day in front of a computer in Galway, and a good job will at least temporarily be there for him when he graduates. It had better be. He's already the father of an eighteen-month-old little boy. Marriage? Out of the question.

Tom Ruane and his brother sold their petrol station. It has been replaced by a convenience store that may remind American visitors of what they came here to forget. The long-deserted shed that served as their tractor repair facility now houses an exercise and fitness salon. Maura Burke retired as well, selling her pub license for (it is rumored) several hundred thousand pounds. That license cost her £1,500 thirty years ago. The new owner will tear out the old bar and replace it with something ghastly, of that I am assured. Frank Broderick suffered several strokes and lives intermittently at his sister's or a nursing home (when they'll have the cantankerous old buck). Gossip also has it that Robbie Harty hopes to sell two magnificent pastures of the demesne for building lots. This breaks my heart.

But some things never change. The woman out back tried to sell the old Persse bell tower to an American, who wanted to dismantle this noble monument to aristocratic excess and reerect it over his driveway in County Meath. Unfortunately, this poor woman couldn't locate her deed (if in fact she ever had one) and, as Godfrey Skrine said to me years ago, "couldn't bespeak another." This financial disappointment hastened her death and has delayed, if only temporarily, the imminent disappearance of this artifact.

At 4 this afternoon, all of these ominous developments led me to an irrevocable decision: I would sell Moyode and move on. At 6 p.m. I changed my mind. All will turn to ruin once again, as Yeats wrote so memorably, and I will be here to survey the wreckage.

NOTES

ABBREVIATIONS

AC *The Annals of Clonmacnoise, Being Annals of Ireland from the Earliest Period to AD 1408, Translated into English AD 1627 by Connell Mageoghagan*, ed. Denis Murphy (Dublin: Dublin University Press, 1896).

Calendar State Papers *Calendar of the State Papers, Relating to Ireland, 1509–1670*, 24 vols. (London: Her Majesty's Stationery Office, 1860–1911).

Calendar State Papers, Reigns of *Calendar of the State Papers Relating to Ireland of the Reigns of Henry VIII, Edward VI, Mary, and Elizabeth, 1509–1603*, ed. Hans Claude Hamilton, 11 vols. (Nendeln, Liechtenstein: Kraus Reprint, 1974).

Carew *Calendar of the Carew Manuscripts, Preserved in the Archiepiscopal Library at Lambeth, 1515–1574*, ed. J. S. Brewer and W. Bullen, 6 vols. (London: Longmans, 1867–1873).

FM *Annals of the Kingdom of Ireland, by the Four Masters, from the Earliest Period to the Year 1616*, ed. and trans. John O'Donovan, 7 vols. (Dublin: Hodges, Smith, 1856).

IHS *Irish Historical Studies.*

Ireland Goddard Henry Orpen, *Ireland Under the Normans 1169–1216*, 4 vols. (Oxford: Clarendon Press, 1968).

JCKAS *Journal of the County Kildare Archaeological Society.*

JGAHS *Journal of the Galway Archaeological and Historical Society.*

JRSAI *Journal of the Royal Society of Antiquaries of Ireland.*

New History *A New History of Ireland*, ed. F. J. Byrne, Art Cosgrave, Dáibhí Ó Cróinín, J. R. Hill, F. X. Martin, T. W. Moody, and W. E. Vaughan, 7 vols. (Oxford: Clarendon Press, 1972–1996).

"Ordnance Survey" John O'Donovan, "Letters Containing Information Relative to the Antiquities of the County of Galway, Collected During the Progress of the Ordnance Survey in 1839," typescript, Bray, 1928, vol. 1.

State Papers *State Papers, King Henry VIII, Correspondence Between the Governments of England and Ireland, 1538–1546*, part 3, cont. (London: Her Majesty's Commission, 1834).

FRONT MATTER

ix *"There were yielded out of Connaught . . . ":* "A Poem on Ireland," trans. Paul Walsh, *Ériu* 7, 1 (1915), p. 73.

INTRODUCTION

1 *"He smelleth the battle afar off . . . ":* Job 39:25.

1 *"A pimple on the chin of the world":* Cummian, abbot of Durrow (?), as quoted in Kathleen Hughes, *The Church in Early Irish Society* (London: Methuen, 1966), p. 107.

CHAPTER 1

5 *"A castle of many rooms . . . ":* Sir Nicholas White, 1580, in Richard Bagwell, *Ireland Under the Tudors* (London: Longmans, Green, 1885–1890), vol. 3, p. 47.

5 *Champaign country and delineation of Moyode: The Topographical Poems of John O'Dubhagain and Giolla Na Naomh O'Huidhrin,* trans. John O'Donovan (Dublin: Irish Archaeological and Celtic Society, 1862), pp. xliv, lxi; *The Tribes and Customs of Hy-Many, Commonly Called O'Kelly's Country,* trans. John O'Donovan (Dublin: Irish Archaeology Society, 1843), pp. 68, 70; *FM,* vol. 3, p. 276a (1235); "Ordnance Survey," October 10, 1838, p. 161.

5 Tuath *and Cóiceda:* Francis J. Byrne, *Irish Kings and High-Kings* (London: Batsford, 1973), pp. 7–8, 45–47. See also James Charles Roy, *The Road Wet, the Wind Close: Celtic Ireland* (Dublin: Gill and Macmillan, 1986), pp. 71–72.

11 *Nineteenth-century Persse estate:* John Bateman, *The Great Landowners of Great Britain and Ireland, a List of All Owners of Three Thousand Acres and Upwards, Worth £3,000 Year* (London: Harrison, 1883), p. 357.

12 *Loughrea:* Hely Dutton, *A Statistical and Agricultural Survey of the County of Galway* (Dublin: Royal Dublin Society, 1824), pp. 328–331.

18 *The First Crusade:* Guibert de Nogent, in Con Costello, "Ireland and the Crusades," *Irish Sword* 9, 37 (1970), p. 264. Later chroniclers of Hibernicized Norman families (as opposed to native Celtic septs) did claim extensive involvement of their patrons with various crusades. William de Burgo, for example, was grafted to the family tree of Baldwin de Burgo, king of Jerusalem, in 1118, and the de Burgo coat of arms—a yellow field with red cross—was given a suitably graphic explanation: A de Burgo having killed a noted Saracen warrior, Richard the Lion Heart picked up the infidel's yellow shield and traced a red cross with the dead

man's still warm blood, saying to de Burgo, "These, knight, are your arms forever"; Costello, ibid. G. V. Martyn, "Random Notes on the History of the County of Mayo, and with Special References to the Barony of Kilmaine," *JGAHS* 12, 3-4 (1923), pp. 92–93. See also "History of the Burkes," trans. Thomas O'Reilly, *JGAHS* 14, 1-2 (1928), pp. 33–37 (ll. 8–22).

Chapter 2

21 *"A race madly fond of war"*: Greek geographer Strabo (63? B.C.–24? A.D.), trans. J. J. Tierney, "The Celtic Ethnography of Posidonius," *Proceedings of the Royal Irish Academy* 60 (1959–1960), p. 267.

25 *"The year of Christ, 1070 . . . "*: *FM*, vol. 2, p. 897.

26 *"Woe to brothers in a barbarous nation"*: Giraldus Cambrensis, "The Topography of Ireland," trans. Thomas Forester, *The Historical Works of Giraldus Cambrensis*, ed. Thomas Wright (London: George Bell & Sons, 1905), p. 137. See also *The Annals of Lough Cé: A Chronicle of Irish Affairs from A.D. 1014 to A.D. 1590*, trans. William M. Hennessy (London: Longman, 1871), vol. 1, pp. 317–319.

26 *The Celtic race "most greatly admires . . . "*: Bellum Gallicium, quoted in Tierney, "Celtic Ethnography," p. 274.

26 *Celtic coronations were profoundly sexual:* Byrne, *Irish Kings*, p. 17; James Carney, *Studies in Irish Literature and History* (Dublin: Dublin Institute for Advanced Studies, 1955), pp. 333–336; Tomás Ó Máille, "Medb Chruachna," *Zeitschrift für Celtische Philologie* 17 (1927), pp. 129–146; T. K. O'Rahilly, "On the Origin of the Names Érainn and Ériu," *Ériu* 14 (1946), pp. 14–28; H. Wagner, "Studies in Early Celtic Traditions," *Ériu* 26 (1975), p. 12; Roy, *The Road Wet*, pp. 64–71.

27 *The Turoe Stone*: M. Redington, "Stone at Turoe," *JGAHS* 2, 2 (1902), p. 118; H. T. Knox, "The Turoe Stone and the Rath of Feerwore, Co. Galway," *JGAHS* 9, 3 (1916), pp. 190–193; Joseph Raftery, "The Turoe Stone and the Rath of Feerwore," *JRSAI* 74 (1944), pp. 23–52.

27 *Celtic warriors "regard their lives as naught"*: Diodorus Siculus, in Tierney, "Celtic Ethnography," p. 249.

27 *Irish warriors:* Alfred P. Smyth, *Celtic Leinster—Towards an Historical Geography of Early Irish Civilization A.D. 500–1600* (Blackpool: Irish Academic Press, 1982), p. 107.

28 *Chain mail and armor:* John Hunt, *Irish Medieval Figure Sculpture, 1200–1600: A Study of Irish Tombs with Notes on Costume and Armour* (Dublin: Irish University Press, 1974), vol. 1, pp. 21–32.

28 *A Norman motte the mark of conquest:* Lynn Nelson, *The Normans in South Wales, 1070–1171* (Austin: University of Texas Press, 1966), pp.

114–117; R. E. Glasscock, "Land and People, c. 1300," *New History*, vol. 2, pp. 214–221; John Beeler, "Castles and Strategy in Norman and Early Angevin England," *Speculum* 31, 4 (October 1956), pp. 581–601; Tom McNeill, "Early Castles of Earth and Timber," *Castles in Ireland: Feudal Power in a Gaelic World* (London: Routledge, 1997), pp. 56–74.

29 *Dimensions of motte and bailey:* Goddard Henry Orpen, "The Mote of Oldcastle and the Castle of Rathgorgin," *JGAHS* 9,1 (1915), p. 39.

29 *Annals of Lough Cé: Annals of Lough Cé*, vol. 1, p. 311.

33 *"Foreigners in one mass of iron":* Thomas O'Gorman, "Some Remarks on O'Connor's Tomb at Roscommon," *Journal of the Kilkenny and South-East of Ireland Archaeological Society* 5 (1864–1866), p. 550.

33 *Normans as "heroes": FM*, vol. 2, p. 1173.

34 *Normans turned instead to the horse:* William J. Corbett, "The Development of the Duchy of Normandy and the Norman Conquest of England," *The Cambridge Medieval History*, eds. J. R. Tanner, C. W. Previté-Orton, and Z. N. Brooke (Cambridge: Cambridge University Press, 1964), vol. 5, p. 484. See also Lynn White, "Stirrup, Mounted Shock Combat, Feudalism, and Chivalry," *Medieval Technology and Social Change* (Oxford: Clarendon Press, 1962), pp. 1–38.

35 *William cared more for beasts of prey than he did for his children: The Chronicle of Henry of Huntingdon*, trans. Thomas Forester (London: H. G. Bohn, 1853), p. 218.

35 *The hunt:* Georges Duby, *A History of French Civilization*, trans. Richard Howard (New York: Random House, 1964), p. 43.

35 *Norman equipage:* Ibid., pp. 43–44.

36 "*The Augustus of the West Europe*": FM, 2, p. 1119.

37 *Markgraf*: John Beeler, *Warfare in Feudal Europe, 730–1200* (Ithaca, N.Y.: Cornell University Press, 1971), p. 20.

37 *Feudal levy of the Count de Champagne:* Ibid., p. 37.

37 *Norman duchy:* Corbett, "Development of the Duchy of Normandy," p. 483. According to David Douglas, "Better described as a creation of history than of nature"; *The Norman Experience* (London: Fontana Books, 1972), p. 26.

38 *The Normans, with their "untamable temper," and following:* Anna Comnena, *The Alexiad of the Princess Anna Comnena, Being the History of the Reign of Her Father, Alexius I, Emperor of the Romans, 1081–1118 A.D.*, trans. Elizabeth Dawes (New York: Barnes and Noble, 1967), pp. 37, 347.

39 *William "harried" the north of England:* Corbett, "Development of the Duchy of Normandy," p. 507; Douglas, *The Norman Experience*, pp. 73–74; David C. Douglas, *William the Conqueror* (Berkeley: University of California Press, 1964), pp. 219–220.

39 *"Blood ran down the steps of the sanctuary"*: *Chronicle of Henry of Huntingdon*, p. 215.

39 *Marshal, the "flower of chivalry":* See Georges Duby, *William Marshal, the Flower of Chivalry,* trans. Richard Howard (New York: Pantheon Books, 1985). See also *Ireland,* vol. 2, pp. 199–234.

39 *"By the love of Christ, Madame . . . ":* Duby, *William Marshal,* p. 61.

40 *Boutez en avant!:* The town of Buttevant in Cork takes its name from this war cry; L. Russell Muirhead, *Ireland* (London: Ernest Benn, 1962), p. 214.

40 *Norman tactics: The Song of Dermot and the Earl, an Old French Poem from the Carew Manuscript No. 596 in the Archiepiscopal Library at Lambeth Palace,* trans. Goddard Henry Orpen (Oxford: Clarendon Press, 1892), pp. 51–53 (ll. 664–691); John Beeler, *Warfare in England, 1066–1189* (Ithaca, N.Y.: Cornell University Press, 1966), and Beeler, *Warfare in Feudal Europe,* pp. 60–119.

40 *Norman treachery: FM,* vol. 3, p. 481; Seán MacAirt, ed., *The Annals of Inisfallen* (Dublin: Dublin Institute for Advanced Studies, 1951), pp. 395–397. Well into Elizabethan times, warnings against the dangers of negotiating in the open were commonplace: "Item, he shall not assemble the Queen's people upon hills, or parley on hills," Privy Council Book, *FM,* vol. 3, p. 573i.

40 *"An incredible sore and incurable disease" and following:* Comnena, *The Alexiad,* p. 26. For Norman use of terror, see Giraldus Cambrensis, "The History of the Conquest of Ireland," *The Historical Works,* pp. 209–211.

40 *Normans in southern Italy:* See Edmund Curtis, *Roger of Sicily and the Normans in Lower Italy, 1016–1154* (New York: G. P. Putnam's Sons, 1912); Ferdinand Chalandon, "The Conquest of South Italy and Sicily by the Normans," in "The Norman Kingdom of Sicily," *Cambridge Medieval History,* vol. 5, pp. 163–207.

41 *Normans "must be bent and bowed . . . ": Master Wace, His Chronicle of the Norman Conquest, from the Roman de Rou,* trans. Edgar Taylor (London: Pickering, 1837), p. 274.

41 *Even Guiscard believed in God, or at least Dante thought so:* Dante compares Guiscard with Charlemagne in *The Comedy of Dante Alighieri, the Florentine—Cantica III, Paradise,* trans. Dorothy Sayers and Barbara Reynolds (Harmondsworth: Penguin, 1971), canto 18, ll. 43–48, p. 215. See also Douglas, *The Norman Experience,* p. 109.

41 *The "contrasted emotions" of these times:* Douglas, *The Norman Experience,* p. 17.

42 *Normans could walk away from ambition:* See James Charles Roy, "St. Patrick's Purgatory," *Canadian Journal of Irish Studies* 10, 1 (June 1984), pp. 7–40.

43 *The "unendurable grail":* Norman Mailer, *The Armies of the Night* (New York: Signet, 1968), p. 51.

47 *William's levy in 1066:* Corbett, "Development of the Duchy of Normandy," pp. 498, 512.

47 *Increase in William's wealth:* Douglas, *William the Conqueror,* pp. 269–270.

47 *The Anglo-Norman kingdom:* Douglas, *The Norman Achievement,* pp. 112–114.

47 *William's earliest career:* Douglas, *William the Conqueror,* pp. 15–82.

48 *"King Henry crossed over to Ireland . . . ": The Chronicle of Florence of Worcester,* trans. Thomas Forester (London: H. G. Bohn, 1854), pp. 294, 301.

49 *Hervey de Montmorency "a man of fallen fortunes . . . ":* Cambrensis, "Conquest of Ireland," p. 189.

49 *Strongbow's nickname:* A. J. Otway-Ruthven, *A History of Medieval Ireland* (London: Ernest Benn, 1968), p. 42.

49 *The de Clare family out of favor at court:* Nelson, *Normans in South Wales,* pp. 133–134; Otway-Ruthven, *History of Medieval Ireland,* p. 42; Edmund Curtis, *A History of Medieval Ireland from 1086 to 1513* (London: Methuen, 1938), p. 46; *Ireland,* vol. 1, pp. 85–90.

49 *Strongbow bitter yet fearful, and character of:* Curtis, *Medieval Ireland,* pp. 38–40, 46; Cambrensis, "Conquest of Ireland," p. 205n. See also Nelson, "The Cambro-Norman Reaction: The Invasion of Ireland," *Normans in South Wales,* pp. 131–150; *Ireland,* vol. 1, pp. 191–192.

50 *Dermot's mission to Henry II: Song of Dermot and the Earl,* pp. 21–23 (ll. 254–265); *Ireland,* vol. 1, pp. 77–85; F. X. Martin, "Diarmait Mac Murchada and the Coming of the Anglo-Normans," *New History,* vol. 2, pp. 43–66.

50 *One of Henry's little jokes: "Ironica magis quam vera,"* Cambrensis, "Conquest of Ireland," p. 207; Otway-Ruthven, *History of Medieval Ireland,* p. 45.

51 *Abbess of Kildare: AC,* p. 193.

51 *Dervorgilla's affair: Song of Dermot and the Earl,* pp. 5–11 (ll. 22–99); Cambrensis, "Conquest of Ireland," p. 184; *AC,* p. 193; *Ireland,* vol. 1, pp. 39–75.

52 *"Three contemporary sources described it . . . ": Song of Dermot and the Earl;* Cambrensis, "Conquest of Ireland"; and *FM,* as well as other native annals. See also F. X. Martin, "Allies and an Overlord, 1169–72," *New History,* vol. 2, pp. 67–97; Robin Frame, *Ireland and Britain, 1170–1450* (London: Hambledon Press, 1998), pp. 1–14; J. R. S. Phillips, "The Anglo-Norman Nobility," *The English in Medieval Ireland: Proceedings of the First Joint Meeting of the Royal Irish Academy and the British Academy, Dublin, 1982,* ed. J. F. Lydon (Dublin: Royal Irish Academy, 1984), pp. 87–104.

53 *"Strike, barons, strike!":* See *Song of Dermot and the Earl,* p. 143 (l. 1927), "the traitors are quite naked"; p. 243 (l. 3330), "the Irish, who had no

armor." See also Katherine Simms, *From Kings to Warlords: The Changing Political Structure of Gaelic Ireland in the Later Middle Ages* (Woodbridge, Sussex: Boydell Press, 1987), pp. 125–126.

53 *Normans preferred "the hard field and open ground": Song of Dermot and the Earl*, pp. 51–53 (ll. 664–691).

53 *The Norman on foot was a cumbersome warrior:* Comnena, *The Alexiad*, p. 129.

53 *Irish as warriors: Song of Dermot and the Earl*, p. 149 (ll. 2011–2014); p. 117 (ll. 1576–1577). Later invaders also came to fear inland travel through forests. As the French chronicler Jean Creton wrote regarding Richard II's disastrous expedition against Leinster chieftains in 1395, "The woods are so dangerous." Smyth, *Celtic Leinster*, p. 109.

54 *Dermot bit off the lips, ears, and nose of his foe:* Cambrensis, "Conquest of Ireland," p. 193.

54 *Dermot died "of an insufferable and unknown disease . . . ": FM*, vol. 2, p. 1183.

54 *True intent of the Normans became clear:* Curtis, *Medieval Ireland*, pp. 52–53.

59 *Yeats called Athenry a forlorn place:* Aggie Qualter, *Athenry, History from 1780, Folklore Recollections* (Athenry: N.p., 1989), p. 57.

59 *Henry II's expedition to this island in 1171: Ireland*, vol. 1, pp. 247–284; J. F. O'Doherty, "Historical Revision," *IHS* 1, 2 (1938), pp. 156–157; F. X. Martin, "Overlord Becomes Feudal Lord, 1172–85," *New History*, vol. 2, pp. 98–126; Nelson, *Normans in South Wales*, p. 149.

60 *Strongbow called "prudent": Song of Dermot and the Earl*, p. 113 (l. 1309).

61 *Hugh de Lacy's grants:* Curtis, *Medieval Ireland*, pp. 62–64.

61 *Another Norman "at the summit of power":* Cambrensis, "Conquest of Ireland"; Otway-Ruthven, *History of Medieval Ireland*, p. 59. See also *Ireland*, vol. 2, pp. 5–23; Seán Duffy, "John de Courcy and the Men of Cumbria," *Colony and Frontier in Medieval Ireland: Essays Presented to J. F. Lydon*, ed. T. B. Barry, Robin Frame, and Katherine Simms (London: Hambledon Press, 1995), pp. 1–28.

63 *President Reagan's trip to Ireland: New York Times*, June 2, 1984, pp. 1, 6; June 3, 1984, pp. 1, 12–13; June 4, 1984, pp. 1, 8.

64 *People "barking in your face": The Patrician Texts in the Book of Armagh*, trans. Ludwig Bieler (Dublin: Dublin Institute for Advanced Studies, 1979), p. 131.

65 *Prophecy of the druid Lochru:* Ibid., p. 77.

Chapter 3

67 *"His voice had become hoarse . . . ":* Cambrensis, "Conquest of Ireland," p. 197.

66 *"The conquest limpeth":* Richard Stanyhurst, *Chronicles* (1577), in D. B. Quinn, *The Elizabethans and the Irish* (Ithaca, N.Y.: Cornell University Press, 1966), p. 57.

67 *Queen Eleanore and "chivalry":* Sidney Painter, *French Chivalry: Chivralic Ideas and Practices in Medieval France* (Ithaca, N.Y.: Cornell University Press, 1957), pp. 28–64, 95–148.

68 *The value of Isabel's dowry:* Sidney Painter, *William Marshal: Knight-Errant, Baron, and Regent of England* (Baltimore, Md.: Johns Hopkins University Press, 1933), pp. 77–79.

69 *John a competent monarch:* Sidney Painter, "The Royal Administration," *The Reign of King John* (Baltimore, Md.: Johns Hopkins University Press, 1966), pp. 93–150; F. X. Martin, "John, Lord of Ireland," *New History*, vol. 2, pp. 127–155.

69 *John "a mere boy":* Cambrensis, "Conquest of Ireland," p. 315. See also *Ireland*, vol. 2, pp. 91–108.

69 *New settlers "cut throats, murderers, and lewd fellows":* Cambrensis, "Conquest of Ireland," p. 285.

69 *"They rudely pulled them by the beards . . . ":* Ibid., p. 315.

69 *The chanson de geste of William Marshal: Histoire de Guillaume le Maréchal*, ed. Paul Meyer (Paris: Société de l'Histoire, 1891–1901), not yet translated into English. See Painter, *William Marshal*, pp. 130–131.

69 *William de Burgo:* Martin J. Blake, "William de Burgh, Progenitor of the Burkes in Ireland," *JGAHS* 7, 2 (1911), pp. 83–101; *Ireland*, vol. 2, pp. 179–198.

70 *Parchment grant:* Michael Dolley, *Anglo-Norman Ireland, c. 1100–1318* (Dublin: Gill and Macmillan, 1972), p. 91. See also James Lydon, "The Expansion and Consolidation of the Colony, 1215–54," *New History*, vol. 2, pp. 161–166.

71 *"Out, dunghill . . . ": King John* 4.3.87. See also Painter, *William Marshal*, p. 194.

71 *Children of de Burgo's marriage:* "The child that sucketh the milk of the nurse must of necessitie learne his first speech of her," Edmund Spenser, *A View of the Present State of Ireland*, ed. W. L. Renwick (Oxford: Clarendon Press, 1970), p. 67.

71 *King John commanded his vassal to relinquish property or prisoners:* R. Dudley Edwards, "Anglo-Norman Relations with Connacht, 1169–1224," *IHS* 1, 2 (1938), pp. 149–150; Dolley, *Anglo-Norman Ireland*, p. 105.

71 *"William de Burgo took the spoyles of all the Churches of Connaught . . . ": AC*, p. 220.

72 *The "plain of great assemblies, no small kingship": Topographical Poems*, p. 69.

72 *William buried at Athassel Priory:* Martin J. Blake, "The Abbey of Athenry," *JGAHS* 2, 2 (1902), p. 77. See also Robert Cochrane, "Notes

on the Augustinian Priory of Athassel, County Tipperary," *JRSAI* 39 (1909), pp. 278–289.

72 *John's Irish policy:* Curtis, *Medieval Ireland*, p. 96.

72 *Palatine lordships:* Painter, *William Marshal*, pp. 77–78; *Oxford English Dictionary*, 2nd ed., s.v. "palatine."

77 *Richard de Burgo:* H. T. Knox, "Occupation of the County of Galway by the Anglo-Normans After 1237," *JRSAI* 32 (1902), pp. 132–138; Goddard Henry Orpen, "Richard de Burgh and the Conquest of Connaught," *JGAHS* 7, 1 (1911–1912), pp. 129–147; *Ireland*, vol. 3, pp. 158–224.

77 *Richard de Burgo's "enormous" fine:* Otway-Ruthven, *History of Medieval Ireland*, p. 98. For Richard the Lion Heart's ransom, see Painter, *William Marshal*, p. 98.

77 *Predatory dealings with the O'Connors:* For overview, see Helen Perros, "Crossing the Shannon Frontier: Connacht and the Anglo-Normans, 1170–1224," *Colony and Frontier*, pp. 117–138.

78 *An encounter as savage as it was insignificant: FM*, vol. 3, p. 319.

78 *In Moyode itself "they committed great depredations": FM*, vol. 3, p. 277.

78 *The "English left the country without peace or tranquility": FM*, vol. 3, p. 277.

78 *Conquest of Connaught, 1235:* Curtis, *Medieval Ireland*, pp. 132–133.

78 *"Dermot, son of Manus, went into the house of the English . . . ": FM*, vol. 3, p. 289.

78 *The de Berminghams:* Blake, "Abbey of Athenry," pp. 71–75; H. T. Knox, "The Bermingham Family of Athenry," *JGAHS* 10, 3-4 (1919), pp. 139–153; Goddard Henry Orpen, "Notes on the Bermingham Pedigree," *JGAHS* 9, 4 (1916), pp. 195–205.

78 *"In such manner, know ye all, was the country planted . . ." and preceding: The Song of Dermot and the Earl*, p. 233 (ll. 3202–3207), p. 231 (ll. 3178–3182).

78 *Athenry, "the ford of kings":* H. T. Knox and "A Colleague," "Notes on the Burgus of Athenry, Its First Defenses, and Its Town Walls," *JGAHS* 11, 1 (1920), p. 1; "Ordnance Survey," October 10, 1838, p. 155.

79 *The Laws of Breteuil:* Nelson, *Normans in South Wales*, pp. 169–171; Mary Bateson, "The Laws of Breteuil," *English Historical Review* 15 (1900), pp. 73–78, 302–318, 496–523, 754–757; 16 (1901), pp. 92–110, 332–345. See also Jocelyn Otway-Ruthven, "The Character of Norman Settlement in Ireland," *Historical Studies* 5 (Philadelphia: Dufour, 1965), pp. 75–83.

79 *Rathgorgin Castle:* Orpen, "Mote of Oldcastle," pp. 33–44; M. Redington, "Notes on the Ordnance Survey Letters Relating to the Barony of Dunkellin—v., Killeeneen Parish," *JGAHS* 6 (1909–1910), pp. 146–147; Patrick Holland, "The Anglo-Norman Landscape in County Galway;

Land-Holdings, Castles and Settlements," *JGAHS* 49 (1997), pp. 159–161; McNeill, *Castles in Ireland*, p. 136; "Ordnance Survey," October 10, 1838, pp. 160–161.

80 *Garrisoned with "brave knights of great worth": The Song of Dermot and the Earl*, p. 235 (l. 3227).

80 *Progress was a notion unheard of in Ireland:* Curtis, *Medieval Ireland*, p. 117.

80 *Athenry Castle:* Harold G. Leask, *Irish Castles and Castellated Houses* (Dundalk: Dundalgen Press, 1964), pp. 36–39; Knox et al., "Notes," pp. 13–21; McNeill, *Castles in Ireland*, pp. 130–135.

80 *Archaeological dig at Athenry Castle:* Cliona Papazian, "Excavations at Athenry Castle, Co. Galway," *JGAHS* 43 (1991), pp. 1–45.

80 *Rory O'Connor was caught nude:* See A. T. Lucas, "Washing and Bathing in Gaelic Ireland," *JRSAI* 95 (1965), pp. 65–114.

81 *The filth, gloom, smoke, and din of these castles:* Duby, *French Civilization*, p. 42.

82 *Prisoners torn apart by horses: FM*, vol. 3, p. 427.

82 *Richard's castle building:* McNeill, *Castles in Ireland*, pp. 101–103, 130–137.

82 *"I put myself under your safeguard, O Champion . . . ":* "Unpublished Irish Poems: XXVI—an Irritable Genius," ed. Osborn Bergin, *Studies: An Irish Quarterly Review of Letters, Philosophy, and Science* 13 (June 1924), pp. 245–246; *FM*, vol. 3, pp. 180–181, n. e; Frank O'Connor, *A Short History of Irish Literature: A Backward Look* (New York: Putnam, 1967), p. 17.

83 *Roscommon Castle:* McNeill, *Castles in Ireland*, pp. 96–100; Brian de Breffny, *Castles of Ireland* (London: Thames and Hudson, 1977), pp. 194–195.

84 *The kind of battering ram that "might make a hole in the walls of Babylon":* Comnena, *The Alexiad*, p. 342.

84 *"Fear and dismay": FM*, vol. 3, p. 337.

84 *Moyode, "the green plain of the grassy sod":* P. W. Joyce, *The Origin and History of Irish Names of Places* (Dublin: Éamonn de Búrca, 1995), vol. 2, p. 382; E. W. L. Holt, "An Abridged Transcript of the Letters Relating to Parishes in, or Partly in, the Barony of Dunkellin, Co. Galway: With Prefatory Note," *JGAHS* 5, 3 (1909–1910), p. 147.

85 *De Burgo carousing with O'Connor "in one bed, cheerfully and happily": FM*, vol. 3, p. 387. See also *Ireland*, vol. 4, pp. 107–126.

85 *Celts "wallowing upon the skins of wild animals . . . ":* Diodorus Siculus, in Tierney, "Celtic Ethnography," p. 252.

85 *"The Age of Christ": FM*, vol. 3, p. 411.

85 *No English or Irish could separate the two nor "keep them from annoying each other": AC*, p. 247.

85 *"These sort of men . . . ":* See Art Cosgrove, "Ireland Beyond the Pale, 1399–1460," *New History*, vol. 2, p. 574; G. A. Hayes-McCoy, "The Completion of the Tudor Conquest and the Advance of the Counter-Reformation, 1571–1603," *New History*, vol. 3, p. 102; G. A. Hayes-McCoy, "The Gallóglach Axe," *JGAHS* 17, 1-2 (1937), pp. 101–121; Simms, *From Kings to Warlords*, pp. 121–124.

86 *Searching for Dolphins:* Edward MacLysaght, *More Irish Families* (Blackpool: Irish Academic Press, 1982), p. 82.

87 *The Dolphins have disappeared:* Estate maps sold from Portumna Castle in 1948 that enumerated properties owned by the earl of Clanricard around 1791 list only three Dolphins in the whole area. Patrick Egan, "The Town of Loughrea in 1791," *JGAHS* 24, 3-4 (1951), pp. 95–110.

89 *Richard, the Red Earl: Ireland*, vol. 4, pp. 133–158.

91 *"Richard, the Red Earl, son of Walter, Earl of Ulster . . . ": FM*, vol. 3, p. 447.

91 *The de Clares:* Painter, *William Marshal*, pp. 78–79.

91 *The Bruce invasion: AC*, pp. 268–282; Diarmuid Mac Iomhair, "Bruce's Invasion of Ireland and First Campaign in County Louth," *Irish Sword* 10, 40 (1972), pp. 188–212; Robin Frame, "The Bruces in Ireland, 1315–18," *IHS* 19, 73 (March 1974), pp. 3–37; *Ireland*, vol. 4, pp. 160–206.

91 *"Men ate each other in Ireland": AC*, p. 282.

91 *Richard in attendance to the king, 1302–1304:* See James Lydon, "Edward I, Ireland and the War in Scotland, 1303–1304," *England and Ireland in the Later Middle Ages: Essays in Honor of Jocelyn Otway-Ruthven*, ed. J. Lydon (Blackpool: Irish Academic Press, 1981), pp. 62–85.

93 *"Abashed": AC*, p. 272.

93 *Moyode "was wasted and destroyed" and following: FM*, vol. 3, p. 513.

93 *De Burgo "was without force or power . . . ": AC*, p. 275.

94 *William "the Grey" de Burgo:* Martin J. Blake, "Notes on the Persons Named in the Obituary Book of the Franciscan Abbey at Galway," *JGAHS* 7, 1 (1911–1912), pp. 1–12; Nolan, "Athenry Abbey," pp. 75–77.

95 *A "fierce and spirited engagement": FM*, vol. 3, p. 513.

95 *"Many sons of Kings . . . ": Annals of Lough Cé* (1316), in Blake, "Notes," p. 6.

95 *Town seal of Athenry:* "Ancient Seal and Mace of Athenry," *JRSAI* 3, fourth series (1874–1875), pp. 371–373. See also W. F. Wakeman, "The Mace of the Ancient Corporation of Athenry, County Galway," *JRSAI* 29 (1899), pp. 109–110.

95 *Bermingham's Court never emerged as a Windsor Castle:* Nelson, *Normans in South Wales*, p. 170.

96 *"He is a carpenter . . . ": FM*, vol. 3, p. 339.

96 *William, the Brown Earl: Ireland*, vol. 4, pp. 238–243, 245–249.

96 *William the Grey's sons:* Blake, "Notes," pp. 23–27, with images; Thomas O'Reilly, "Historia et Genealogia Familiae De Burgo," *JGAHS* 13, 3 (1922), p. 57; *FM*, vol. 3, pp. 550–551; H. T. Knox, "Establishment of the MacWilliamship," *The History of the County of Mayo to the Close of the Sixteenth Century* (Dublin: Hodges, Figgis, 1908), pp. 142–198.

100 *De Burgos's inland borough towns were built "whiles they had their swords in their hands":* Oliver St. John, "A Description of Connaght in the Year 1614," *Carew*, 1871, pp. 295–296. See also Edmund Hogan, *The Description of Ireland, and the State Thereof as It Is at This Present in Anno 1598* (Dublin: M. H. Gill, 1878), p. 131.

100 *Towns came to epitomize an English aura:* Galway and Athenry "boasted themselves to be strongholds of the English blood and speech"; Edmund Curtis, "The Spoken Languages of Medieval Ireland," *Studies: An Irish Quarterly Review of Letters, Philosophy, and Science* 8 (June 1919), p. 241.

100 *Athenry a mere "waste town": Carew*, 1870, p. 174.

100 *The town "all ruined save the walls":* Hogan, *Description of Ireland*, p. 131.

100 *Galway enjoyed varying periods of prosperity:* James Hardiman, *The History of the Town and County of the Town of Galway, from the Earliest Period to the Present Time, 1820* (Galway: Connacht Tribune, 1958), pp. 64–73, 81, 398–414; G. V. Martyn, "Random Notes on the History of the County of Mayo, and with Special References to the Barony Kilmaine (continued)," *JGAHS* 13, 1-2 (1924), p. 36; M. D. O'Sullivan, "Glimpses of the Life of Galway Merchants and Mariners in the Early Seventeenth Century," *JGAHS* 15, 3-4 (1931–1933), pp. 129–140. For general background, see also *Galway, History and Society: Interdisciplinary Essays of the History of an Irish County*, eds. G. Moran and R. Gillespie (Dublin: Geography Publications, 1996); M. D. O'Sullivan, *Old Galway: The History of a Norman Colony in Ireland* (Cambridge: W. Heffner and Sons, 1942), pp. 77, 398–414; Diarmuid O Cearbhaill, ed., *Galway: Town and Gown, 1484–1984* (Dublin: Gill and Macmillan, 1984).

100 *Galway, site of intrigue and Spanish plots:* M. D. O'Sullivan, "The Fortification of Galway in the Sixteenth and Early Seventeenth Centuries," *JGAHS* 16, 1-2 (1934), pp. 1–47.

101 *Christopher Columbus in Galway:* Samuel Eliot Morison, *Admiral of the Ocean Sea: A Life of Christopher Columbus* (Boston: Little, Brown, 1942), p. 25.

101 *Eventual decline:* J. G. Simms, "Connaught in the Eighteenth Century," *IHS* 11 (1958–1959), pp. 124–125.

101 *Relations between Galway City and surrounding clans:* D. B. Quinn, "'Irish' Ireland and 'English' Ireland," *New History*, vol. 2, p. 625.

102 *More than one earl of Clanricard pawned his jewels:* M. D. O'Sullivan, "The Wives of Ulick, 1st Earl of Clanricard," *JGAHS* 21, 3-4 (1945), p. 183.

103 *"Degenerative" status of many Old English lords:* G. A. Hayes-McCoy, "The Royal Supremacy and Ecclesiastical Revolution, 1534–47," *New History*, vol. 3, p. 39.

103 *Richard II's expeditions:* Edmund Curtis, *Richard II in Ireland 1394–5, and Submissions of the Irish Chiefs* (Oxford: Clarendon Press, 1927); J. F. Lydon, "Richard II's Expeditions to Ireland," *JRSAI* 93, 2 (1963), pp. 141–149.

103 *The House of Kildare:* D. B. Quinn, "The Hegemony of the Earls of Kildare, 1494–1520," *New History*, vol. 2, pp. 638–661; Steven G. Ellis, "Tudor Policy and the Kildare Ascendancy in the Lordship of Ireland, 1496–1534," *IHS* 20, 79 (March 1977), pp. 235–271.

104 *Bards who "made men of the country to believe they be descended of Alexander the Great . . . ":* "Smyth's Information for Ireland," *Ulster Journal of Archaeology*, 1st series, vol. 6 (1858), p. 166, in Quinn, *Elizabethans*, p. 43.

105 *"Silken Thomas":* Laurence McCorristine, *The Revolt of Silken Thomas: A Challenge to Henry VIII* (Dublin: Wolfhound Press, 1987).

105 *"Intestine commotion": FM*, vol. 5, p. 1681.

106 *Kerns "think no man dead until his head be off":* Thomas Gainsford, "The Glory of England," 1618, in Quinn, *Elizabethans*, p. 168.

106 *Coyne and livery:* It was a "protection racket," according to Hiram Morgan, "The End of Gaelic Ulster: A Thematic Interpretation of Events Between 1534 and 1610," *IHS* 26, 101 (May 1988), p. 9; Simms, *From Kings to Warlords*, p. 119.

106 *Kildare's daughter*: "The Book of Howth," Carew, 1871, p. 181.

107 *"No wilder men of Ireland be than they":* Sir Thomas Cusack, lord chancellor of Ireland, to the duke of Northumberland, May 8, 1552, *Carew*, 1867, p. 236.

107 *Kildare motivated by "a private grudge":* Sir John Davis, Knight, *Historical Relations: or, A Discovery of the True Causes Why Ireland Was Never Entirely Subdued, nor Brought Under Obedience of the Crown of England Until the Beginning of the Reign of King James I* (Dublin: Andrew Cook, 1704), p. 16; Donough Bryan, *Gerald Fitzgerald, the Great Earl of Kildare, 1456–1513* (Dublin: Talbot Press, 1933), p. 236.

107 *The Battle of Knockdoe "such as had not been known in latter times": FM*, vol. 5, p. 1277; "The Book of Howth," pp. 181–186; G. A. Hayes-McCoy, *Irish Battles* (London: Longmans, Green, 1969), pp. 48–67. See also H. T. Knox, "The Effigy of William Burke," *JGAHS* 1, 2 (1902), pp. 107–109; Henry S. Crawford, "The Burke Effigy at Glinsk, Co. Galway," *JRSAI* 37 (1907), pp. 307–308; Hunt, *Irish Medieval Figure Sculpture* vol. 1, p. 150; vol. 2, plate 169.

107 *A handgun used at Knockdoe:* "The Book of Howth," p. 185. Handguns were clearly available and in use before Knockdoe; see G. A. Hayes-McCoy, "The Early History of Guns in Ireland," *JGAHS* 18, 1-2 (1938), pp. 43–65.

107 *"One broken battalion":* *FM*, vol. 5, p. 1279.

107 *"The field became rough from the heaps of carnage . . . ":* Ibid.

107 *Viscount Gormanston's suggestion:* "We have done one good work, and if we do the other we shall do well. We hath for the most part killed our enemies, and if we do the like with all the Irishmen that we have with us, it were a good deed," "The Book of Howth," p. 185. See also *FM*, vol. 5, p. 1279, note z.

109 *What were the Tudors to do with Ireland?:* D. B. Quinn, "The Reemergence of English Policy as a Major Factor in Irish Affairs, 1520–34," *New History*, vol. 2, pp. 662–664; Hayes-McCoy, "The Royal Supremacy," pp. 40–43; Quinn, *Elizabethans*, pp. 7–13; Nicholas Canny, *The Elizabethan Conquest of Ireland: A Pattern Established 1565–76* (Hassocks, Sussex: 1976), pp. 30–33.

Chapter 4

113 *"The wars here . . . ":* Captain John Zouch, c. 1580, in Bagwell, *Ireland Under the Tudors*, p. 40.

113 *Tom Ruane's father:* Qualter, *Athenry*, pp. 39–40.

116 *"Clanricard's great plain":* *FM*, vol. 5, p. 1583.

117 *Burkes enjoy "imperial jurisdiction in their rooms":* Hayes-McCoy, "The Royal Supremacy," p. 42.

117 *"Barbarous" tanistry:* Spenser, *Present State of Ireland*, p. 7.

117 *"Enclose and husband" the Irish countryside:* Wentworth, earl of Strafford, in C. V. Wedgwood, *The King's Peace, 1637–1641* (New York: Book of the Month, 1991), p. 59.

117 *Seasonal herding "a very idle life . . . ":* Spenser, *Present State of Ireland*, p. 157.

117 *The Tudors wished a radical transformation . . . :* Quinn, "The Reemergence of English Policy," pp. 662–687.

117 *"Allure the Irish to obedience":* Lord Deputy and Council to Henry VIII, May 15, 1543, *State Papers*, p. 455.

118 *Palesmen create Henry king of Ireland:* Lord Deputy and Council of Ireland to Henry VIII, 1541, *State Papers*, p. 306; Canny, *Elizabethan Conquest*, pp. 31–33.

118 *Lord Leonard Grey:* Hayes-McCoy, "The Royal Supremacy," pp. 43–45.

118 *Chieftains "who would not be ordered":* Grey to Henry VIII, July 26, 1538, *State Papers*, p. 58.

118 *MacWilliam Burke, "who did much hurt to the town of Galway":* Ibid., p. 60.

118 *"Braking" castles with cannon:* Ibid., p. 147. See also J. P. Nolan, "The Castles of Clare Barony," *JGAHS* 1, 1 (1900–1901), p. 42; Hayes-McCoy, "Early History of Guns in Ireland," pp. 43–65.

118 *Castles turned over to Ulick Burke "for money":* Ormond to R. Cowley, July 20, 1538, *State Papers,* p. 55.

118 *Ulick was "sure to the King":* Sir Thomas Cusack to the Council in England, undated, 1541, *State Papers,* p. 327.

118 *Ulick, "The Beheader":* G. E. Cokayne, *The Complete Peerage of England, Scotland, Ireland, Great Britain and the United Kingdom, Extant or Dormant* (London: St. Catherine's Press, 1913), vol. 3, p. 228; John Smith de Burgh, eleventh earl of Clanricard, *Memoirs and Letters of Ulick, Marquis of Clanricarde, and Earl of St. Albans; Lord Lieutenant of Ireland, and Commander in Chief of the Forces of King Charles the First in the Kingdom, During the Rebellion, Governor of the County and Town of Galway, Lord Lieutenant of the County of Kent, and Privy Counsellor in England and Ireland* (London: J. Hughes, 1757), p. x.

118 *"Bourken Country":* Lord Leonard Grey to Henry VIII, July 26, 1538, *State Papers,* p. 60. See also D. B. Quinn and K. W. Nichols, "Ireland in 1534," *New History,* vol. 3, pp. 13–14.

118 *"Small gifts and honest persuasion":* St. Leger to Henry VIII, February 21, 1541, *State Papers,* pp. 289–290.

119 *Surrender and regrant:* For an overview, see W. F. Butler, "The Policy of Surrender and Regrant," *JRSAI* 43 (1913), pp. 47–65, 99–127.

119 *"To the King's greatest dishonor . . . ":* "Diverse abuses and enormities, among others, noted and collected by the King's Council of Ireland, against the Right Honorable Lord, Lord Leonard Grey, Viscount Grane, late the King's Deputy in Ireland," *State Papers,* p. 251.

119 *The Burkes could speak no English:* Curtis, "Spoken Languages of Medieval Ireland," p. 243.

119 *Traveling "up and down the country like a priest":* Sir Henry Sidney to Walsingham, undated, 1583, in "Sir Henry Sidney's Memoir of His Government in Ireland," *Ulster Journal of Archaeology,* 1st series, vol. 3 (1855), p. 97; Canny, *Elizabethan Conquest,* p. 471.

119 *The Beheader "so apt to offend . . . ":* Henry VIII to the Lord Deputy and Council of Ireland, and reply, undated, 1541, *State Papers,* pp. 303, 309; *Carew,* 1868, p. 119.

120 *The King's Artillery:* Nolan, "Castles of Clare Barony," p. 13.

120 *"Improving the savage quarters under his rule":* Lord Deputy and Council to Henry VIII, May 15, 1543, *State Papers,* p. 455.

120 *He wished to be "a grand captaine . . . ":* "Petition of the Lord FitzWilliam Bourke to Sir Anthony St. Leger, Lord Deputy, and the

Council," October 9, 1544, *Carew*, 1867, p. 210; *State Papers*, undated, 1542, pp. 359–361.

120 *"No":* "An Abregement of the Irisshmens Requestes," undated, 1543, *State Papers*, pp. 463–464; Lord Deputy and Council to Henry VIII, May 15, 1543, *State Papers*, pp. 456–457.

121 *Moyode a "fair champaign country": Carew*, 1867, p. 237.

121 *"To your most Excellent Highness . . ." and reply:* McWilliam to King Henry VIII, March 12, 1541, and Henry VIII to McWilliam, undated, 1541, *State Papers*, pp. 290–291, 300–302.

122 *The dowry of Ulick's granddaughters consisted of cattle:* O'Sullivan, "The Wives of Ulick," p. 178.

122 *The "chieftest man in Connaught . . . ": Carew*, 1867, p. 308; Robert Crowley, "For the Reformation of Ireland," undated, *State Papers*, p. 347.

122 *Dame Marie Lynch "was of a civil and English order":* O'Sullivan, "The Wives of Ulick," p. 178; "Documents Relating to the Wardenship of Galway," *Analecta Hibernica* 14 (December 1944), p. 100.

122 *Plate and jewelry suitable for pawning:* O'Sullivan, "The Wives of Ulick," p. 180.

123 *Clanricard a holding of over 200,000 acres:* Martyn, "Random Notes (cont.)," p. 84.

123 *Connaught more vulnerable to a King's wrath:* Canny, *Elizabethan Conquest*, p. 2.

123 *The Queen's Closet:* "Creations," July 1, 1543, *Carew*, 1867, pp. 203–204.

123 *John Malte, tailor's bill and following:* "The Kinges Majestie gave them theire robes of estate, and all things belonging thereunto, and payd all manner of duties belonging to the same," *State Papers*, p. 474; January 4, 1578, *Calendar State Papers, Reigns of, 1574–1585*, p. 128.

123 *Ulick "came home safe": FM*, vol. 5, p. 1477.

124 *"An ape will be an ape . . . ":* Captain Nicholas Dawtrey, June 1594, in Quinn, *Elizabethans*, p. 247. Dame Marie herself referred to her late husband as a man of "wylde government"; Martyn, "Random Notes (cont.),"p. 37.

123 *Clanricard:* Cokayne, *Complete Peerage*, p. 228a.

124 *The earl's "ale cup . . . ":* O'Sullivan, "The Wives of Ulick," p. 181.

124 *At the gates of Athenry, Ormond lost five horsemen . . . :* Lord Justice and Council of Ireland to St. Leger, March 24, 1544, *State Papers*, p. 491; *FM*, vol. 5, p. 1489.

124 *Burkes lived "diabolically, without marriage":* Sir Thomas Cusack to the Council in England, undated, 1541, *State Papers*, p. 326.

124 *Ormond confessed to bewilderment: Carew*, 1867, p. 211.

124 *"Between them both the whole country was wasted":* Sir Thomas Cusack, Lord Chancellor of Ireland, to the Duke of Northumberland, May 8, 1553, *Carew*, 1867, pp. 237–238.

125 *"Within one fortnight, having put certain gentlemen to execution . . . ":* Ibid.

125 *Earl's amatory inclinations "recall those of the poultry yard":* Cokayne, *Complete Peerage*, p. 230.

125 *The second, from whom "he had got thre sons . . . ":* Ibid., p. 230.

125 *Connaught, a place "that was not worthy . . . ":* Sir Edward Fitton, November 6, 1573, *Calendar State Papers, Reigns of, 1509–1573*, p. 528, in Quinn, *Elizabethans*, p. 36.

125 *"Poor Ireland, worse to worse":* George Dowdall, Archbishop of Armagh, July 1558, in Quinn, *Elizabethans*, p. 123.

127 *Irish tower houses:* Leask, *Irish Castles*, pp. 75–112; H. G. Leask, "The Irish Tower-House Castle," *Proceedings of the Belfast Natural History and Philosophical Society* 3 (1945–1946), pp. 28–34; McNeill, *Castles in Ireland*, pp. 201–229. The many articles and publications by Leask on Irish towers and castles are enumerated in a "List of Published Works," *JRSAI* 96, 1 (1966), pp. 1–6.

127 *Moyode Castle a minimum security building:* Nolan, "Castles of Clare Barony," p. 17.

127 *Castle lists:* J. P. Nolan, "Galway Castles and Owners in 1574," *JGAHS* 1, 2 (1901), p. 121.

127 *The Dolphinage:* Ibid.; A. Martin Freeman, ed., *The Compossicion Book of Connaught* (Dublin: Stationery Office, 1936), p. 46; Orpen, "Mote of Oldcastle," pp. 42–43; Holland, "Anglo-Norman Landscape," pp. 164–165.

128 *A hog:* W. A. McComish, "Survival of the Irish Castle in an Age of Cannon," *Irish Sword* 9 (1969–1970) pp. 16–21; "General Attack and Defense of Castles," in Nolan, "Castles of Clare Barony," pp. 24–26; *FM*, vol. 5, pp. 1846–1847.

129 *Yeats:* "We had fed the heart on fantasies/ The heart's grown brutal from the fare"; "The Stare's Nest by My Window," *Meditations in Time of Civil War*, in *Selected Poems and Two Plays of William Butler Yeats*, ed. M. L. Rosenthal (New York: Macmillan, 1962), p. 107.

129 *"The lady of the house meets you . . ." and following:* Luke Gernon, "A Discourse of Ireland, circa 1620," in C. Litton Falkiner, *Illustrations of Irish History and Topography, Mainly of the Seventeenth Century* (New York: Longmans, Green, 1904), pp. 360–361. See also Katherine Simms, "Guesting and Feasting in Gaelic Ireland," *JRSAI* 108 (1978), pp. 67–100; H. F. McClintock, "Some Hitherto Unpublished Pictures of Sixteenth Century Irish People and the Costumes Appearing in Them," *JRSAI* 83 (1953), pp. 105–155; Anne Chambers, *Chieftain to Knight: Tibbott-ne-Long Bourke (1567–1629)* (Dublin: Wolfhound Press, 1983).

131 *"I satisfied his curiosity . . . ":* Walter Fitzgerald, "Ballydams in the Queen's County, and the Bowen Family," *JCKAS* 7 (1912–1913), p. 13.

136 *"Rendering their names famous":* *FM*, vol. 5, p. 1565.

137 *Elizabeth had the same three options as her father:* Canny, *Elizabethan Conquest*, pp. 30–44. See also Bernadette Cunningham, "Natives and Newcomers in Mayo, 1560–1603," in R. Gillespie and G. Moran, eds., *'A Various County,' Essays in Mayo History 1500–1900* (Westport, County Mayo: Foil Seaccháin Náisiúnta Teoranta, 1987), pp. 24–43.

137 *"I could wish it sunk into the sea:* Earl of Essex to Elizabeth II, undated, 1560, *Carew*, 1867, p. 302, in Canny, *Elizabethan Conquest*, p. 30.

137 *Henry VIII's "new error and heresy" and following: FM*, vol. 5, p. 1445.

137 *"There is no order, nor justice in the country . . . ":* Captain Francisco de Cuellar, quoted in Bagwell, *Ireland Under the Tudors*, p. 186.

137 *Sidney's schemes:* Bernadette Cunningham, "The Composition of Connaught in the Lordships of Clanricard and Thomond, 1577–1641," *IHS* 24, 93 (May 1984), pp. 1–14.

137 *Richard's arbitrary exercise of authority tended to "fare well for his friends . . . ":* Sir Henry Sidney to Privy Council, April 27, 1576, *Carew*, 1868, p. 50.

139 *Dunkellin Castle:* M. Redington, "Notes on the Ordnance Survey Letters Relating to the Barony of Dunkellin: i—Killeely Parish," *JGAHS* 7, 2 (1911–1912), pp. 68–70; "Ordnance Survey," October 6, 1838, p. 142.

139 *Caher na Earle:* James Charles Roy, "Caher na Earle (The Earl's Chair)," *JGAHS* 52 (2000), pp. 144–154.

140 *Dearth of salmon:* Ciaran Tierney, "War of Words Erupts over Sea Trout Crux," *Connacht Tribune*, October 16, 1992, p. 24; Michael Finlan, "Sea-Trout Claim Seen as Myth," *Irish Times*, October 16, 1992, p. 7.

141 *Turloughs:* R. Lloyd Praeger, *The Natural History of Ireland* (London: Collins, 1950), pp. 103–104; F. O'Gorman, *The Irish Wildlife Book* (Dublin: Irish Wildlife Publications, 1979), pp. 58–60.

141 *"All this talk of bird life drying up is madness . . ." and following:* Kevin O'Sullivan, "Dunkellin Drainage," *Connacht Tribune*, October 16, 1992, pp. 1, 24.

141 *The Abbey of SS. Peter and Paul "a noble ruin":* Blake, "Abbey of Athenry," p. 65. See also Harold G. Leask, *Irish Churches and Monastic Buildings: Gothic Architecture to A.D. 1400* (Dundalk: Dungalgan Press, 1966), pp. 126–128.

142 *Cloister destroyed, belfry collapsed:* R. A. S. Macalister, "The Dominican Church at Athenry," *JRSAI* 43, 3 (1913), p. 198.

142 *The tooth shrine of St. Patrick:* Raghnall Ó Floinn, *Irish Shrines and Reliquaries of the Middle Ages* (Dublin: National Museum of Ireland, 1994), p. 20.

142 *The Book of Durrow: AC*, p. 96. See also James Charles Roy, *Islands of Storm* (Dublin: Wolfhound Press, 1991), pp. 230–238, 297.

142 *"I gave order for the making of a bridge at Athlone . . . ":* Margaret MacCurtain, *Tudor and Stuart Ireland* (Dublin: Gill and Macmillan, 1972), p. 100.

143 *"Stir no sleeping dogs":* Correspondence between Lord Justice Arnold and Sir Robert Cecil, "Bears and Bandogs," January 20, 1565, and February 1565, *Calendar State Papers, Reigns of, 1509–1573*, pp. 252–254.

143 *Fitton's sweep:* Martyn, "Random Notes (cont.)," pp. 38–41.

143 *A yearly rent of 26 shillings, 6 pence:* Macalister, "Dominican Church," p. 197.

144 *"Those graceless imps":* Martyn, "Random Notes (cont.)," p. 40.

145 *"Here was the sepulchre of their fathers . . . ":* Curtis, *Medieval Ireland*, p. 196.

145 *"Younger brothers and bastards scorn all endeavors save liberty . . . ":* Thomas Gainsford, "The Glory of England," 1618, in Quinn, *Elizabethans*, p. 167.

145 *Burkes "stolen across the Shannon . . . ":* J. P. Prendergast, *The Cromwellian Settlement of Ireland* (Dublin: Mellifont Press, 1922), p. 31n. See also Hayes-McCoy, "Tudor Conquest," pp. 101–102.

145 *Richard "confined in a close prison . . . ": FM*, vol. 5, p. 1689.

145 *"Noisy were the ravens . . . ":* Ibid., p. 1673.

145 *Athenry "a woeful spectacle . . . ":* Sidney to the English Privy Council, April 1576, in Blake, "Athenry Abbey," p. 87.

145 *"Break and raze the house . . . ":* Sir Henry Malbie to the Earl of Leicester, September 30, 1581, *Carew*, 1868, p. 324.

145 *"These most wicked sons . . . ":* Malbie to Leicester, January 29, 1581, and March 23, 1581, *Carew*, 1868, pp. 320–321.

147 *"That man is not well bent":* Malbie to Leicester, June 11, 1580, *Carew*, 1868, p. 264.

147 *William's execution: FM*, vol. 4, p. 1753; Bagwell, *Ireland Under the Tudors*, p. 93.

147 *"My perpetual curse":* Martyn, "Random Notes (cont.)," p. 43; Bagwell, *Ireland Under the Tudors*, p. 103.

147 *Ulick and John do "come upon their knees craving . . ." and following:* Malbie to Leicester, August 27, 1582, *Carew*, 1868, p. 330.

147 *"Disquiet" Connaught:* Malbie to Leicester, January 29, 1581, *Carew*, 1868, p. 320.

147 *"It was with difficulty . . ." and following: FM*, vol. 5, p. 1805.

147 *John's murder "odious":* Don Philip O'Sullivan Bear, *Ireland Under Elizabeth: Chapters Towards a History of Ireland in the Reign of Elizabeth. Being a Portion of the History of Catholic Ireland*, trans. Matthew Byrne (London: Kennikat Press, 1970), p. 59. See also *Carew*, 1873, p. 416.

148 *John, "that good man": FM*, vol. 5, p. 1805.

148 *"He had always a treasonable mind . . . ":* John Browne to Hatton and Walsingham, November 19, 1583; Bagwell, *Ireland Under the Tudors*, p. 120.

148 *Ulick "stood fast":* Sir Geoffrey Fenton to Sir Robert Cecil, December 12, 1599, *Calendar State Papers: 1599–1600, February*, p. 316.

149 *"He knows he is not able to bear head against them":* Sir Arthur Savage to Sir Robert Cecil, June 4, 1600, *Calendar State Papers, 1600, March–October,* p. 214.

149 *"They were to me a great trouble . . . ":* Bingham to Loftus, August 30, 1586, in Bagwell, *Ireland Under the Tudors,* p. 154.

149 *They responded with ugly fits of ill temper:* H. T. Knox, "Sir Richard Bingham's Government of Connaught," *JGAHS* 4, 3-4 (1905), pp. 161–176, 181–197; 5, 1 (1907–1908), pp. 1–27; *FM,* vol. 5, p. 1819.

149 *O'Brien, "an arch traitor . . . ": FM,* vol. 5, p. 1819.

149 *"This slimy land . . . ":* Sir John Perrott to Sir George Carew, April 27, 1582, in Bagwell, *Ireland Under the Tudors,* p. 160.

150 *Ulick's manor in the Pale:* Henry VIII to the Lord Deputy and Council of Ireland, July 9, 1543, *State Papers,* p. 475; "Answers Given by the Queen to Sundry of Her Subjects in Ireland," July 16, 1559, *Carew,* 1867, pp. 282, 300.

151 *"The exotic and strange character of their equipment . . . ": FM,* vol. 6, p. 2001.

152 *The war had three distinct phases:* Quinn, *Elizabethans,* pp. 132–135.

152 *Friars attempt "to seduce the Earl":* Sir Geoffrey Fenton to Sir Robert Cecil, March 31, 1600, *Calendar State Papers: 1600, March-October,* p. 63.

152 *England had need for "men of stomach":* Fenton to Cecil, December 12, 1599, *Calendar State Papers: 1599, April–1600, February,* p. 316.

153 *The English deemed the earl merely jealous:* Bagwell, *Ireland Under the Tudors,* p. 205.

153 *"Without ready money, he will not deliver a cow":* Sir Conyers Clifford to the Privy Council, October 25, 1598, *Calendar State Papers: 1598, January–1599, March,* p. 315.

153 *"Our daily expectation is to be hurted . . . ":* Sir Robert Napper to Sir Robert Cecil, November 18, 1599, *Calendar State Papers: 1599, April–1600, February,* pp. 259–260.

153 *Lady Clanricard sends two "boardes" of wine to O'Donnell:* "Intelligence out of Connaught," December 12, 1599, ibid., p. 318.

153 *O'Donnell passed "without any blow . . ." and following:* Sir George Carew to Sir Robert Cecil, June 27, 1600, *Calendar State Papers: 1600, March-October,* p. 265.

153 *The Irish stuck their swords into masonry joints . . . :* Knox et al., "Notes," p. 8.

154 *Rewards would give others "comfortable examples . . . ":* Elizabeth to Clanricard, January 9, 1600, *Calendar State Papers: 1599, April–1600, February,* pp. 392–393.

154 *Ulick's son, Richard, sent to England as a pledge, and following:* Richard to Walsingham, September 8, 1588, and Bingham to Walsingham, May 23, 1589, *Calendar State Papers: 1588, August–1592, September,* pp. 27, 188.

154 *Ulick's eulogy: FM*, vol. 4, p. 2237.

154 *"If I might be so happy . . . ":* Baron Dunkellin to Lord Deputy Mountjoy, March 19, 1600, *Calendar State Papers: 1600, March-October*, p. 54.

154 *"He has given his word to Tyrone!":* Fenton to Cecil, March 31, 1600, ibid., p. 62.

155 *Battle of Curlew Mountains: FM*, vol. 6, pp. 2127–2137; O'Sullivan, *Old Galway*, p. 138.

156 *Richard in charge of "the battle": Calendar State Papers: 1599, April–1600, February*, p. 113.

156 *"Vile and base men":* Bagwell, *Ireland Under the Tudors*, p. 337.

156 *"Braking from them in a fury":* John Dymmok, "A Brief Relation of the Defeat in the Corleus, the 15 of August 1599," *Irish Archaeological Society*, 1843, p. 46; *FM*, vol. 6, p. 2135.

156 *His body "passed not in one direction . . . ": FM*, vol. 6, p. 2133.

156 *"Barbarous for the latin . . . ": FM*, vol. 6, p. 2137.

156 *Dunkellin "had a narrow escape":* Philip O'Sullivan-Beare, *Ireland Under Elizabeth. Chapters Towards a History of Ireland in the Reign of Elizabeth. Being a Portion of the History of Catholic Ireland by Don Philip O'Sullivan Bear*, trans. Matthew J. Byrne (Dublin: Sealy, Bryers & Walker, 1903), p. 128.

156 *"Dispossess a base sister of mine":* Earl of Clanricard to the Earl of Essex, August 25, 1599, *Calendar State Papers: 1599, April–1600, February*, p. 138.

157 *"These beginnings will have a worser end . . . ":* Sir Francis Shane to Sir Robert Cecil, April 8, 1600, *Calendar State Papers: 1600, March to October*, p. 84.

157 *"It is to be feared . . . ":* Sir Geoffrey Fenton to Sir Robert Cecil, January 21, 1600, *Calendar State Papers: 1599, April–1600, February*, p. 412.

157 *What if father and son should "list? . . . ":* Sir Francis Shane to Sir Robert Cecil, April 8, 1600, *Calendar State Papers: 1600, March to October*, p. 84.

157 *"I cannot but acquaint your lordship . . . ":* Baron Dunkellin to Lord Deputy Mountjoy, March 19 and May 2, 1600, *Calendar State Papers: 1600, March-October*, pp. 53, 146.

157 *"I do believe him . . ." and following:* Lord Deputy Mountjoy to Sir Robert Cecil, May 2, 1600, *Calendar State Papers: 1600, March-October*, p. 141.

158 *Talk of foreign intervention "threw the Irish into great jollity":* Sir Henry Malbie to the Earl of Leicester, June 11, 1580, *Carew*, 1868, p. 270.

158 *Battle of Kinsale:* "The Lord Mountjoy's Letter to the Council of Dublin," December 26, 1601, *Trevelyan Papers, Part II, A.D. 1446–1643* (London: Camden Society, 1863), pp. 104–106; Hayes-McCoy, *Irish Battles*, pp. 144–173; John J. Silke, *Kinsale: The Spanish Intervention in Ireland at the End of the Elizabethan Wars* (Liverpool: Liverpool University Press, 1970), p. 144; "The Tudor Conquest," pp. 129–137; *FM*, vol.

6, pp. 2281–2291. Thomas Stafford, *Pacata Hibernia; or, A History of the Wars in Ireland, During the Reign of Queen Elizabeth, Especially Within the Province of Munster Under the Government of Sir George Carew and Compiled by his Direction and Appointment* (London: Downey, 1896), vol. 2, pp. 58–59, most explicitly gives credit to Richard. Stafford, however, was a publicist of sorts for Carew and portrayed Carew's rival, Mountjoy, in a negative light when possible. See Frederick M. Jones, "The Spaniards and Kinsale 1601," *JGAHS* 21, 1-2 (1944), pp. 1–43.

158 *"I cannot dissemble how confident I am . . . ":* Quinn, *Elizabethans*, p. 138.

159 *Richard Clanricard created a scene: Carew*, 1870, p. 193.

159 *O'Neill's column "thinned and discomforted": FM*, vol. 6, p. 2287.

159 *"Manifest was the displeasure of God":* Ibid., p. 2289.

159 *"The Earl had many fair escapes . . . ":* "Journal of Such Services as Were Done Since the 13th of December, When Sir Oliver St. John Left the Camp," *Carew*, 1870, p. 194; Fynes Moryson, *An Itinerary, Containing His Ten Yeeres Travell Through the Twelve Dominions of Germany, Bohmerland, Sweitzerland, Netherland, Denmarke, Poland, Italy, Turkey, France, England, Scotland and Ireland* (Glasgow: James MacLehose and Sons, 1907–1908), vol. 2, p. 245.

163 *Richard, fourth earl of Clanricard:* Cokayne, *Complete Peerage*, pp. 230–231; Aaron Crossly, *The Peerage of Ireland: or, An Exact Catalogue of the Present Nobility* (Dublin: Thomas Hume, 1725), p. 32.

163 *The French ambassador thought him ignorant:* He "has neither understanding nor conduct to lift himself high"; Bagwell, *Ireland Under the Tudors*, p. 454.

163 *The earl considered "a goodly, personable gentleman":* Ibid.

163 *"A shrouded figure . . . ":* Lytton Strachey, *Elizabeth and Essex: A Tragic History* (New York: Harcourt, Brace, 1928), p. 268. Strachey's treatment of Lady Essex did not extend far beyond the more glamorous figures of her first two husbands. The moment she married Clanricard, she "vanishes from interest."

164 *"Good my lord, hasten my leave . . . ":* Clanricard to Viscount Cranbourne, February 26, 1605, *Calendar State Papers: 1603–1606*, p. 263.

164 *"All quiet, very poor . . . ":* Clanricard to Sir Robert Cecil, May 25, 1604, *Calendar State Papers: 1603–1606*, p. 176.

164 *"3000 barrels of corn . . . ":* "Petition of Earl of Clanricade to the King," August 7, 1626, *Calendar State Papers: 1625–1632*, pp. 147–148.

164 *Richard lived "in very honorable fashion" and following:* Sir John Davys to Sir Robert Cecil, December 8, 1604, *Calendar State Papers: 1603–1606*, p. 212. Twenty-eight years later, Clanricard called the just deceased Frances "so good a wife and so great an assistant"; Clanricard to Sir Henry Lynch, April 27, 1632; Bernadette Cunningham, ed., "Clanricard

Letters: Letters and Papers, 1605–1673, preserved in the National Library of Ireland, Manuscript 3111," *JGAHS* 48 (1996), p. 193.

165 *Portumna:* See David Newman Johnson, "Portumna Castle: A Little-Known Early Survey and Some Observations," *Settlement and Society in Medieval Ireland: Studies Presented to F. X. Martin, O.S.A.*, ed. John Bradley (Kilkenny: Boethius Press, 1988), pp. 477–503; de Breffny, *Castles of Ireland*, pp. 187–189; Mark Bence-Jones, *Burke's Guide to Country Houses: Ireland* (London: Burke's Peerage, 1978), pp. 233–234; H. T. Knox, "Portumna and the Burkes," *JGAHS* 6, 2 (1909), pp. 107–109; Maurice Craig, "Portumna Castle, County Galway," *The Country Seat: Studies in the History of the British Country House Presented to Sir John Summerson on His Sixty-Fifth Birthday, Together with a Select Bibliography of His Published Writings*, eds. H. Colvin and J. Harris (London: Allen Lane, 1970), pp. 36–41. A new collection of interpretative essays, Jane Fenlon, ed., *Clanricard's Castle, Portumna*, is slated to be published in early 2001 (Dublin: Four Courts Press).

165 *"Disorder reigns in many things" and following:* Sir Thomas Rotherham to Lord Clanricade, January 12, 1626, *Calendar State Papers: 1625–1632*, p. 20.

165 *"If you do not come . . . ":* Justice Osbaldeston to Earl of Clanricarde, February 1, 1626, *Calendar State Papers: 1625–1632*, pp. 89–90.

165 *In case the earl had to be shipped back "to keep the natives in order" and following:* "My Lord's Memorial concerning the Earl of Clanricade's appointment unto Ireland," November 1, 1625, *Calendar State Papers, 1625–1632*, p. 45.

165 *The province "very tottering and unassured":* Sir Arthur Chichester to Salisbury, June 13, 1610, *Calendar State Papers: 1608–1610*, p. 462.

165 *"There is talk of a plantation here . . . ":* Justice Osbaldeston to Earl of Clanricarde, February 1, 1626, *Calendar State Papers: 1625–1632*, pp. 89–90.

166 *"I should rather put my hand in the fire":* Clanricard to Sir Henry Lynch, March 9, 1624/5, "Clanricard Letters," p. 179.

166 *The history of Ireland is the story of property:* T. W. Moody, "Early Modern Ireland," *New History*, vol. 3, pp. xlviii–l.

166 *Where Walter Raleigh failed . . . :* Hugh Kearney, *Strafford in Ireland, 1633–4* (Manchester: Manchester University Press, 1959), p. 126. See also T. O. Ranger, "Richard Boyle and the Making of an Irish Fortune, 1588–1614," *IHS* 10, 39 (1957), pp. 257–297.

167 *To "line Connaught thoroughly with English and Protestants":* Strafford to Charles II, September 10, 1636, *The Earl of Strafforde's Letters and Dispatches*, ed. William Knowler (London: William Bowyer, 1739), vol. 2, p. 34.

167 *Theories of plantations:* Nicholas Canny, "The Attempted Anglicization of Ireland in the Seventeenth Century: An Exemplar of 'British History,'" *The Political World of Thomas Wentworth, Earl of Strafford, 1621–1641*, ed. J. F. Merritt (Cambridge: Cambridge University Press, 1996), pp. 157–186; William F. T. Butler, *Confiscation in Irish History* (London: Kennikat Press, 1970).

167 *Wentworth and Connaught:* Aidan Clarke, "The Government of Wentworth, 1632–40," *New History*, vol. 3, pp. 243–269; *The Old English in Ireland, 1625–42* (London: MacGibbon & Kee, 1966), pp. 90–108; Richard Bagwell, *Ireland Under the Stuarts and During the Interregnum* (London: Longmans, Green, 1909), vol. 1, pp. 245–254.

167 *Ireland "unsound and rotten at the heart":* Strafford to Charles II, September 10, 1636, *Strafforde's Letters*, vol. 2, p. 34.

167 *The reign of King Charles:* See Wedgwood, *The King's Peace*, pp. 152–153, 165–166.

168 *"Himself first, his people afterwards":* Kearney, *Strafford in Ireland*, p. 60.

168 *The "Graces":* Aidan Clarke, *The Graces 1625–41* (Dundalk: Dundalgan Press, 1968).

169 *"It would be both to King and Subject . . . ":* Strafford to Charles II, August 24, 1635, *Strafforde's Letters*, vol. 1, p. 450.

169 *"Some nice points of moth eaten records":* Kearney, *Strafford in Ireland*, p. 91.

169 *"By reason of continual wars and rebellions . . ." and following:* Strafford, "A Brief of His Majesty's Title to the Counties of Roscommon, Sligo, Mayo and Galway, in the Province of Connaught," *Strafforde's Letters*, vol. 1, pp. 455, 458.

170 *The Lord Deputy "cast himself in his riding boots upon very rich beds":* Clarke, *Old English*, p. 97.

171 *"What great nonsense . . . ": "Ex magno conamine magno nugus";* ibid., p. 95.

171 *The jury "most obstinately and perversely . . . ":* Strafford to Mr. Secretary Coke, August 25, 1635, *Strafforde's Letters*, vol. 1, p. 451.

171 *"A great and wicked man":* See Wedgwood, *The King's Peace*, pp. 151–153.

171 *A "business of so great weight . . . ":* Strafford to Coke, August 25, 1635, *Strafforde's Letters*, vol. 1, p. 451.

171 *The sheriff's "pertinacious carriage":* Ibid.

171 *"We conceive to seize for his Majesty their lands":* Ibid., p. 453.

171 *"There is scarce a Protestant freeholder to be found . . . ":* Ibid., p. 451.

171 *The powers of Clanricard "are greater than in reason of state ought to be allowed . . ." and following:* Ibid., p. 454.

172 *"I came very lately from my lord of St. Alban's funeral . . . ":* Earl of Danby to Strafford, November 27, 1635, in Kearney, *Strafford in Ireland*, p. 93; Bagwell, *Ireland Under the Stuarts*, vol. 1, p. 250.

172 *"I am absolutely innocent . . . ":* Strafford to Earl of Danby, December 31, 1635, *Calendar State Papers: 1633–1647*, p. 119; Bagwell, *Ireland Under the Stuarts*, vol. 1, p. 250.

173 *Slurry:* "A far cry from the postcard image of the West"; *Connacht Tribune*, August 26, 1994, p. 10.

174 *Career of Ulick de Burgh: Letter-Book of the Earl of Clanricarde, 1643–47*, ed. John Lowe (Dublin: Irish Manuscripts Commission, 1983), pp. xvii–xxvi.

175 *"Rumours of my estate being questioned . . . ":* Clanricade to Strafford, March 26, 1638, *Strafforde's Letters*, vol. 2, p. 155.

175 *"He could not tell how fit it might be . . . ":* Archbishop William Laud to Strafford, September 12, 1636, *The Works of the Most Reverend Father in God, William Laud, D. D. Sometime Lord Archbishop of Canterbury* (Oxford: John Henry Parker, 1860), vol. 7, p. 284.

175 *The king would procure "all that is of right belonging them . . . ":* Strafford to Clanricard, May 23, 1638, *Strafforde's Letters*, vol. 2, p. 173.

175 *"You do not lack for friends":* Secretary Winde Bank to Earl of Clanricard, undated, *Calendar State Papers: 1647–1660*, p. 360.

176 *"St. Albans has moved the King":* Laud to Strafford, *Works of the Most Reverend Father*, pp. 283–284.

177 *The rebellion of 1641:* Patrick J. Corish, "The Rising of 1641 and the Catholic Confederacy, 1641–5," *New History*, vol. 3, pp. 289–316.

177 *Massacre at the bridge of Shrule:* W. E. Lecky, *A History of Ireland in the Eighteenth Century* (London: Longmans, Green, 1892), p. 90.

179 *The politics of Galway town, 1642:* Hardiman, *History of Galway*, pp. 113–127; S. O'Riordan, "Rinuccini in Galway," *JGAHS* 23, 1-2 (1948–1949), pp. 27–28; James Hogan, ed., *Letters and Papers Relating to the Irish Rebellion Between 1642–46* (Dublin: Stationery Office, 1936), pp. 103–111; O'Sullivan, *Old Galway*, pp. 234–267.

179 *"I have had no rest since the rebellion broke out":* Clanricard, November 15, 1641, *Calendar State Papers: 1633–1647*, p. 349.

179 *"He still had more conversation with heretics than with Catholics":* Edward, Earl of Clarendon, *The History of the Rebellion and Civil Wars in England Begun in the Year 1641*, ed. W. Dunn Macray (New York: Oxford University Press, 1992), vol. 5, p. 266.

179 *Ormond and Rinuccini:* O'Riordan, "Rinuccini in Galway," pp. 19–51; Patrick J. Corish, "Ormond, Rinuccini, and the Confederates, 1645–9," *New History*, vol. 3, pp. 317–335. See also E. P. Duffy, "Clanricarde and the Duke of Lorraine," *JGAHS* 31 (1964–1965), pp. 71–99.

179 *"Duty and moderation":* See Lecky, *History of Ireland*, pp. 90–92.

179 *The animosity of Confederates for Clanricard:* See the polemic "Aphorismical Discovery of Treasonable Faction," written c. 1652–1660, in John T. Gilbert, ed., *A Contemporary History of Affairs in Ireland from*

1641 to 1652 (Dublin: Irish Archaeological and Celtic Society, 1879–1880).

180 *"He trusts no one but himself . . . ":* O'Riordan, "Rinuccini in Galway," p. 36.

180 *Cromwell:* Patrick J. Corish, "The Cromwellian Conquest, 1649–53," *New History*, vol. 3, pp. 336–352.

180 *"My estate in this Kingdom . . . ":* Clanricard to Lord Cottington, February 12, 1644, *Letter-Book*, p. 39.

181 *Clanricard's last weeks of command:* Eamon Duffy, "The Siege and Surrender of Galway 1651–1652," *JGAHS* 39 (1982–1983), pp. 115–142.

181 *"The Earl may transport himself with eight servants . . . ":* "Order by the Parliamentary Commissioners in Ireland," December 6, 1652, *Calendar State Papers: 1647–1660*, p. 653.

181 *Portumna passes to Henry Cromwell:* Prendergast, *Cromwellian Settlement*, p. 163; J. P. Dalton, "The Abbey of Kilnalahan," *JGAHS* 6, 4 (1909–1910), pp. 210–211; P. B. Ellis, *Hell or Connaught! The Cromwellian Colonization of Ireland, 1652–1660* (Belfast: Blackstaff Press, 1975), pp. 185, 196.

181 *Those who had "adventured" monies:* Patrick J. Corish, "The Cromwellian Regime, 1650–60," *New History*, vol. 3, pp. 353–375. See also Martin J. Blake, "A Transplanter's Decree of Final Settlement, by the Loughrea Commissions in Cromwell's Time," *JGAHS* 3, 3 (1904), pp. 148–153; Samuel Johnson, *A Dictionary of the English Language* (London: Longman, Rees, Orme, Brown and Green, 1827), vol. 1: "What think you then of 'an adventurer'?/ I moan some wealthy merchant."

182 *Plight of Philip Fitzgerald:* Prendergast, *Cromwellian Settlement*, p. 153; Jerome Fahey, *The History and Antiquities of the Diocese of Kilmacduagh* (Dublin: M. H. Gill and Son, 1893), p. 298. See also J. G. Simms, "The Restoration, 1660–85," *New History*, vol. 3, pp. 420–429.

182 *The sixth earl, his feud with Ann, widow of Ulick:* "Documents Relating to the Case of Anne, Marchioness of Clanricade," June 20, 1661, *Calendar State Papers: 1660–1662*, pp. 360–362.

183 *"The Princess of Babylon" and following:* Anthony Hamilton, *Memoirs of the Count de Grammont*, trans. Horace Walpole (New York: Dodd, Mead, 1928), pp. 83, 192.

183 *Somerhill: A Short History of Somerhill, Tonbridge* (Tonbridge, 1952); *A General Account of Tunbridge Wells and Its Environs: Historical and Descriptive* (London: G. Pearch, 1771), pp. 37–39; John Britton, *Descriptive Sketches of Tunbridge Wells and the Calverley Estate* (London, 1832); Margaret Barton, *Tunbridge Wells* (London: Faber and Faber, 1937); Arthur Oswald, *Country Houses of Kent* (London: Country Life, 1936), pp. 41–42. See also A. J. Finberg, *The Life of J. M. W. Turner, R. A.* (Oxford: Clarendon Press, 1961), pp. 169, 180; John Walker, *Joseph Mallord William Turner* (New York: Harry N. Abrams, 1983), pp. 68–69.

187 *"James, the pile of shit . . . ": Songs Ascribed to Raftery, Being the Fifth Chapter of the Songs of Connacht*, ed. Douglas Hyde (Shannon: Irish University Press, 1973), p. 319.

187 *"Your countrymen, Madame, are skilled in the art of running away . . . "*: Peter B. Ellis, *The Boyne Water: The Battle of the Boyne, 1690* (London: Hamish Hamilton, 1976), p. 123; Richard Doherty, *The Williamite War in Ireland, 1688–1691* (Dublin: Four Courts Press, 1998), p. 124.

187 *James returns to France:* Matthew O'Conor, *Irish Brigades; or, Memoirs of the Most Eminent Irish Military Commanders Who Distinguished Themselves in the Elizabethan and Williamite Wars in Their Own Country, and in the Service of France and Spain* (Dublin: Duffy, 1855), p. 112.

188 *The Battle for Athlone:* Diarmuid Murtagh, "The Siege of Athlone," *JRSAI* 83 (1953), pp. 58–81.

188 *The Battle of Augrim:* Hayes-McCoy, *Irish Battles*, pp. 238–272; G. A. Hayes-McCoy, "The Battle of Aughrim, 1691," *JGAHS* 20 (1942), pp. 1–30; J. G. Simms, "The War of the Two Kings, 1685–91," *New History*, vol. 3, pp. 478–508; Piers Wauchope, *Patrick Sarsfield and the Williamite War* (Blackpool: Irish Academic Press, 1992), pp. 218–236.

188 *"To bury his body or win"*: Richard Murphy, *The Battle of Aughrim* (London: Faber and Faber, 1968), p. 37.

188 *"We have them . . . "*: Hayes-McCoy, *Irish Battles*, pp. 262, 265; "Battle of Aughrim," p. 26; *A Jacobite Narrative of the War in Ireland, 1688–1691*, ed. John T. Gilbert (New York: Barnes & Noble, 1971), p. 141; J. G. Simms, *Jacobite Ireland, 1685–91* (Toronto: Toronto University Press, 1969), p. 224.

188 *Bloody Knife:* Evan S. Connell, *Son of the Morning Star: Custer and the Little Bighorn* (San Francisco: North Point Press, 1984), p. 12. The future king James II was unmoved by carnage, however sudden or unexpected. Samuel Pepys records in his diary for June 8, 1665, that during a naval engagement with the Dutch, a cannonball struck off the head of Richard Boyle (son to the earl of Cork), redirecting it into the face of James, knocking him to his feet "as some say." The poet Andrew Marvell wrote that James "distains" the distraction and continued commanding the fleet without losing composure. See *The Diary of Samuel Pepys* (London: Macmillan, 1920), p. 317; James Fenton, "Goodbye to All That," *New York Review of Books*, June 20, 1996, p. 59.

189 *Luttrell's Pass: A Jacobite Narrative*, pp. 143–146; O'Conor, *Irish Brigades*, pp. 168–169.

189 *Richard, eighth earl of Clanricard, at the Boyne: Jacobite Narrative*, p. 99.

189 *John Burke, the future ninth earl:* At Aughrim he went by the title Lord Bophin. Richard and John's other brother, Lord Galway, was killed during the battle. John D'Alton, "A List of the Considerable Irish Officers Killed and Taken at Aughrim, July 12, 1691," *Illustrations, Historical and*

Genealogical, of King James's Irish Army List (1689) (Dublin: Private subscription, n.d.), p. 784; Simms, *Jacobite Ireland*, p. 227. *A Jacobite Narrative* claims that Lord Galway "was despatched by the foreigners after quarter given, as 'tis said" (p. 141).

190 *Clanricard "inherited neither the courage nor the loyalty of his ancestor . . . ":* Cokayne, *Complete Peerage*, p. 233. See also de Burgh, *Memoirs and Letters of Ulick*, p. xvii; D'Alton, "A List," pp. 130–159; Lewis Innes, *The Life of James the Second, King of England, Collected out of Memoirs Writ of His Own Hand. Together with the King's Advice to His Son, and His Majesty's Will* (London: Longman, Hurst, Rees, Orme, and Brown, 1816), vol. 2, p. 459; J. G. Simms, "The Surrender of Galway," *Jacobite Ireland*, pp. 230–239; Harman Murtagh, "Galway and the Jacobite War," *Irish Sword* 12, 46 (1975), pp. 1–4.

190 *"Acquitted of all treasons and attainders . . . ":* Cokayne, *Complete Peerage*, p. 234. See also J. G. Simms, "Connacht," pp. 116–133; de Burgh, *Memoirs and Letters of Ulick*, p. xvii.

190 *Battle of Fontenoy:* Charles Petrie, "The Irish Brigade at Fontenoy," *Irish Sword* 1 (1949–1953), pp. 166–172.

190 *Sir William Scawen:* J. G. Simms, *The Williamite Confiscation in Ireland, 1690–1703* (London: Faber and Faber, 1956), p. 155. See also Karl S. Bottigheimer, *English Money and Irish Land* (Oxford: Clarendon Press, 1971).

190 *Death of Henry Luttrell:* Wauchope, *Patrick Sarsfield and the Williamite War*, p. 302. Some scholars have claimed that Luttrell's assassination had more to do with a sexual scandal than it did with his alleged treachery at Aughrim.

Chapter 5

193 *"Dean Dudley . . . ":* James L. Pethica and James Charles Roy, eds., *"To the Land of the Free from This Island of Slaves": Henry Stratford Persse's Letters from Galway to America, 1821–1832* (Cork: Cork University Press, 1998), p. 143.

193 *Remaining Norman mottes:* T. B. Barry, "Monumental Destruction," *Irish Times*, April 16, 1980, p. 10.

193–96 *Gleanings from the local paper: Connacht Tribune*, June 24, 1994, pp. 1, 11; July 22, 1994, pp. 1, 5, 12; August 5, 1994, pp. 7, 11, 20; August 19, 1994, pp. 18, 20; August 26, 1994, pp. 1, 1A, 22.

196 *Celts "high spirited" . . . :* Strabo, in Tierney, "Celtic Ethnography," p. 267

196 *Seaweed industry:* Qualter, *Athenry*, p. 31; *Connacht Tribune*, June 24, 1994, p. 11.

198 *Frank has nothing bad to say about the Persses:* Others have, however. See Qualter, *Athenry*, pp. 13–14.

199 *The will of Burton Walter Persse:* "Fifty pounds to my Workman Ned Maher provided he is in my service at my decease. . . . Any person who under the trust of this will should take a vested interest in any portion of my property, being at the time a Roman Catholic, that interest which he or she would have taken shall not take effect, but shall be deemed to have lapsed as if such person had predeceased me." Dated September 8, 1933; Dublin, Principal Registry 1935.

200 *"Excrementum mundi":* Helen C. Walshe, "Enforcing the Elizabethan Settlement: The Vicissitudes of Hugh Brady, Bishop of Meath, 1563–84," *IHS* 36, 104 (November 1989), p. 353.

200 *"Minister of God's Word" and property "displaced, despoyled, robbed, and deprived":* Depositions of Reverend Edward Persse (February 9, 1641) and his servant Shane Blane (February 10, 1643), reproduced in *The Persse Story* (New Haven, Conn.: N.p., 1988), pp. 78–79.

200 *Dudley "a scoundrel":* Elizabeth Coxhead, *Lady Gregory: A Literary Portrait* (London: Secker & Warburg, 1961), pp. 1–2.

201 *"An eminent cleric": Calendar of the Manuscripts of the Marquess of Ormonde, K.P., Preserved at Kilkenny Castle* (London: Historical Manuscripts Commission, 1911), new series 6, pp. 311–312.

201 *"His grace the Duke of Ormond hath spoke . . . ":* Persse to Henry Gascoigne, October 10, 1682, ibid., p. 461.

202 *"Fortunate, if not distinguished":* Fahey, *History and Antiquities*, p. 322.

202 *"Interbreeding of almost Habsburgian dimensions":* M. D. de Burgh Collins Persse, *De Burgh Fitzpatrick Persse (1840–1921) and His Family: An Essay in Anglo-Irish and Australian History* (Corio, Victoria: N.p., 1971), part 1, p. 14.

202 *"I am credibly informed . . . ":* Persse to Francis Marsh, Archbishop of Dublin, December 22, 1684, *Calendar Ormonde Manuscripts*, pp. 311–312.

203 *Persse Lodge:* Alf Mac Lochlainn, "Some Place Names in Larkin's 1819 Map of Galway," *JGAHS* 50 (1998), p. 212.

203 *"The Irish Meynell":* Francis Humphrey De Trafford, ed., *The Foxhounds of Great Britain and Ireland: Their Masters and Huntsmen* (London: Walter Southwood, 1906), p. 284; de Burgh Collins Persse, *De Burgh Fitzpatrick Persse*, p. 13. See also *British Hunts and Huntsmen, Containing a Short History of Each Fox and Stag Hunt in the British Isles, Together with Biographical Records of Masters Past and Present, and Some Members of Each Hunt. Compiled in Conjunction with "The Sporting Life: England (North), Scotland, and Ireland"* (London: Biographical Press, 1911), p. 378.

204 *"The Hibernian Hero":* "Memoirs of the Hibernian Hero and Miss P—m," *Town and Country Magazine* 5 (1773), pp. 233–238.

204 *An incriminating "latchkey":* Cokayne, *Complete Peerage,* p. 237. See also Desmond Roche, "The Later Clanricards," *Clanricard Country and the Land Campaign* (Galway: Woodford Heritage Group, 1987), pp. 17–29; *An Inquiry into the Truth of the Accusations Made Against the Marquis of Clanricarde, on the Cause of Handcock v. Delacour, Lately Heard in the Irish Court of Chancery* (London: W. H. Dalton, 1848); W. Baring Pemberton, *Lord Palmerston* (London: Batchworth Press, 1954), pp. 254–256.

205 *"Nearly all the inhabitants of the district are Catholics . . . ":* M. de La Tocnaye, *Rambles Through Ireland* (London: G. G. & J. Robinson, 1799), vol. 2, p. 16, quoted in J. G. Simms, "Connaught," p. 118.

207 Spalpeens *and hiring fairs:* Qualter, *Athenry,* pp. 25–27.

209 *Esker, "a house of refuge":* Blake, "Athenry Abbey," p. 66. See also P. J. Dowling, *The Hedge Schools of Ireland* (Cork: Mercier Press, 1968).

209 *"Christmas Box" and following:* Eustás Ó Héideáin, ed., *The Dominicans in Galway 1241–1991* (Galway: Dominican Priory, 1991), p. 16.

213 *William Persse:* James Mitchell, "Colonel William Persse," *JGAHS* 30, 3-4 (1963), pp. 49–89.

214 *A "strange madness":* Earl of Charlemont, *The History of the Proceedings and Debates of the Volunteer Delegates* (Dublin, 1784), p. 35, quoted in ibid., p. 69.

215–18 *Correspondence of Henry Stratford Persse: Henry Strafford Persses's Letters,* pp. 66, 81, 89–94, 96, 98, 103, 104, 116, 122, 157.

216 *Persse's Irish Whiskey:* Begun in 1815, this distillery remained in business until 1914. See de Burgh Collins Persse, *De Burgh Fitzpatrick Persse,* p. 17; E. B. McGuire, *Irish Whiskey: A History of Distilling, the Spirit Trade and Excise Controls in Ireland* (Dublin: Gill and Macmillan, 1973), pp. 359–360; Marguerite Hayes-McCoy, "The Eyre Documents in University College Galway," *JGAHS* 23 (1949), pp. 147–149. See also "H. S. Persse (Limited), Nun's Island Distillery, Galway, Ireland," *Galway Vindicator and Connaught Advertiser,* February 29, 1896: Net average profit between 1891 and 1895 was nearly £12,000 yearly on production of about 400,000 gallons.

216 *Moyode House:* de Burgh Collins Persse, *De Burgh Fitzpatrick Persse,* p. 23; Bence-Jones, *Burke's Guide,* p. 220; Qualter, *Athenry,* pp. 11–14.

217 *"I asked a peasant who had a dozen pretty children . . . ":* La Tocnaye, *Rambles Through Ireland,* p. 15.

219 *The usual flood of panegyrics . . . : Galway Express,* September 10, 1859.

219 *The will of Burton Sr.:* "The Last Will and Testament and Three Codicils of Burton Persse Esquire," dated September 1, 1859; Dublin, Her Majesty's Court of Probate, Principal Registry 1859, T18213A.

219 *Landlords required their rents . . . ":* Padraig G. Lane, "The Impact of the Encumbered Estates Court upon the Landlords of Galway and Mayo," *JGAHS* 38 (1981–1982), pp. 45–58.

219 *The Great Famine killed off more than a million Irish peasants:* Kerby Miller, *Emigrants and Exile: Ireland and the Irish Exodus to North America* (Oxford: Oxford University Press, 1985), p. 280.

221 *Absentee landlords drained out of Ireland £6 million in rents alone, 1842:* Cecil Woodham-Smith, *The Great Hunger, Ireland 1845–9* (London: New English Library, 1968), p. 16.

221 *The Moyode Cup:* A foreign visitor to Athenry in 1828 commented on the wild local racing scene, "altogether a strange spectacle, well suited to a half-savage nation." He also noted of Athenry in general that "no village in Poland is more poverty-stricken." Hermann Rasche, "'. . . A Strange Spectacle . . . ': German Travellers in the West 1828–1858," *JGAHS* 47 (1995), pp. 91–92.

221 *"Oh! That this were for Ireland!":* Wauchope, *Patrick Sarsfield and the Williamite War,* p. 298.

222 *He was the kind of man an Elizabethan soldier would have hanged:* Quinn, *Elizabethans,* p. 126.

223 *"Going to mass of me, God was gracious . . . ":* "Mary Hynes, or the Posy Bright," *Songs Ascribed to Raftery,* pp. 331–335. See also William Butler Yeats, "Dust Hath Closed Helen's Eye," *The Celtic Twilight, and a Selection of Early Poems,* ed. Walter Starkie (New York: New American Library, 1962), pp. 45–51.

224 *Seefin Hill:* The inscription is probably a stanza from Raftery's "Anthony Daly," *Songs Ascribed to Raftery,* pp. 123–133. See also Qualter, *Athenry,* pp. 22–23.

226 *The Blazers:* Mary L. Persse, comp., *Birth of "The Blazers," and the Mastership of Mr. Burton R. P. Persse: How the Famous Hunt Got Its Name, Being Extracts from the Country Gentleman and the Connacht Tribune from 1883 to 1935* (Barnstable: A. E. Barnes, n.d.); De Trafford, *Foxhounds of Great Britain and Ireland,* pp. 283–285; *British Hunts and Huntsmen,* pp. 378–395.

227 *Burton's "fine seat" and following: British Hunts and Huntsmen,* p. 387.

228 *Moyode "magnificently furnished . . . ":* de Burgh Collins Persse, *De Burgh Fitzpatrick Persse,* pp. 23–24.

229 *Persse sells his pack and hunts in England: Birth of "The Blazers,"* p. 11.

230 *Obituary notice, Burton Persse:* "Know ye not that a great man has this day fallen in Israel," *Galway Express,* May 30, 1885.

230 *The astronomical sum of £40,000:* de Burgh Collins Persse, *De Burgh Fitzpatrick Persse,* p. 24.

230 *"Clanrackrent":* Desmond Roche, "Lord Clanricarde," *A Forgotten Campaign, and Aspects of the Heritage of South-East Galway* (Galway: Woodford Heritage Group, 1986), pp. 13–19; Duke de Stackpoole, *Irish and Other Memories* (London: A. M. Philpot, 1922), pp. 1-4; Bateman, *Great Landowners,* p. 91.

230 *Andy Dolphin:* He "belonged to an old family but lived in a very rough-and-ready fashion," Stackpoole, *Irish and Other Memories,* pp. 15–17.

230 *Ascendancy balls: Galway Express,* October 31, 1885.

231 *The Wyndham Act:* Mark Bence-Jones, *Twilight of the Ascendancy* (London: Constable, 1987), pp. 91–93; Roy Foster, *Modern Ireland, 1600–1972* (London: Allen Lane, 1988), pp. 414, 425n; Ann Morrow, *Picnic in a Foreign Land* (London: Grafton, 1989), p. 146; F. S. L. Lyons, "The Aftermath of Parnell, 1891–1903," *New History,* vol. 6, pp. 95–99, 158–163. For background, see W. E. Vaughan, *Landlords and Tenants in Mid-Victorian Ireland* (Oxford: Clarendon Press, 1994).

231 *Chain mail still in use:* W. Burgis, *Ancient Helmets and Examples of Mail. A Catalogue of the Objects Exhibited in the Rooms of the Royal Archaeological Institute of Great Britain and Ireland, June 3–16, 1880* (London: Archaeological Journal, 1881), p. 110. See also Robert Day, "On a Hauberk of Chain Mail, and Silvered Badge Found in the Phoenix Park, Dublin," *JRSAI* 14, 1, fourth series (1876), pp. 94–98.

231 *"Nowhere to call home":* "There was a time when County Galway was peopled by a numerous and hospitable gentry who spent money freely. Perhaps too freely, as they had to admit when the bad times came in 1879, and continued for some years, with indifferent seasons for farmers. After the Land League was formed, and rents were forcibly reduced by agitation, intimidation and British legislation; when, owing to various incidents involved in the 'Plan of campaign,' much foreclosing of mortgages took place, many of these families were ruined, and gradually disappeared from the country." Stackpoole, *Irish and Other Memories,* p. 1. See also Mark Bence-Jones, "The Changing Picture of the Irish Landed Gentry," *Burke's Genealogical and Heraldic History of the Landed Gentry of Ireland* (London: Burke's Peerage, 1958), pp. xviii–xxi.

232 *Ireland did not deserve the velvet glove:* General Sir John Maxwell, in Dorothy Macardle, *The Irish Republic* (Dublin: Corgi Books, 1968), p. 169.

233 *The west "awake" and following on Liam Mellows:* Charles Greaves, *Liam Mellows and the Irish Revolution* (London: Lawrence and Wishart, 1971), pp. 73–101, 386–387.

235 *The Twelve Apostles:* Qualter, *Athenry,* p. 33. See also Peadar O'Dowd, "Some Galway and Other Memories from Ballykinlar Camp 1921," *JGAHS* 48 (1996), pp. 153–160.

241 *Death of Tom Egan:* Qualter, *Athenry,* p. 16; "Nora O'Brien Talks to Paul McNamara," *Athenry Journal* 2, 2 (August 1966), p. 32.

241 *Frank Shawe-Taylor shot dead:* Stackpoole, *Irish and Other Memories,* p. 32.

245 *Roxborough burned:* de Burgh Collins Persse, *De Burgh Fitzpatrick Persse,* p. 12.

Chapter 6

249 "*The end of the world I knew*": Dermot Hynes, 1996.

249 "*They were the pity of all creation*" *and following . . . :* Qualter, *Athenry*, pp. 29, 30, 60.

249 *In 1875 smallpox ravaged the town:* Ibid., p. 30. See also Anne Walsh, "Smallpox in Athenry 1875," *JGAHS* 48 (1996), pp. 143–152.

253 *Kilconierin Church:* Patrick Kennedy, "Historical Aspects of Kilconieron Church," private letter of January 17, 1952; Redington, "Notes on the Ordnance Survey Letters," p. 147; "Ordnance Survey," October 10, 1838, p. 160.

260 *Firmum in vita nihil:* Bernard Burke, *The General Armory of England, Scotland, Ireland, and Wales: Comprising a Registry of Armorial Bearings from the Earliest to the Present Time* (London: Burke's Peerage, 1961), p. 291.

261 *The old Persse bell tower:* James Charles Roy, "Triumphal Gateway, Moyode Castle, County Galway," *JGAHS* 49 (1997), pp. 194–201.

261 *All will turn to ruin once again:* W. B. Yeats, "To Be Carved on a Stone at Thoor Ballylee," *W. B. Yeats, the Poems*, ed. D. Albright (London: Dent, 1990), p. 298.

SELECT BIBLIOGRAPHY

This book is not intended to be a definitive history of Ireland but a brisk canter through high spots and low of an Irish story often too colorful and dramatic for its own good. I have thus dispensed with the customary full-length bibliography. There are so many fine books on nearly every aspect of Irish history that readers who wish to delve further into a particular era or event will quite easily find their way.

Having said that, however, I cannot obscure my reliance on the scholarship of many who have worked these fields before me. I mention some of these below, as well as many of the better books for a general readership that I have enjoyed over the years. Experts will notice many omissions.

For the most part, this abridged bibliography follows the same chronological order as the book's narrative, beginning with broad surveys.

The most accessible works on Irish history are *The Gill History of Ireland* (Dublin: Gill & Macmillan, 1972–1990) in its several volumes and T. W. Moody and F. X. Martin, eds., *The Course of Irish History* (Cork: Mercier Press, 1984). The old-fashioned *Cambridge Medieval History* series, in particular volumes 5 through 8 (Cambridge: Cambridge University Press, 1926–1936) still reward study, and the ongoing *New History of Ireland* (Oxford: Clarendon Press, 1972–1996), a masterpiece of Irish scholarship, is indispensable, though at times heavy going for the uninitiated.

The value of books by Norman Douglas and the French historian Georges Duby to the understanding of Normandy cannot be overestimated. *The Norman Achievement* (London: Collins/Fontana, 1972) by Douglas is a fine summary of the Norman character, and Duby's *History of French Civilization* (New York: Random House, 1967) a lucid primer. *William Marshal, the Flower of French Chivalry* (New York: Pantheon, 1985), also by Duby, is that rarest of prizes, a major examination by a renowned continental historian of someone who really mattered in the Norman world of Ireland.

The literature on William the Conqueror is legion. Douglas's fine biography, *William the Conqueror* (Berkeley: University of California Press, 1964), lists many sources.

I found especially illuminating two books on the Normans of the Welsh marches: Lynn Nelson, *The Normans in South Wales, 1070–1171* (Austin: University of Texas Press, 1966), and Janet Meisel's *Barons of the Welsh Frontier: The Corbet, Pantulf, and Fitz Warin Families, 1066–1272* (Lincoln: University of Nebraska Press, 1980).

G. H. Orpen's four-volume *Ireland Under the Normans, 1169–1333* (Oxford: Clarendon Press, 1911–1920) is still regarded as the primary work on the invasion and its consequences. At times fatiguing in detail, the book offers a wealth of fact and narrative that is still impressive, though historians today are questioning Orpen's alleged sympathy with the invaders. Edmund Curtis's *History of Medieval Ireland from 1086 to 1513* (London: Methuen, 1938) and A. J. Otway-Ruthven's *History of Medieval Ireland* (London: Ernest Benn, 1968) are also necessary for the serious student. Both Maurice Sheehy's *When the Normans Came to Ireland* (Cork: Mercier Press, 1975) and Richard Roche's *Norman Invasion of Ireland* (Tralee: Anvil, 1970) are good in detailing the first years of the Norman incursion. Alfred P. Smyth, *Celtic Leinster—Towards an Historical Geography of Early Irish Civilization A.D. 500–1600* (Blackrock: Irish Academic Press, 1982), is an unusual look at the milieu of the much-maligned Dermot MacMurrough, and the Irish annals, in many varied editions, always reward study (see James Charles Roy, *The Road Wet, the Wind Close: Celtic Ireland* [Dublin: Gill & Macmillan, 1986], p. 206).

Again, there are many excellent biographies of the various Plantagenets. I found W. L. Warren's *Henry II* (Berkeley: University of California Press, 1973) to be very good, likewise his later book, *King John* (Berkeley: University of California Press, 1978). John Gillingham's *Richard the Lion Heart* (London: Weidenfeld and Nicolson, 1978) devastates the currently fashionable portrait of Richard as a probable homosexual, and Kate Norgate's *John Lackland* (New York: AMS Press, 1970) is about as fair a treatment as its subject will allow.

The eminent Irish historian James Lydon wrote extensively on the medieval period of Ireland's history, and his several books remain available in most academic libraries. T. B. Barry, R. Frame, and K. Simms, eds., *Colony and Frontier in Medieval Ireland: Essays Presented to J. F. Lyon* (London: Hambledon Press, 1995), reflects the high scholarship of teacher and pupils alike.

Tudor and Elizabethan studies abound, many highly specific to Ireland and narrowly focused. Both Nicholas Canny's *Elizabethan Conquest of Ireland* (Hassocks: Harvester Press, 1976) and D. B. Quinn's *Elizabethans and the Irish* (Ithaca, N.Y.: Cornell University Press, 1966) are representative in style, historical detail, and impeccable insight. To single out one or two from the many dozens I consulted, however, would be unfair to the honest labor of so many dedicated scholars, and so I abstain. I can only say again that a close reading of the various academic journals mentioned below will develop an impressive array of leads.

General histories of the sixteenth century, wherein the escapades of Burkes and Clanricards obliquely intrude, are probably best represented in the works of Richard Bagwell, in particular *Ireland Under the Tudors* (London: Longmans, Green, 1885–1890), and his later work, *Ireland Under the Stuarts and During the Interregnum* (London: Longmans, Green, 1909–1916). Many others are listed in Richard Berleth, *The Twilight Lords, an Irish Chronicle* (New York: Knopf, 1978), itself a very stylish book on the Elizabethan wars. Sean O'Faolain's *Great O'Neill* (Cork: Mercier Press, 1970) is also deservedly well known.

The acknowledged master on the subject of early and medieval Irish architecture is the late Harold Leask, who labored for years as an inspector of national monuments for the government. His *Irish Castles and Castellated Houses* (Dundalk: Dundalgen Press, 1964), along with numerous articles and pamphlets, many handsomely illustrated with diagrams and line drawings, are models of erudite scholarship. W. A. McComish, "The Survival of the Irish Castle in an Age of Cannon," in vol. 9 of *The Irish Sword* (1969, pp. 16–22), is also useful. As the combination in subject matter of Irish castles and the poet William Butler Yeats are irresistible to me, Mary Hanley's little book on Yeats's tower, *Thoor Ballylee* (Dublin: Dolmen Press, 1965), is a personal favorite. See also Seamus Heaney's essay "W. B. Yeats and Thoor Ballylee," in James Pethica, ed., *Yeats's Poetry, Drama, and Prose* (New York: Norton, 2000), pp. 429–439.

For the Battle of Kinsale (and, for that matter, those of the Boyne and Aughrim), consult G. A. Hayes-McCoy, *Irish Battles* (London: Longmans, 1969). Hayes-McCoy is probably the most esteemed military historian in Ireland.

C. V. Wedgwood's two-volume work on Charles II, *The King's Peace, 1637–41* and *The King's War, 1641–47* (New York: Book of the Month, 1972), are to my mind some of the most elegant and insightful histories ever written. Her works on Wentworth, in particular *Thomas Wentworth, First Earl of Strafford 1593–1641: A Revaluation* (London: J. Cape, 1961), are also excellent, as is Hugh Kearney's *Strafford in Ireland, 1633–4* (Manchester: Manchester University Press, 1959).

The letters of Richard, fourth earl of Clanricard, were recently edited by Bernadette Cunningham and published in *JRSAI* 48 (1996), pp. 162–208. The woes of his son, Ulick, the fifth earl of Clanricard, during the calamitous decade of the 1640s can be read to best advantage in John Lowe, ed., *Letter-Book of the Earl of Clanricard 1643–47* (Dublin: Irish Manuscript Commission, 1983). Eamon Duffy has contributed some very good articles to *JGAHS* on Clanricard's mostly futile maneuverings during this same time frame (see *JGAHS* 31 [1964–1965], pp. 71–99 and 39 [1983–1984], pp. 115–142). S. O'Riordan covered the topic in "Rinuccini in Galway, 1647–49," *JGAHS* 23, 1-2 (1948), pp. 19–51. Edward, earl of Clarendon's *History of the Rebellion and Civil Wars in England* (Oxford: Clarendon Press, 1888) is the most famous reference work for these particular episodes of English and Irish history, though modern works, which abound, are generally sounder. See Peter Young and Richard Holmes, *The English Civil War 1642–51* (London: Erye Methuen, 1974); J. P. Kenyon, *The Civil Wars of England* (New York: Knopf, 1988); and Michael Perceval-Maxwell, *The Outbreak of the Irish Rebellion of 1641* (Montreal: McGill-Queens University Press, 1994). James Scott Wheeler's *Cromwell in Ireland* (New York: St. Martin's Press, 1999) provides in full detail the account its title promises.

I found Theo Aronson's *Kings Over the Water, the Saga of the Stuart Pretenders* (London: Cassell, 1979) an enjoyable analysis of James II. There are many others. Robert Shepherd, *Ireland's Fate: The Boyne and After* (London: Aurum Press, 1990), and Piers Wauchope, *Patrick Sarsfield and the Williamite War* (Dublin: Irish Academic Press, 1992), are both fine general-readership books on this catastrophic period in Irish history. William of Orange is well treated by Henri and Barbara van der Zee in *William and Mary* (New York: Macmillan, 1973). A useful essay by D. W. Hayton, "The Williamite Revolution in Ireland, 1688–91," can be found in J. Israel, ed., *The Anglo-Dutch Moment: Essays on the Glorious Revolution and Its World Impact* (Cambridge: Cambridge University Press, 1991), pp. 184–214. All students of this period must consult the works of J. G. Simms, in particular *Jacobite Ireland, 1685–91* (London: Routledge & Kegan Paul, 1969).

The 1700s, an era of Protestant dominance in Ireland, is amply represented in academic literature, in particular volumes 5 and 6 of the aforementioned *New History of Ireland*. These books, and specialist literature in general pertaining to this century, are often dense with detail, however, and casual readers may find themselves lost on the moors without a guide. R. F. Foster's *Modern Ireland, 1600–1972* (London: Allen Lane, 1988) is far better suited for the generalist. J. G. Simms, "Connaught in the

Eighteenth Century," *Irish Historical Studies* 11 (1958–1959), pp. 116–133, presents a fine overview of the province during this time frame. The Rising of 1798 is best viewed in Thomas Pakenham, *The Year of Liberty: The Story of the Great Irish Rebellion of 1798* (Englewood Cliffs, N.J.: Prentice-Hall, 1969).

A sampling of Raftery's poetry can be found in Douglas Hyde's *Songs Ascribed to Raftery* (Shannon: Irish University Press, 1973). See also W. B. Yeats, *The Celtic Twilight, and a Selection of Early Poems*, ed. Walter Starkie (New York: New American Library, 1962), in particular pp. 45–51.

The only scholarly article to be found on the Persse family is J. Mitchell's enterprising "Colonel William Persse," *JGAHS* 30, 3-4 (1963), pp. 49–89. The newly uncovered letters of William's fourth son, Henry Stratford Persse, were edited for publication; see James Pethica and James Charles Roy, eds., *"To the Land of the Free from This Island of Slaves": Henry Stratford Persse's Letters from Galway to America, 1821–1832* (Cork: Cork University Press, 1998). Because Lady Gregory, a Roxborough Persse, had such a profound influence on the literary history of Ireland, her biographers have generally worked in a few pages, often illuminating, on her childhood in County Galway. Elizabeth Coxhead's two books *Lady Gregory, Selected Plays* (London: Putnam, 1962) and *Lady Gregory: A Literary Portrait* (London: Secker & Warburg, 1961) are good examples. See also James Pethica, ed., *Lady Gregory's Diaries, 1892–1902* (Oxford: Oxford University Press, 1996).

Garland Publishing in New York recently undertook an ambitious series of reprints in nineteenth-century Irish fiction, masterfully assembled by Robert Le Wolff of Harvard, that total seventy-seven novels by twenty-two writers. Readers might wish to read novelists such as Maria Edgeworth (*The Absentee*, 1812) and Anthony Trollope (*The Landleaguers*, 1883) for their sometimes accurate and sometimes imaginary depictions of Ascendancy life.

As the Persses of Moyode were best known for their addiction to field and blood sports, it is not surprising that general histories of various hunts in Great Britain should give them considerable mention. A typical entry can be found in *British Hunts and Huntsmen, Containing a Short History of Each Fox and Stag Hunt in the British Isles, Together with Biographical Records of Masters Past and Present, and Some Members of Each Hunt* (London: Biographical Press, 1911).

Cecil Woodham-Smith's internationally known work *The Great Hunger* (London: H. Hamilton, 1962) is justifiably regarded as the premier book for a general audience on the famine of the 1840s. Specialist literature abounds, much of it on account of the 150th anniversary of those grim years. Kerby Miller's *Emigrants and Exiles: Ireland and the Irish Exodus to North America* (Oxford: Oxford University Press, 1985) typifies the high degree of endeavor that has characterized scholarship on the famine.

Mark Bence-Jones is certainly the most accomplished commentator on the Protestant Ascendancy, both past and present, being a member of it himself. His *Twilight of the Ascendancy* (London: Constable, 1987) is a handsome look at the life and times of the big house, Dublin society in general, and the land agitation that brought it all to disaster. Burke's *Guide to Irish Mansions* (London: Burke's Peerage, 1978), which Bence-Jones compiled and wrote, is likewise a monument to both an excellent memory and his affection for the topic. One of the most striking books of photography in recent years is Simon Marsden's *In Ruins, the Once Great Houses of Ireland* (New York: Knopf, 1980), utilizing the eerie skeletons of Irish mansions to great effect. Andrew

Bush's *Bonnettstown, a House in Ireland* (New York: Abrams, 1989) deals with much the same subject matter, though with more restraint and circumspection. Autobiographies of Ascendancy survivors, usually full of eccentricities and self-absorption, are in fashion today. Annabel Davis-Goff's *Walled Gardens: Scenes from an Anglo-Irish Childhood* (New York: Knopf, 1989) is representative of this genre.

There are hundreds of books on the Irish Easter Rising, civil war, and Troubles. Charles Greaves's biography *Liam Mellows and the Irish Revolution* (London: Lawrence and Wishart, 1971) deals extensively with Moyode and the disturbances in Galway. For the behavior of British irregulars, see Richard Bennett, *The Black and Tans* (Boston: Houghton Mifflin, 1960), and for the civil war, Calton Younger, *Ireland's Civil War* (London: Frederick Muller, 1968).

To get the feel of Ireland during the economic doldrums of the 1930s through the 1950s, readers should turn to the novels and short stories of Edna O'Brien and William Trevor. More anthropological and folklorist treatments can be found in Conrad Arensberg, *The Irish Countryman* (New York: Natural History Press, 1968), and E. Estyn Evans, *Irish Heritage* (Dundalk: Dundalgan Press, 1977).

For the history of Connaught in general, the reader can do no better than sweep through issues of the various Irish academic journals in the hope of finding the many nuggets of specialist fact and insight that lie everywhere in their pages. Recommended in particular are *Ériu*, *The Irish Sword*, *Studia Hibernica*, *Celtica*, *Irish Historical Studies*, *Égise*, and the *Journal of the Royal Society of Antiquarians of Ireland*, along with their American and Canadian counterparts, *Éire-Ireland*, *New Hibernia Review*, and the *Canadian Journal of Irish Studies*. The most rewarding of all, for the purposes of this book, was the *Journal of the Galway Archaeological and Historical Society*. Articles by H. T. Knox, Martin Blake, M. D. O'Sullivan, J. P. Nolan, and countless others yielded tremendous amounts of obscure and fascinating material.

For Galway City, James Hardiman's *History of the Town and County of the Town of Galway, from the Earliest Period to the Present Time, 1820* (Galway: Connacht Tribune, 1958), and M. D. O'Sullivan's *Old Galway: The History of a Norman Colony in Ireland* (Cambridge: W. Heffner and Sons, 1942), are two well-respected sources. A recently published collection of papers that will interest all students of the region is R. Gillespie and G. Moran, eds., *Galway History and Society: Interdisciplinary Essays on the History of an Irish County* (Dublin: Geography Publications, 1996). H. T. Knox's *History of County Mayo to the Close of the Sixteenth Century* (Dublin: Hodges, Figgis & Co., 1908) is an antiquarian delight.

The Loughrea and Athenry region of County Galway is by comparison rather bare in source materials. Listed below are most of the books, articles, and pamphlets I consulted, however meager.

Works Specific to Athenry and Loughrea

Bigger, F. J. "The Franciscan Friary of Killconnell in the County of Galway. Its History and Its Ruins." *JGAHS* 1, 2 (1901), pp. 145–167; 2, 1 (1902), pp. 3–20.

Blake, Martin J. "The Abbey of Athenry." *JGAHS* 2, 2 (1902), pp. 65–90.

Bourke, Eamonn. *Burke People and Places*. Whitegate, Co. Clare: De Búrca, 1984.
Cody, Eamon. "An Archaeological Survey of the Barony of Athenry, County Galway." Thesis, University College Galway, 1989.
Fahey, J. *The History and Antiquities of the Diocese of Kilmacduagh*. Dublin: H. M. Gill & Son, 1893.
Fallon, Padraic. *Poems*. Dublin: Dolmen Press, 1974.
______. *Poems and Versions*. Manchester: Carcanet New Press, 1983.
______. *"Erect Me a Monument of Broken Wings": An Anthology of Writings by and on Padraic Fallon*. Ed. Brian Fallon. Athenry: V. P. Shields, 1992.
Finerty, Martin. *Punann Arsa: The Story of Athenry, County Galway*. Ballinasloe: N.p., 1951.
Gorman, T., C. Stanley, M. Lyons-Hynes, D. Roche, and S. McEneany, eds. *Clanricarde Country and the Land Campaign*. Galway: Woodford Heritage Group, 1987.
Healy, Ann. *Athenry: A Brief History*. Tuam: Connacht Tribune, 1989.
Holland, Patrick. "The Anglo-Norman Landscape in County Galway, Land-Holdings, Castles and Settlements." *JGAHS* 47 (1997), pp. 159–193.
Kennedy, Patrick. "Historical Aspects of Kilconierin Church." Private letter, January 17, 1952.
Knox, H. T., and "A Colleague." "Notes on the Burgus of Athenry, Its First Defenses, and Its Town Walls." *JGAHS* 11, 1 (1920), pp. 1–26.
Macalister, R. A. S. "The Dominican Church at Athenry." *JRSAI* 43, 3 (1913), pp. 195–222.
Mahony, Edmund. *The Galway Blazers: Memoirs*. Galway: Kenny's, 1979.
______. *Falcons and Foxhounds*. Galway: Kenny's, 1984.
McCaffrey, Peter. "A Contribution to the Archaeology of the Barony of Dunkellin, County Galway." Thesis, University College Galway, 1952.
McNeill, Charles. "Remarks on the Walls and Church of Athenry." *JGAHS* 11, 3-4 (1920), pp. 132–141.
Monahan, Phelim. *The Old Abbey Loughrea, 1300–1650*. N.p., n.d.
______. *The Carmelite Abbey, Loughrea, County Galway*. Galway: Corrib, 1983.
O Donaill, Padraig. *The Story of Esker, 1707–1905*. N.p., n.d.
O'Donovan, John. "Letters Containing Information Relative to the History and Antiquities of the County of Galway, Collected During the Progress of the Ordnance Survey in 1839." Typescript, 3 vols., Bray, 1928.
Ó Héideáin, Eustás, ed. *The Dominicans in Galway 1241-1991*. Galway: Dominican Priory, 1991.
O'Regan, Finburr, ed. *The Lamberts of Athenry: A Book on the Lambert Families of Castle Lambert and Castle Ellen, Co. Galway. A Study of the Townland's Association with them and Their Edward Carson Connection*. Galway: Lambert Project Society, 1999.
Orpen, Goddard Henry. "The Mote of Oldcastle and the Castle of Rathgorgin." *JGAHS* 9, 1 (1915), pp. 33–44.
Papazian, Cliona. "Excavations at Athenry Castle, Co. Galway." *JGAHS* 43 (1991), pp. 1–45.
Persse, Mary L., comp. *Birth of "The Blazers," and the Mastership of Mr. Burton R. P. Persse, Being Extracts from the County Gentleman and the Connacht Tribune from 1883 to 1935*. Barnstable: A. E. Barnes, n.d.

Persse, Michael D. de Burgh. *De Burgh Fitzpatrick Persse (1840–1921) and His Family: An Essay in Anglo-Irish and Australian History*. Corio, Victoria: N.p., 1971 and 1972.

Qualter, Aggie. *Athenry, History from 1780, Folklore Recollections*. Athenry: N.p., 1989.

Roy, James Charles. "Triumphal Gateway, Moyode Castle, County Galway." *JGAHS* 49 (1997), pp. 194–201.

______. "Caher na Earle (The Earl's Chair)." *JGAHS* 52 (2000), pp. 144–154.

Rynne, Etienne. *Athenry: A Medieval Irish Town*. Athenry: Athenry Historical Society, 1992. (Professor Rynne has also authored an entire host of brochures and pamphlets on Athenry Castle, Priory, Market Cross, de Bermingham's grave, town walls and gates, and other topics. All reward study.)

Shiel, M. J., ed. *A Forgotten Campaign, and Aspects of the Heritage of South-East Galway*. Galway: Woodford Heritage Group, 1986.

Westropp, T. J. "Athenry." *JRSAI* 25 (1895), pp. 297–302.

ACKNOWLEDGMENTS

This book would not have been possible without the generosity of countless people from Athenry, friends and strangers alike. Some may object to my depiction of this old town as a place of gloom and downtrodden fortunes—especially given the economic boom of the 1990s—but I hope the cantankerous observations of an outsider will be seen for what they are: simply one person's opinion. I am hopeful that anyone I may have offended will accept my sincere regrets and offer, with typical Irish largess, some measure of forgiveness. It is to my benefit, certainly, that only in Ireland are Americans truly welcome.

To those who appear in this book, my thanks. To those who do not but assisted me in so many other ways, either by researching the many arcane queries with which I peppered them or else "led me out to the back" searching up some ruin or artifact known only to them, I cannot begin to repay my debt other than to acknowledge them here: the late Carmen Broderick; John Coen; Martin Connors; Christy Corless; Brigitte Coughlan; Melanie Daly; Brendan Glynn; Stan Lawless; Willie McDonnagh; Michael Morrissey; Jerome Mahony; Tomas O'Brien; Father Eustás Ó Héideáin, O.P.; Mary Joe O'Dea; Elizabeth Ruane; Michael Ryan; Pat Ryan; Eileen Sweeney; and Joe Sweeney.

Although mentioned once or twice in the text, I must again acknowledge my debt to the late Major Walter Joyce, a fund of antiquarian knowledge for the central Galway area and a writer who should have been published long, long ago.

In the United States, I am grateful to Timothy Horgan, John Windsor Persse III, and James Rogers, editor of *New Hibenia Review*, for his intervention on my behalf with various recalcitrant administrators. As usual, Katherine Dibble and the staff of the Boston Public Library were always ready, when needed, to track down those long mis-shelved volumes that no one, in a hundred years, has ever called to see. And unlike several other private libraries in the Boston area, that of Boston College bent over backward to cooperate on many laborious searches. The National Library of Ireland, the Library of University College Galway, and the little town library of Athenry were likewise extraordinarily helpful.

To the following, acknowledgment is made for permission to reproduce various pieces of artwork from their collections: the representation of Dermot MacMurrough is to be found in a margin of *The History of the Conquest of Ireland* by Giraldus Cambrensis (c. 1200) and is published courtesy of the National Library of Ireland; images from the eleventh-century Bayeux Tapestry, by special permission of the City of Bayeux; William "The Grey" de Burgo, by kindness of the Board of Trinity College, Dublin; Street Market, Athenry, from the Valentine Collection of the National Library of Ireland; Frances Walsingham, reproduced by permission of Viscount De L'Isle, from his private collection, Penshurst Place, Kent; the engraving of Ulick, fifth earl of Clanricard, by courtesy of the National Portrait Gallery, London; Turner's *Somer Hill, Tunbridge*, courtesy the National Gallery of Scotland; Spy's cartoon of Lord Clanricard © British Museum; Liam Mellows, from the *Illustrated London News* Picture Library; detail from the 1835 ordnance survey map by permission of the Irish government, permit 5570.

For permission to photograph and reproduce the hitherto unpublished portrait of Dean Dudley Persse, I am most grateful to Coralie Persse, his direct descendant, now living in San Francisco. The miniature of Burton Persse, "The Irish Meynell," was provided by his direct descendant Michael D. de Burgh Collins Persse of Corio, Victoria, in Australia. I acknowledge his helpfulness in many other of my queries as well. The photograph of Burton Robert Persse in hunting attire was kindly provided by the late Mrs. John Windsor Persse of Hamden, Connecticut, who likewise made available to me the letters of Henry Stratford Persse. Her spirit of generosity and many other favors I gratefully acknowledge. To the County Club, Galway, my apologies for the disruption caused in October of 1992 when the enormous presentation portrait of Burton Persse by Charles Augustus Henry Lutyens (1829–1915, the father of the architect Sir Edwin Lutyens) was photographed. The Reverend Canon J. Robinson deserves special thanks for his courtesy in facilitating access to the tomb of William Marshal in the Temple, London, on a day when that church was, inexplicably, closed. And my thanks to Frank Broderick, friend and neighbor, for rousting out the old picture of Moyode House. The little boy standing by the horse was Frank's father.

My appreciation to Margaret Uniacke for the photograph of Thomas, and to both her and Frances O'Brien for the extraordinary afternoon of October 24, 1992, spent in the company of Nora Egan.

The illustrations of motte and bailey and a Norman knight were by Edwin Tunis and first appeared in his book *Weapons, a Pictorial History* (New York: Thomas Y. Crowell Company, 1954), a present on my seventh birthday from my parents, whose encouragement of my varied interests I will never forget. Both are © 1954 by Edward Tunis and reprinted by permission of Curtis Brown, Ltd. The schematic diagram of a fifteenth-century tower house (actually, Clara Castle in County Kilkenny) is the work of Harold Leask and reproduced by permission of his publisher, Dundalgan Press. Maps are by Jane Crozen. The Great Seal of Athenry was first described in the *Journal of the Royal Society of Antiquaries of Ireland* and the detail that appears in this book is based on the illustration found opposite p. 371 of vol. 3, 1874–1875, reproduced by kind permission of the society. For several decades, no one in Athenry had the slightest idea where the seal and its equally venerable companion, the town mace, were to be found (rumor had it they were on the Isle of Wight). Thanks to Professor Etienne Rynne, resident authority on Athenry, both were finally located and arrangements made for their return to the village, where they are now on display.

For the record, "The Fields of Athenry" is the title of a very popular ballad by Pete St. John, Walton MNF Ltd. and Celtic Songs.

My thanks to Jan V. Roy for all her work on the line drawings, and again to Laura Henderson and Elizabeth Welch for their yeoman efforts to bring order to the various drafts they reviewed. Ralph Brown's input was also highly valued. Bill Lane did everything asked of him, once more, and a special appreciation to Christina Ward.

The editorial and production teams at Westview Press are true professionals in every sense of that term. Thank you to Carol Jones, Michelle Trader, and Meegan Finnegan. My copyeditor, Alice Colwell, again embarrassed me profoundly with all the mental and grammatical errors she detected in the manuscript. My admiration for her work in the trenches is highly placed. At the top of the pyramid stands Rob Williams. I have never had a better editor.

And finally, one or two points of clarification: Before the many Persses all over the world rush to their stationery boxes to dash off feverish letters of correction that Moyode House was never called by that name but always "Moyode Castle," let me admit that I accept the point entirely. When faced with two distinct buildings lying within 300 yards of each other, both known by the name "Moyode Castle," I arbitrarily decided for purposes of clarity to call the Persse mansion Moyode House as apart from the sixteenth-century tower of Moyode Castle, which is the centerpiece of this book. I am likewise aware that Rathgorgin Castle and the motte and bailey of Oldcastle lie in two separate townlands, not one, despite their proximity to each other. Again, to avoid unnecessary confusion, I assigned them a single geographical assignation. These are minor points—and there are others—but they do not, I believe, affect the accuracy of my larger picture.

JCR
April 18, 2000
Newburyport, Massachusetts

INDEX

fn refers to footnote on page indicated
(notes) refers to page indicated in Notes section.